Reed Carlson
Unfamiliar Selves in the Hebrew Bible

Ekstasis

Religious Experience
From Antiquity to the Middle Ages

Edited by
John R. Levison

Editorial Board
David Aune, Jan Bremmer, John Collins,
Dyan Elliott, Amy Hollywood, Sarah Iles Johnston,
Gabor Klaniczay, Paulo Nogueira,
Christopher Rowland and Elliot R. Wolfson

Volume 9

Reed Carlson

Unfamiliar Selves in the Hebrew Bible

Possession and Other Spirit Phenomena

DE GRUYTER

ISBN 978-3-11-154277-5
e-ISBN (PDF) 978-3-11-067003-5
e-ISBN (EPUB) 978-3-11-067006-6
ISSN 1865-8792

Library of Congress Control Number: 2021945469

Bibliographic information published by the Deutsche Nationalbibliothek
The Deutsche Nationalbibliothek lists this publication in the Deutsche Nationalbibliografie;
detailed bibliographic data are available in the Internet at http://dnb.dnb.de.

© 2024 Walter de Gruyter GmbH, Berlin/Boston
This volume is text- and page-identical with the hardback published in 2022.

www.degruyter.com

To the memories of

Marguerite Ann Annoni
and
Gracy Ann Carlson

2 Corinthians 4:13

Contents

Abbreviations of Sources —— IX

Textual Conventions —— XIII

Acknowledgments —— XV

1	**The Ghost of a Self** —— 1	
1.1	A Murder in Brookfield, Connecticut —— 1	
1.2	Argument —— 5	
1.3	Terminology —— 7	
1.4	Methods —— 10	
1.5	The Organization of this Book —— 24	

2 Raising the Specter —— 27
2.1 Co-Creating with Spirits Among Cuban *Espiritistas* —— 27
2.2 Chapter Overview —— 29
2.3 Saul's Spirit Sickness —— 30
2.4 The Spirit Medium of Endor —— 46
2.5 Conclusions —— 59

3 Getting into the Spirit —— 60
3.1 The Myriad Modes of Talking to the Dead Among Gullah/Geechee Women —— 60
3.2 Chapter Overview —— 62
3.3 Spirit Language —— 62
3.4 Descriptions of Spirit Possession —— 72
3.5 Myths About Spirits —— 80
3.6 Conclusions —— 90

4 When a Spirit Moves —— 91
4.1 The Exorcism of Robert Brigges —— 91
4.2 Chapter Overview —— 94
4.3 Abiding Spirits —— 95
4.4 Migrating Spirits —— 105
4.5 Conclusions —— 121

5   In Good Spirits — 123
5.1   Umbanda Public Possession Ceremonies — 123
5.2   Chapter Overview — 126
5.3   Spirit Possession in a Medical Idiom — 127
5.4   Unfamiliar Selves — 141
5.5   Holy Spirits as Preventative Care — 153
5.6   Conclusions — 159

Bibliography — 162
Primary Sources — 162
Secondary Sources — 162

Index of Ancient Sources — 189

Subject and Author Index — 197

Abbreviations of Sources

1QapGen	Genesis Apocryphon
1QH[a]	Hodayot or Thanksgiving Hymns
1QS	Serek Hayaḥad or Community Rule
AB	Anchor Bible
ABD	*Anchor Bible Dictionary*. Edited by David Noel Freedman. 6 vols. New York: Doubleday, 1992
ACSS	African Christian Studies Series
AGJU	Arbeiten zur Geschichte des antiken Judentums und des Urchristentums
AJEC	Ancient Judaism and Early Christianity
AJSR	*Association for Jewish Studies Review*
AMD	Ancient Magic and Divination
AmEthno	*American Ethnologist*
ANEM	Ancient Near East Monographs
AnthCon	*Anthropology of Consciousness*
AnthHor	Anthropological Horizons
AnthT	*Anthropology Today*
AOAT	Alter Orient und Altes Testament
AQ	*Anthropological Quarterly*
ARAnth	Annual Review of Anthropology
AS	Aramaic Studies
BASOR	*Bulletin of the American Schools of Oriental Research*
BBR	*Bulletin for Biblical Research*
BHS	*Biblia Hebraica Stuttgartensia*. Edited by Karl Elliger and Wilhelm Rudolph. Stuttgart: Deutsche Bibelgesellschaft, 1983
BI	*Biblical Illustrator*
BibInt	*Biblical Interpretation*
BibInters	Biblical Intersections
BibOr	Biblica et Orientalia
BJRL	*Bulletin of the John Rylands University Library of Manchester*
BN	*Biblische Notizen*
BrJPsych	*British Journal of Psychology*
BT	*The Bible Translator*
BTB	*Biblical Theology Bulletin*
BThSt	Biblisch-theologische Studien
BZAW	Beihefte zur Zeitschrift für die alttestamentliche Wissenschaft
CBQ	*Catholic Biblical Quarterly*
CBR	*Currents in Biblical Research*
CCRM	Cross Cultural Research and Methodology
CCS	*Clinical Case Studies*
CD	Damascus Document
CQS	Companion to the Qumran Scrolls
CSCD	Cambridge Studies in Christian Doctrine
CSCS	Cambridge Studies in Cultural Systems

CSCO	Corpus Scriptorum Christianorum Orientalium
CSHSMC	Comparative Studies of Health Systems and Medical Care
CSRS	Comparative Studies in Religion and Society
DCLY	Deuterocanonical and Cognate Literature Yearbook
DDD	*Dictionary of Deities and Demons in the Bible*. Edited by Karel van der Toorn, Bob Becking, and Pieter W. van der Horst. Leiden: Brill, 1995. 2nd rev. ed. Grand Rapids: Eerdmans, 1999
DJD	Discoveries in the Judaean Desert
DSD	*Dead Sea Discoveries*
EDSS	*Encyclopedia of the Dead Sea Scrolls*. Edited by Lawrence H. Schiffman and James C. VanderKam. 2 vols. New York: Oxford University Press, 2000
EHLL	*Encyclopedia of Hebrew Language and Linguistics*. Edited by Geoffrey Khan, Shmuel Bolozky, Steven E. Fassberg, Gary A. Rendsburg, Aaron D. Rubin, Ora R. Schwarzwald, and Tamar Zewi. 4 vols. Leiden: Brill, 2013.
EHPI	Études d'Histoire et de Philosophie Ireligieuses
Ekstasis	Ekstasis: Religious Experience from Antiquity to the Middle Ages
EJL	Early Judaism and its Literature
ER	*Encyclopedia of Religion*. Edited by Lindsay Jones. 2nd ed. 15 vols. Detroit: Macmillan Reference USA, 2005.
Ethnos	*Ethnos: Journal of Anthropology*
Ethos	*Ethos: Journal of the Society for Psychological Anthropology*
EvT	Evangelische Theologie
ExpTim	*Expository Times*
FAT	Forschungen zum Alten Testament
FAT2	Forschungen zum Alten Testament 2. Reihe
FRLANT	Forschungen zur Religion und Literatur des Alten und Neuen Testaments
GH	Gender & History
HALOT	*The Hebrew and Aramaic Lexicon of the Old Testament*. Ludwig Koehler, Walter Baumgartner, and Johann J. Stamm. Translated and edited under the supervision of Mervyn E. J. Richardson. 4 vols. Leiden: Brill, 1994 1999
HAU	HAU: Journal of Ethnographic Theory
HeyM	Heythrop Monographs
HistJ	*The Historical Journal*
HSM	Harvard Semitic Monographs
HT	History Today
HTR	Harvard Theological Review
HTS	Harvard Theological Studies
HUCA	Hebrew Union College Annual
IBHS	*An Introduction to Biblical Hebrew Syntax*. Bruce K. Waltke and Michael O'Connor. Winona Lake, IN: Eisenbrauns, 1990
IEJ	Israel Exploration Journal
Int	Interpretation
IOS	Israel Oriental Studies
JAAR	Journal of the American Academy of Religion
JAJSup	Journal of Ancient Judaism Supplements
JANES	The Journal of the Ancient Near Eastern Society
JAOS	Journal of the American Oriental Society

JBL	Journal of Biblical Literature
JETS	Journal of the Evangelical Theological Society
JJS	Journal of Jewish Studies
JMC	Journal of Material Culture
JPCC	Journal of Pastoral Care & Counseling
JPT	Journal of Pentecostal Theology
JPTSup	Journal of Pentecostal Theology Supplement Series
JQR	Jewish Quarterly Review
JR	Journal of Religion
JRAf	Journal of Religion in Africa
JRAI	Journal of the Royal Anthropological Institute
JRH	Journal of Religious History
JSJ	Journal for the Study of Judaism
JSJSup	Supplements to the Journal for the Study of Judaism
JSNT	Journal for the Study of the New Testament
JSNTSup	Journal for the Study of the New Testament Supplement Series
JSOT	Journal for the Study of the Old Testament
JSOTSup	Journal for the Study of the Old Testament Supplement Series
JSP	Journal for the Study of the Pseudepigrapha
JSS	Journal of Semitic Studies
JSSR	Journal for the Scientific Study of Religion
JTrauSt	Journal of Traumatic Stress
LAT	Latin America Studies
LHBOTS	Library of Hebrew Bible/Old Testament Studies
LotS	Life of the Spirit
LSTS	Library of Second Temple Studies
MHRC	Mental Health Religion & Culture
MRLLA	Magical and Religious Literature of Late Antiquity
MT	Masoretic Text
NA^{28}	*Novum Testamentum Graece*, Nestle-Aland, 28th ed.
NDAW	New Directions in Anthropological Writing
NJPS	*Tanakh: The Holy Scriptures: The New JPS Translation according to the Traditional Hebrew Text*
NovTSup	Supplements to Novum Testamentum
NovaRel	Nova Religio
NRSV	New Revised Standard Version
NTS	New Testament Studies
Numen	Numen: International Review for the History of Religions
OBO	Orbis Biblicus et Orientalis
OG	Old Greek
OTE	Old Testament Essays
OTL	Old Testament Library
OtSt	Oudtestamentische Studiën
PCNA	Psychiatric Clinics of North America
PGHI	Publications of the German Historical Institute.
PP	Past & Present
PsyT	Psychological Trauma: Theory, Research, Practice, and Policy

RB	Revue Biblique
RBL	Review of Biblical Literature
RBS	Resources for Biblical Study
RevQ	Revue de Qumran
RGRW	Religions in the Graeco-Roman World
SAM	Studies in Ancient Medicine
SAN	Studia Aarhusiana Neotestamentica
SAST	Suomen Antropologisen Seuran Toimituksia
SBL	Society of Biblical Literature
SBLDS	Society of Biblical Literature Dissertation Series
SBLSS	Society of Biblical Literature Symposium Series
SBT	Studies in Biblical Theology
SBTS	Sources for Biblical and Theological Study
SDSSRL	Studies in the Dead Sea Scrolls and Related Literature
SemeiaSt	Semeia Studies
SHR	Studies in the History of Religions
SIDA	Scripta Instituti Donneriani Aboensis
SJOT	Scandinavian Journal of the Old Testament
SJT	Scottish Journal of Theology
SPCK	Society for Promoting Christian Knowledge
SMBRH	Studies in Modern British Religious History
SSA	Seminar Studies in Anthropology
SSM	Social Science & Medicine
STDJ	Studies on the Texts of the Desert of Judah
STS	Semitic Texts and Studies
SynTh	Syndicate Theology
TBN	Themes in Biblical Narrative
TDOT	Theological Dictionary of the Old Testament. Edited by G. Johannes Botterweck and Helmer Ringgren. Translated by John T. Willis et al. 8 vols. Grand Rapids: Eerdmans, 1974–2006
TPRR	Transcultural Psychiatric Research Review
TSAJ	Texts and Studies in Ancient Judaism
UCOP	University of Cambridge Oriental Publications
VT	Vetus Testamentum
VTSup	Supplements to Vetus Testamentum
WBBC	Wiley Blackwell Bible Commentaries
WBC	Word Biblical Commentary
WM	World of Music
WO	Die Welt des Orients
WUNT	Wissenschaftliche Untersuchungen zum Neuen Testament
WUNT2	Wissenschaftliche Untersuchungen zum Neuen Testament 2. Reihe
WW	Word and World
ZAW	Zeitschrift für die Alttestamentliche Wissenschaft
ZTK	Zeitschrift für Theologie und Kirche

Textual Conventions

In writing for a scholarly but not necessarily a specialist audience, I have endeavored to provide as much technical detail about the primary texts as is necessary without obscuring the general trajectory of my main arguments. The information provided here summarizes the conventions followed in the book.

Unless otherwise noted, translations from the Hebrew Bible and New Testament are based on the NRSV. Where I modify a translation, I provide the NRSV rendering in a footnote.

In texts where the versification between the NRSV and Masoretic Text differ, I use the MT.

I include Hebrew words and phrases in parentheses that are pertinent to the discussion and include diacritical marks only when they are relevant to my argument.

I use "OG" (short for Old Greek) to refer to the ancient Jewish translations of the texts of the Hebrew Bible into Greek (sometimes referred to as the Septuagint or LXX).

For translations of the Dead Sea Scrolls and other Second Temple Jewish literature, I provide citation information at the first occurrence. Hebrew characters that appear within brackets are missing from the document. Those appearing under a small circle are damaged. Both are reconstructed in the cited sources.

Finally, throughout this book I render the tetragrammaton in English using the traditional "the LORD." In Hebrew, I use [ה׳].

Acknowledgments

This book would not have come together without assistance from several generous institutions and advice from an array of wise people.

First, I am grateful for grants from Harvard Divinity School, the Episcopal Church Foundation, the Fulbright Scholar Program, and the Louisville Institute, which helped fund my research and writing. Saint Peter's Episcopal Church in Cambridge also invested openhandedly in me during the two years that I served there as a teaching priest while completing my degree.

What a blessing it has been to have landed at United Lutheran Seminary. My faculty colleagues, administrators, and coworkers have cheerfully supported me in this project since my hiring. In particular, Kyle Schiefelbein-Guerrero and Evan Boyd read portions of a late version of the manuscript and provided valuable feedback. Additionally, the library staff of ULS has been a treasure, working miracles in the midst of a pandemic to get me the resources I needed. I am especially thankful also to the students who took my elective course "Spirit(s), Angels, and Demons in the Bible" and from whom I learned so much.

In addition to financial and research support, this project has also benefited from comments and suggestions collected from several conferences and workshops where I have presented my works in progress. These venues included three sections of the Society of Biblical Literature: Religious Experience in Antiquity, Philology in Hebrew Studies, and Contextual Biblical Interpretation. Additionally, the Society for Pentecostal Studies has heard several different parts of this project, and each presentation was followed by constructive and spirited discussion. Further, two Harvard workshops—Hebrew Bible and Jewish Studies—helped me find clarity around my research question at early stages. It is impossible to choose which Harvard courses contributed the most toward this book, but I must mention a New Testament seminar on spirit possession taught by Giovanni Bazzana. I am indebted also to Nathan MacDonald and Paul Michael Kurtz for the feedback they provided me when I shared a portion of this book in the Old Testament Seminar at the University of Cambridge.

Three phenomenal editors helped me get this manuscript done: Aaron Sanborn-Overby at De Gruyter patiently pushed me through, Carol Wise's careful copyediting improved every page, and Evan Christensen was an adept research assistant, wrangling bibliographic software and helping me assemble the index. If it is true that the devil is in the details, I have benefited from the best editorial exorcists.

Several others read large sections of this book and provided me with invaluable critiques. These include Anne Monius (whom I will always remember as a remarkable teacher and intellectual), Andrew Teeter, Giovanni Bazzana, and Carol Newsom. Each has left a particular mark on me as an academic and as a person. Special recognition is due also to Jack Levison, who has been an especially encouraging and productive dialogue partner over the course of this project. In particular, I am grateful that Jack invited me to submit my manuscript for publication with De Gruyter in the Ekstasis series; I could not think of a better place to share this work.

We do not always get to call our classmates our friends and mean it, but that is my good fortune. For their camaraderie and humor, as well as for reading some of my worst ideas and graciously sharing their much better ones, I am grateful to Nicholas Schaser, Eric Jarrard, and Ethan Schwartz. Also, it needs to be said in print that I do not deserve a teacher and friend as generous as Matthew Rasure, whose considerable insights are scattered throughout this book.

The dissertation upon which this book is based was written under the direction of Jon Levenson. Teaching and researching with not only skill and confidence but also integrity and humility, Jon is a model for the kind of scholar I strive to become.

Personal acknowledgments are due to my family, especially to my parents, Rodney and Melody Carlson (my first and best teachers), and to my sister, Allyson Martinez (my first classmate and often a teacher, too). My son, Anthony Carlson, was born while I was writing my dissertation, and he continued to inspire me as I revised it for this book. I cannot say he has always made writing easy, but he has made it worth it. Finally, my spouse, Britta Meiers Carlson, has been my generous teammate and a critical interlocutor. I am blessed in having her as both a beloved partner and a vocational companion. I doubt there is single idea in this book that I did not test on her first, and she has always responded tirelessly with encouragement, sound judgment, and so much love.

This book is dedicated to the memory of my grandmothers. Having grown up a fifth-generation Pentecostal Christian through both my parents, I thought that I was journeying far from my roots when I became an Episcopal priest and started a doctorate in divinity school. Yet here is a book I have written about spirits and the Bible—just like Marguerite and Gracy taught me.

Despite the significant support and advice that I have received from those named here and others I have missed, mistakes and shortcomings remain in this book, and these are entirely my own. Likewise, for anything in this project that is commendable, exhortative, or true—

—לא לנו [ה׳] לא לנו כי־לשמך תן כבוד

Reed Carlson
Season after Pentecost 2021
Saint Paul, Minnesota

1 The Ghost of a Self

1.1 A Murder in Brookfield, Connecticut

The first recorded modern murder in rural Brookfield, Connecticut, occurred during the early evening on February 16, 1981. Nineteen-year-old Arne Cheyenne Johnson reportedly stabbed and killed Alan Bono on the lawn of a kennel business. To the police who arrested Johnson several hours after the event, the case seemed unambiguous: Allegedly, the two men had been arguing about Johnson's girlfriend, Deborah Glatzel, who rented an apartment from Bono. Early reports of the incident summarized that both men had been drinking heavily and things had apparently gotten out of hand. A few days after the murder, however, a different account took shape: By the time of the trial, the defendant, his family, and several priests from the Catholic Diocese of Bridgeport claimed that Johnson had been possessed by the devil at the time of the killing, and their lawyer intended to argue it in defense.[1] With this, the case became a potential enigma in United States legal history. It also captured the imaginations of enthusiasts of the supernatural around the world.

According to reporters who had interviewed members of the Glatzel family, the possession had started nearly a year earlier, yet not with Johnson but with Deborah's eleven-year-old brother. The boy had reportedly exhibited several of the conspicuous behaviors Western Christians have associated with demon possession for centuries, including spasms, an altered voice, disproportionate strength, and visions of demons. The family had previously enlisted the help of several Catholic priests from their local diocese in what reporters called "lesser exorcisms."[2] In the months after the murder, the Glatzel family provided re-

---

1 Julie Stagis, "Killer's Defense Was Demon Possession," *Hartford Courant*, 12 April 2014, https://www.courant.com/news/connecticut/hc-250-arne-johnson-20140412-story.html; Dudley Clendinen, "Defendant in a Murder Puts the Devil on Trial," *New York Times*, 23 March 1981, http://www.nytimes.com/1981/03/23/nyregion/defendant-in-a-murder-puts-the-devil-on-trial.html?pagewanted=all; and Lynn Darling, "By Demons Possessed," *Washington Post*, 13 September 1981, https://www.washingtonpost.com/archive/lifestyle/1981/09/13/by-demons-possessed/3479fa6b-eee3-4233-a2fc-b9defa403504/. More recently see, Jesse Leavenworth, "Was the 12-year-old Connecticut Boy Featured in 'Conjuring 3' Really possessed? His Brother Says "No" –and the True Horror Story has been his Family's Exploitation," *Hartford Courant*, 2 June 2021, https://www.courant.com/news/connecticut/hc-news-ct-demon-defense-conjuring-3-glatzel-20210602-bmugjsuihndixog222mub2lfaa-story.html.
2 Darling, "By Demons Possessed." A formal exorcism required the authorization of a bishop, which was never given.

porters with several photographs of these rituals, including one in which Johnson held a crucifix to the prostrate boy's forehead, and another in which the crucifix lay broken on the floor while Johnson appeared to be holding the boy down. On at least one of these occasions, Johnson had reportedly challenged a demon to leave the boy and enter him instead, a transfer that the family came to believe eventually took place. All three witnesses to the murder—Johnson's two younger sisters and his girlfriend, Deborah—claimed that Johnson had also showed signs of demon possession in the weeks leading up to the murder. His actions in that moment were therefore not his own.

It did not take long for the remarkable story to gain international attention. Even before the murder, the Glatzel family had enlisted the help of self-proclaimed demonologists Ed and Lorraine Warren, who had made their careers as authors and lecturers on the paranormal. They later helped publicize the case (in the process, speeding sales of their then recent book). Johnson's volunteer attorney, Martin Minnella, elevated international curiosity in the case by publicly announcing his intent to plead "demon possession" as a formal defense in court. As Minnella explained: "The courts have dealt with the existence of God; now they're going to have to deal with the existence of the Devil [sic]."[3]

Minnella's grand theological vision for the case never manifested, however. Within days of the murder, the Catholic diocese stopped commenting publicly on the case. The judge eventually disallowed the demonic possession defense on the grounds that it was unprovable and thus irrelevant. A jury eventually found Johnson guilty of manslaughter, implying that he did not intend to murder Bono but only to injure him. Johnson was sentenced to ten-to-twenty years but served only five. He and Deborah Glatzel eventually married and remained out of the media spotlight.

Despite its anticlimactic conclusion, the case has proven enduringly popular, spawning several books and magazine stories.[4] Based on the events, a made-for-TV movie was aired by NBC in 1983 and Warner Bros. distributed a large budget horror film in 2021.[5] In a recent *Hartford Courant* story revisiting

---

[3] Clendinen, "Devil on Trial."
[4] Lynne Baranski, "In a Connecticut Murder Trial, Will (Demonic) Possession Prove Nine-Tenths of the Law?," *People*, 26 October 1981, https://people.com/archive/in-a-connecticut-murder-trial-will-demonic-possession-prove-nine-tenths-of-the-law-vol-16-no-17/; and Gerald Brittle, *The Devil in Connecticut* (Bantam, 1983).
[5] William Hale, *The Demon Murder Case* (Len Steckler Productions, Dick Clark Productions, 1983) and Michael Chaves, *The Conjuring: The Devil Made Me Do It* (Warner Bros. Pictures 2021).

the case, the attorney, Minnella, maintained his belief in Johnson's demonic possession at the time of the murder.[6]

Like so many modern accounts of contemporary spirit possession, the case of Arne Johnson exhibits familiar characteristics from generations of Western experience with demons, devils, and their misdeeds in the bodies of humans. The descriptions of the young Glatzel boy as communicating in multiple voices, levitating, cursing, and speaking presciently are as at home in accounts of spirit possession in late antiquity as they are in cable television's late-night pseudo-documentaries on the paranormal. The boy's visions of the devil as a hoofed, hairy old man who spoke Latin might just as easily have been relayed by a medieval-era cloistered mystic as by a New England adolescent in the same year as the release of *Raiders of the Lost Ark*. Further, echoes of the New Testament gospels can be heard in this story: The transfer of demonic presence from the boy to Arne is reminiscent of Jesus's expulsion of the demons into swine (Matt 8:28–34/Mark 5:1–20/Luke 8:26–39). The Glatzel boy's violent episodes parallel those of demonized figures in the gospels (e.g., Matt 17:14–21/Mark 9:14–29/Luke 9:37–43).

Certainly, the circumstances surrounding the murder and subsequent court case remain exceptional, but the descriptors at play in this story of spirit possession perpetuate a conventional set of ideas concerning the phenomenon. These attributes remain consistent across similar episodes in North American culture even today—especially among conservative Catholics, Evangelicals, and Pentecostals.[7] Thus, a good deal of what makes the possession of Arne Johnson remarkable is not so much its supernatural aspects as the collision of these strong undercurrents in popular Western demonology with a modern legal system—an institution that found them completely unintelligible.

---

6 Leavenworth, "Was the 12-year-old Connecticut Boy Featured in 'Conjuring 3' Really possessed?"

7 A 2013 poll of 1,000 people living in the United States showed that 57% believed in the existence of the devil and that 51% believed "someone can be possessed by the devil or some other evil spirit." These numbers were highest among "born-again" Christians (devil 86%, possession 72%). Katie Jagel, "Half of Americans Believe in Possession by the Devil," *YouGov*, 17 September 2013, https://today.yougov.com/topics/lifestyle/articles-reports/2013/09/17/half-americans-believe-possession-devil. A 2020 survey of more than 17,000 adults living in the United States found that about half believed that demons exist and about 46% believed in ghosts. Jaimie Ballard, "About Half of Americans Believe Ghosts and Demons Exist," *YouGov*, 30 October 2020, https://today.yougov.com/topics/philosophy/articles-reports/2020/10/30/ghosts-demons-exist-poll-data. For a sociological study of contemporary belief and practices of these phenomena, see Tanya M. Luhrmann, *When God Talks Back: Understanding the American Evangelical Relationship with God* (New York: Vintage Books, 2012).

In this way, the case poignantly illustrates a significant shift in the modern Western imagination concerning spirit phenomena, and it is one that will come under examination throughout this book. Put simply, it was not so long ago that being "possessed by the devil" in a New England court of law was grounds for capital punishment.[8] Yet at some point between colonial Salem and 1980s Connecticut, the same phenomenon came to be seen by some as precisely the opposite: a line of legal defense. As Johnson's attorney, Martin Minnella, remarked to a reporter, "I could put the pope on and he'd tell you that if a guy is demonically possessed, he is not responsible [for his actions]."[9]

The fact that this shift occurred even among those who maintained a belief in the reality of spirit possession demonstrates that more had changed than simply a greater public understanding of the workings of the natural world. Norms around human moral agency, expectations of what constitutes a spirit phenomenon, and conventions about how such things might be recognized had also shifted.

For many laypeople and scholars alike, stories of spirit phenomena like that of Arne Johnson remain some of the most chilling, yet bizarrely fascinating human experiences portrayed in literature. Premodern exorcisms, witch trials, and themes from gothic horror fiction are reliable workhorses in the bookstores and box offices of popular Western culture. The stories gathered and retold under these banners are often intentionally grotesque and/or exploitatively exotic. In academic circles, spirit possession falls within the purview of multiple fields, including history, theology, the study of religion, literary and critical theory, cultural anthropology, and psychology, but the findings of each are not usually shared in interdisciplinary settings. Even among scholars—particularly in the nineteenth and early twentieth centuries—there existed and still persists a temptation to present studies of spirit phenomena and trance experiences as safaris into *another* world, one where the ways of being human are more primitive than what is usually accepted in mainstream Western religions and societies.

The story of the first murder in Brookfield, Connecticut, introduces several of the intersecting themes that this book explores. When we bring the story into conversation with biblical scholarship, it also stages an opportunity to evaluate spirit phenomena in biblical literature along lines other than merely mapping ancient metaphysics and myths. It invites forays into ancient as well as modern notions of the self and of religious experience. It asks how the interpretation of

---

8 I am grateful to Matthew Rasure for making this poignant observation in a private correspondence.
9 Darling, "By Demons Possessed."

biblical texts shaped expectations of spirit phenomena in antiquity and how it still does so today. In this way, a sensational story like the Brookfield murder is helpful for commencing our topic since it embodies so many of the stereotypes readers may assume when encountering a project that concerns spirit possession. The Hebrew Bible actually presents us with very few figures like Arne Johnson, the Glatzel family, and their devil, but it nevertheless contains an expansive and diverse array of phenomena that fit the label of spirit possession. In order to recognize these texts, however, it will be necessary to expand the standard conceptions of spirit possession beyond this familiar template.[10]

1.2 Argument

The central argument of this book addresses a straightforward question: Does the Hebrew Bible depict possession and other similar spirit phenomena?[11] I will demonstrate that it does—though rarely within those paradigms prioritized by Christian tradition and Western intellectual history. I have chosen to focus specifically on the literature of the Hebrew Bible, because so many interpreters have assumed Christian models of spirit phenomena to be a kind of norm or *telos* (e.g., demonic exorcisms and Holy Spirit baptism) when reading the Old Testament. Thus, spirit language and rituals in the Hebrew Bible and in Second Temple Jewish literature have habitually been interpreted as underdeveloped or even anti-pneumatic.[12] These misinterpretations have been offered both by those who

---

[10] This paradigm for spirit possession has been helpfully deconstructed and/or reevaluated by historians and scholars of religion, especially by those who study historic forms of witchcraft and medieval mysticism. See, for example, Stuart Clark, *Thinking with Demons: The Idea of Witchcraft in Early Modern Europe* (Oxford: Oxford University Press, 1999); Nancy Mandeville Caciola, *Discerning Spirits: Divine and Demonic Possession in the Middle Ages* (Cornell University Press, 2015). See also the seminal work Michael T. Taussig, *The Devil and Commodity Fetishism in South America* (Chapel Hill: University of North Carolina Press, 1980).

[11] For this project, I generally prefer the term "Hebrew Bible." However, I endeavor to use "Old Testament" when discussing Christian theological interpretation specifically and "Tanakh" when discussing a postbiblical Jewish faith tradition. See the methodological comments in Jon D. Levenson, "The Hebrew Bible, the Old Testament, and Historical Criticism," in *The Hebrew Bible, the Old Testament, and Historical Criticism: Jews and Christians in Biblical Studies* (Louisville: Westminster John Knox, 1993), 1–32.

[12] Much of the field is currently undergoing a paradigm shift regarding the use of terms like "Bible," "biblical," and "scripture," especially as they relate to Second Temple Judaism. Many texts were treated as scripture in early Judaism and not all of them were included in what we now call the Hebrew Bible. Moreover, the contents of these texts were remarkably fluid and did not achieve a fixed state until well after the Second Temple period. See, for example,

wish to characterize the Old Testament as existing on an inevitable theological trajectory leading into the New Testament, and those pushing against such readings.

The current project overcomes this impasse by utilizing an interdisciplinary method informed by the study of religion, cultural anthropology, and ethnography. Adopting an uncommon but not unprecedented approach in biblical studies, I compare the Hebrew Bible and the literature of early Judaism with ethnographic studies of contemporary possession-practicing communities around the world and, in particular, from the global south and its diasporas. By means of these comparisons, my research reveals a different portrait of possession and other spirit phenomena in the Hebrew Bible. For instance, rather than being practiced individually, spirit possession in many places around the world is corporate. This is in fact how it most regularly appears in early Jewish literature. Likewise, we may expect spirit possession to be an unexpected and regrettable occasion in the lives of those who endure it. Although that description frequently suits an initial experience of spirit possession, many practitioners today are taught to compromise and collaborate with their spirit(s), eventually coming to cultivate possession as an intentional religious practice. Whereas the historic Western fascination with the self as an autonomous, "self-possessed" free agent has helped to generate the stereotype of the spirit-possessed person as out of control and thus morally and rationally compromised. Both in practice today and in the Hebrew Bible, the experiences of a spirit-influenced person encompass a far more varied array of possibilities for conceptualizing the relationship between a "host" and "spirit." Indeed, the complete suspension of a host's personality is often taken as evidence that something has gone very wrong in spirit possession.

Including ethnographic comparative data provides an informative perspective on spirit phenomena from outside biblical studies. With it, we can better measure and account for the considerable degree to which conventional inter-

---

Molly Zahn, *Genres of Rewriting in Second Temple Judaism: Scriptural Composition and Transmission* (Cambridge: Cambridge University Press, 2020); Eva Mroczek, *The Literary Imagination in Jewish Antiquity* (Oxford: Oxford University Press, 2015); Reinhard G. Kratz, *Historical and Biblical Israel: The History, Tradition, and Archives of Israel and Judah* (Oxford: Oxford University Press, 2015); and D. Andrew Teeter, "The Hebrew Bible and/as Second Temple Literature: Methodological Reflections," *DSD* 20.3 (2013): 349–77. Reflective of this trend, my comparative analysis in this book includes extrabiblical Second Temple Jewish texts and recognizes that many current distinctions between these literatures were not yet operative within the communities that composed them. Thus, the spirit phenomena that I identify in the Hebrew Bible are not different in kind from those found in other early Jewish literature.

pretations of spirit phenomena in biblical texts have been moralized and theologized in interpretive traditions both ancient and modern. This aspect of the book will prove especially useful when examining certain theological approaches to understanding these texts, approaches that have proven influential beyond the Protestant intellectual traditions in which they were first promulgated.

A final goal of this project is to account for the profoundly material nature of spirit possession without artificially reducing it through biomedical or other means. Following the anthropological literature, my research suggests that spirit possession in the Bible can be mapped as one of many ellipses in a Venn diagram, which partially overlaps with the circles representing other phenomena including mental health, medicine, addiction, performance, and myth. It is crucial to recognize, however, that no single circle in such a diagram completely encompasses any of the others. Instead, I demonstrate a number of other functions for spirit texts in the Hebrew Bible that do not attempt to "explain away" its complexity. These include expounding spirit possession primarily as a *system of communication* that is utilized to convey a wide range of human experiences.[13]

1.3 Terminology

Since phrases like "spirit possession" have been used variously and sometimes uncritically, it will be helpful to clarify my terminology in this book. Put clinically, the study of spirit possession (sometimes called "possession studies") is the anthropological, ethnographic, and psychological research of altered or unusual states of consciousness (i.e., ASCs).[14] The field focuses on cultures where these states and their associated behaviors are understood as the result of the influence of one or more other personalities. Anthropologists have recognized multiple forms of spirit possession in cultures around the world:

---

[13] The language of a "system of communication" comes from the work of Michael Lambek. See, for example, Michael Lambek, "From Disease to Discourse: Remarks on the Conceptualization of Trance and Spirit Possession," in *Altered States of Consciousness and Mental Health: A Cross Cultural Perspective*, ed. Colleen Ward, CCRM 12 (London: Sage, 1989), 56–57. See more on this below.

[14] On ASCs, see Etzel Cardeña and Michael Winkelman, *Altering Consciousness: Multidisciplinary Perspectives*, 2 vols. (Santa Barbara: Praeger, 2011). There is a risk when using a term like "altered state of consciousness" of normalizing Western notions of awareness and thereby inferring that modes from other cultures are somehow inherently aberrant. In contrast, I use the term here not normatively but as a way of signaling how these phenomena have been understood and studied in fields outside of biblical studies.

> The highest incidence is found in Pacific cultures and the lowest in North and South American Indian cultures. Belief in possession is widespread among peoples of Eurasia, Africa, and the circum-Mediterranean region and among descendants of Africans in the Americas. It occurs more frequently in agricultural societies than in hunting and gathering ones, and women seem to be possessed more often than men.[15]

The term thus extensively overlaps with another used in the anthropological study of religion, "trance," which is sometimes used synonymously with ASC. However, not all trance is spirit possession. Rather, a trance state is typically labeled "spirit possession" when it is indigenously understood as the result of the influence of one or more other personalities, usually a spirit/deity or a deceased ancestor.

Although conventional and relatively simple, this breakdown has proven problematic. Since the eighteenth century, the term "possession" has been integrated into an influential Western paradigm for spirit phenomena that is wrapped up with broader ideas about property, borders, and free will. These ideas do not usually transfer easily into the ancient texts where the term is frequently applied. For example, the Greek term in the New Testament most commonly translated into English as "demon possession," δαιμονίζομαι, is more precisely "being demonized."[16]

The anthropologist Paul Christopher Johnson has explained how modern notions of property came to be associated with spirit possession: For much of the eighteenth through twentieth centuries, anthropologists and scholars of religion operated with a conception of spirit possession that depended on the Enlightenment idea that each person was a kind of economic property that could be possessed by the self or another.[17] The spirit-influenced person, however, was not in control of their own free will and thus incapable of participating in rational religion. Such persons were a risk to society both economically and politically. These underlying assumptions persisted among early anthropologists and theorists of religion, who characterized the various practices of spirit-possession cults in the non-Western world first as "primitive" and then eventually as "uncontrolled" and "mob-like."[18] As Johnson demonstrates, these discourses were instrumental for the systems of thought that came to justify the transatlan-

---

15 Vincent Crapanzano, "Spirit Possession: An Overview," *ER* 13:8687.
16 See the discussion in Giovanni B. Bazzana, *Having the Spirit of Christ: Spirit Possession and Exorcism in the Early Christ Groups* (New Haven: Yale University Press, 2020), 29–31.
17 Paul C. Johnson, "Toward an Atlantic Genealogy of 'Spirit Possession,'" in *Spirited Things: The Work of "Possession" in Afro-Atlantic Religions*, ed. Paul C. Johnson (Chicago: University of Chicago Press, 2014), 23–45.
18 Johnson, "Toward an Atlantic Genealogy," 40.

tic slave trade. Although the various phenomena we call spirit possession today had existed for centuries in Europe, intellectuals developed a framework for possession that characterized it as a supposedly unique feature of the colonized world, where people were possessable, either by spirits or by individual, self-possessed, European men. Johnson's critique thus challenges many of the assumptions about spirit possession inherent in Western scholarship, of which traditional biblical studies is a part. It follows that were I to rely solely on the conventional tools of European biblical studies in this book, my ability to understand how spirit phenomena were depicted in ancient Israelite and early Jewish literature would be severely limited.

A significant risk of utilizing the term spirit possession today is reproducing the morally reprehensible intellectual genealogy that popularized it. But there are compelling reasons to expand and situate the definition of spirit possession rather than exorcise it altogether. First, as Bazzana has demonstrated, spirit possession was already associated with notions of slavery in antiquity.[19] Early modern theorists thus did not invent the association of spirit phenomena with property; they systematized it and put it on a trajectory useful to capitalism. Second, as Michael Lambek illustrates in his response to Johnson, inscribed into the term "spirit possession" is a productive ambiguity.[20] While conventionally understood as *being possessed by a spirit*, the term can also refer to instances of *people possessing spirits*. The elegant vagueness of who is influencing whom in such a relationship reveals how this phrase is remarkably apt for describing the complex subjectivity we see in many instances of spirit phenomena both ancient and modern, as I demonstrate throughout this book.

Conscious of these ethical stakes, I use the term "spirit possession" selectively and treat it as one of many examples of spirit phenomena found in the Hebrew Bible and Second Temple literature. Both in contemporary practice around the world and in the Hebrew Bible, we find a broad spectrum of spirit phenomena, including those better characterized as spirit *collaboration, confluence, consultation*, and *conflict*.[21] Thus, to use the term spirit possession in the conventional

---

[19] One example can be found in Bazzana's discussion of the fifth similitude of the Shepherd of Hermas, *Having the Spirit of Christ*, 127–32. See also, for example, Acts 16:16–18.
[20] Michael Lambek, "Afterword: Recognizing and Misrecognizing Spirit Possession," in *Spirited Things: The Work of "Possession" in Afro-Atlantic Religions*, ed. Paul C. Johnson (Chicago: University of Chicago Press, 2014), 257–76. See also Bazzana, *Having the Spirit of Christ*, 17.
[21] The inadequacy of this terminology (and the limits of the idea of "possession" in particular) has been recognized by anthropologists as well. See the brief but helpful discussion of terminology in Bettina E. Schmidt and Lucy Huskinson, "Introduction," in *Spirit Possession and Trance:*

sense would be too narrow. Yet, to avoid speaking of spirit possession altogether is to avoid grappling with the role that the term has played in characterizing spirit phenomena in the study of religion and biblical studies and to forfeit a productive premodern framework for understanding the relationship between the self and the Other in spirit phenomena experiences.

1.4 Methods

The approach herein adopted is not necessarily novel. Biblical scholars have routinely (if not always productively) engaged with cultural anthropology and ethnography, even in the study of spirit phenomena. Robert Wilson's 1980 *Prophecy and Society in Ancient Israel* stands as a highly influential example.[22] In this investigation into the social world of the prophets, Wilson made use of some of the foremost scholars on spirit possession and trance of his day, including works by Ioan Lewis and Erika Bourguignon.[23] Crucially, however, while many anthropologists and ethnographers have since moved on from the structural-functional approach adopted by Wilson, biblical scholars have yet to produce a similarly updated treatment of spirit phenomena in the Bible.

Other standout predecessors deserve mention. Comparative work on notions of spirits, divination, and prophecy in other ancient Semitic cultures has better equipped the field to recognize similar phenomena in the Hebrew Bible.[24] In ad-

---

New Interdisciplinary Perspectives, ed. Bettina E. Schmidt and Lucy Huskinson (New York: Continuum, 2011), 1–15.

[22] Robert R. Wilson, *Prophecy and Society in Ancient Israel* (Philadelphia: Fortress Press, 1980). See also Robert R. Wilson, "Prophecy and Ecstasy: A Reexamination," *JBL* 98.3 (1979): 321–37.

[23] Ioan M. Lewis, *Ecstatic Religion: A Study of Shamanism and Spirit Possession*, 3rd ed. (New York: Routledge, 2003); 1st ed. (London: Penguin, 1971); and Erika Bourguignon, "The Self, the Behavioral Environment, and the Theory of Spirit Possession," in *Context and Meaning in Cultural Anthropology*, ed. Melford E. Spiro (New York: Free Press, 1965), 39–60.

[24] E.g., Lester L. Grabbe, "Shaman, Preacher, or Spirit Medium?: The Israelite Prophet in the Light of Anthropological Models," in *Prophecy and the Prophets in Ancient Israel*, ed. John Day, LHBOTS 531 (New York: T & T Clark, 2010), 117–32; "Daniel: Sage, Seer … and Prophet?," in *Constructs of Prophecy in the Former & Latter Prophets & Other Texts*, ed. Lester L. Grabbe and Martti Nissinen, ANEM 4 (Atlanta: SBL Press, 2011), 87–94; Martti Nissinen, ed., *Prophecy in Its Ancient Near Eastern Context: Mesopotamian, Biblical, and Arabian Perspectives*, SBLSS 13 (Atlanta: SBL Press, 2000); *Ancient Prophecy: Near Eastern, Biblical, and Greek Perspectives* (Oxford: Oxford University Press, 2017); Ingrid Lilly, "Rûaḥ Embodied: Job's Internal Disease from the Perspective of Mesopotamian Medicine," in *Borders: Terminologies, Ideologies, and Performances*, ed. Annette Weissenrieder, WUNT 366 (Tübingen: Mohr Siebeck, 2016), 323–36; and "Conceptualizing Spirit: Supernatural Meteorology and Winds of Distress in the Hebrew Bible

dition, Pentecostal interpreters and biblical scholars from the global south often exhibit an exceptional sensitivity to spirit phenomena in biblical texts that other researchers operating outside of these contexts may sometimes lack.[25]

The minor resurgence of interest in spirit phenomena among some scholars of New Testament and early Christianity is perhaps the most methodologically relevant precedent for this book. Pieter Craffert, Colleen Shantz, and Troels Engberg-Pedersen have all addressed the subject.[26] Most recent is Giovanni Bazzana's *Having the Spirit of Christ: Spirit Possession and Exorcism in the Early Christ Groups*.[27] Although Bazzana's approach to reading the literature is similar to my own in his use of ethnographic data and philological study, his book has different aims.[28] *Having the Spirit of Christ* is largely diachronic, charting the earliest traditions about Jesus of Nazareth as a spirit-possessed exorcist, recovering Paul's own understanding of spirit possession, and reconstructing the possession practices of the early Pauline communities. My project is more synchronic in nature, focusing on the depiction of spirit phenomena in the Hebrew Bible and tracing how these traditions were later interpreted.

Even with these invaluable predecessors, integrating ethnographic data about possession studies into a book focused on biblical literature introduces

---

and the Ancient Near East," in *Sibyls, Scriptures, and Scrolls: John Collins at Seventy*, ed. Joel Baden, Hindy Najman, and Eibert Tigchelaar, 2 vols., 2018, 826–44. See also Irmtraud Fischer, *Gotteskünderinnen: zu einer geschlechterfairen Deutung des Phänomens der Prophetie und der Prophetinnen in der Hebräischen Bibel* (Stuttgart: Kohlhammer, 2002); and Vicente Dobroruka, *Second Temple Pseudepigraphy: A Cross-Cultural Comparison of Apocalyptic Texts and Related Jewish Literature*, Ekstasis 4 (Berlin: De Gruyter, 2014).

25 Veli-Matti Kärkkäinen, Kirsteen Kim, and Amos Yong, eds., *Interdisciplinary and Religio-Cultural Discourses on a Spirit-Filled World: Loosing the Spirits* (New York: Palgrave Macmillan, 2013); Kirsteen Kim, *The Holy Spirit in the World: A Global Conversation* (London: SPCK, 2007). See also Graham H. Twelftree, *Jesus the Exorcist: A Contribution to the Study of the Historical Jesus*, WUNT2 54 (Tübingen: Mohr Siebeck, 1993); Lee Roy Martin, *The Unheard Voice of God: A Pentecostal Hearing of the Book of Judges*, JPTSup 32 (Blandford Forum: Deo, 2008); Craig S. Keener, "Spirit Possession as a Cross-Cultural Experience," *BBR* 20.2 (2010): 215–35; and Gordon D. Fee, *God's Empowering Presence: The Holy Spirit in the Letters of Paul* (Peabody: Hendrickson, 2009).

26 Pieter F. Craffert, *The Life of a Galilean Shaman: Jesus of Nazareth in Anthropological-Historical Perspective*, Matrix 3 (Eugene: Cascade Books, 2008); Colleen Shantz, *Paul in Ecstasy: The Neurobiology of the Apostle's Life and Thought* (Cambridge: Cambridge University Press, 2009); and Troels Engberg-Pedersen, *Cosmology and Self in the Apostle Paul: The Material Spirit* (Oxford: Oxford University Press, 2010).

27 Bazzana, *Having the Spirit of Christ*.

28 See Reed Carlson, "Review of Bazzana, Giovanni B. Having the Spirit of Christ: Spirit Possession and Exorcism in the Early Christ Groups," *Pneuma* 42.2 (2020): 269–71.

a host of methodological challenges. Below I discuss four elements of my approach in this book.

1.4.1 Spirit Phenomena Before Christianity

One significant emphasis of this book is correcting a trend that has affected many studies of spirit phenomena in biblical literature for the past 150 years. For much of the twentieth century, studies of the diverse spirit phenomena portrayed in ancient Israelite and early Jewish texts have consistently served Christian pneumatological interests.[29] In these programs, spirit phenomena in the Hebrew Bible and Second Temple Jewish literature can sometimes be categorized according to whether or not they anticipate later notions of a Holy Spirit (usually if they are positive or originate from God) or demon possession (usually if they are negative or if they originate from a source other than God).[30] Modes of spirit phenomena that do not fit easily into either of these categories are thus often underemphasized or overlooked altogether.

In adhering to this characterization, twentieth century scholars continued a strategy that had been programmatic since Hermann Gunkel's influential *Die Wirkungen des Heiligen Geistes* (*The Influence of the Holy Spirit*), initially published in 1888.[31] Although readers are more likely to associate Gunkel with the

---

[29] Scholars pursuing this strategy do not always state it so clearly but the ideas most useful to Christian theological interests are often the fruits of their labor. See, for example, Norman H. Snaith, *Distinctive Ideas of the Old Testament* (Eugene: Wipf and Stock, 2009), 143–58; 1st ed. (London: Epworth, 1944); Marie E. Isaacs, *The Concept of Spirit: A Study of Pneuma in Hellenistic Judaism and Its Bearing on the New Testament*, HeyM 1 (London: Heythrop College, 1976); Wilf Hildebrandt, *An Old Testament Theology of the Spirit of God* (Peabody: Hendrickson, 1995); Wonsuk Ma, *Until the Spirit Comes: The Spirit of God in the Book of Isaiah* (London: Bloomsbury, 2009); and William VanGemeren and Andrew Abernethy, "The Spirit and the Future: A Canonical Approach," in *Presence, Power, and Promise: The Role of the Spirit of God in the Old Testament*, ed. David G. Firth and Paul D. Wegner (Downers Grove: IVP Academic 2011), 321–45.

[30] For example, the seminal, six-volume *Anchor Bible Dictionary* has no entry on "spirits" or "spirit possession" but instead has one entry on the "Holy Spirit" supplemented by various other entries like "Demons," and "Evil," as well as on specific figures like "Devil" and "Satan." David Noel Freedman, *ABD*, 6 vols. (New York: Doubleday, 1992). The more recent *Dictionary of Deities and Demons in the Bible* includes an entry on the "Holy Spirit" but separate entries for "Evil Spirit of God" and "Unclean Spirits." See comments in P. Kyle McCarter Jr., "Evil Spirit of God," *DDD*, 319–20.

[31] Hermann Gunkel, *Die Wirkungen des heiligen Geistes, nach der populären Anschauung der apostolischen Zeit und nach der Lehre des Apostels Paulus: eine biblisch-theologische Studie* (Göttingen: Vandenhoeck & Ruprecht, 1888). The work was reprinted with a new preface in 1899 and

History of Religion(s) School or with Form Criticism than with studies of spirit phenomena, this book, Gunkel's first published work, was well-known within his lifetime. Its most significant contribution was to reorient the scholarly task toward what he called the "influences" or "effects" (*Wirkungen*) of spirit experience, rather than the abstract or ontological nature of the Holy Spirit.[32] Reflective of many Protestant biblical scholars of his era, however, Gunkel carried out this program with added layers of anti-Jewish prejudice.

In particular, Gunkel went beyond simply using Christian frameworks to shape his discussion of pre-Christian texts: he also sought to equate spirit phenomena in the Old and New Testaments, while differentiating both from the supposedly intervening Judaism, which he characterized as spiritually dry and anti-pneumatic:

> At the very outset of our investigation we see that Judaism distinguished itself from ancient Israel and from the Christian community by the fact that it produced no or, stated more cautiously, only very few pneumatic phenomena. In essence, then, we are compelled to construct our analogies to New Testament ideas from the Old Testament.[33]

To be sure, Gunkel did not invent this mischaracterization of early Judaism, but he successfully adapted it in an era that notably saw the wider dissemination of Second Temple Jewish literature.[34] The caricature of late Second Temple Judaism

---

again in 1909. Unless otherwise noted, quotations are from *The Influence of the Holy Spirit: According to the Popular View of the Apostolic Age and the Teaching of the Apostle Paul: A Biblical-Theological Study*, trans. Roy A. Harrisville and Philip A. Quanbeck II (Philadelphia: Fortress Press, 1979). See also Clint Tibbs, *Religious Experience of the Pneuma: Communication with the Spirit World in 1 Corinthians 12 and 14*, WUNT2 230 (Tübingen: Mohr Siebeck, 2007), 77–80 and Werner Klatt, *Hermann Gunkel. zu seiner Theologie der Religionsgeschichte und zur Entstehung der formgeschichtlichen Methode*, FRLANT 100 (Göttingen: Vandenhoeck & Ruprecht, 1969), 17–36.

32 Gunkel, *The Influence of the Holy Spirit*, 27–30. *Die Wirkungen des Heiligen Geistes* can be seen as a significant point along a wider trend in continental—and in particular German scholarship—around the turn of the twentieth century toward studies on ecstatic and irrational religion. See Susannah Heschel, "Ecstasy Versus Ethics: The Impact of the First World War on German Biblical Scholarship on the Hebrew Prophets," in *The First World War and the Mobilization of Biblical Scholarship*, ed. Andrew Mein, Nathan MacDonald, and Matthew A. Collins, LHBOTS 676 (London: Bloomsbury, 2019), 187–206; and Suzanne L. Marchand, *German Orientalism in the Age of Empire: Religion, Race, and Scholarship*, PGHI (Cambridge: Cambridge University Press, 2009). I am grateful to Paul Michael Kurtz for sharing with me his insights on this aspect of Gunkel's work.

33 Gunkel, *The Influence of the Holy Spirit*, 21.

34 Thus, for example, Gunkel could list a sampling of spirit phenomena in works like *The Sibylline Oracles, 1 Enoch, 4 Ezra, Jubilees,* and more but could still somehow conclude that, "From

as spiritually dry was supported to some degree by a particular interpretation of certain cues in primary texts (e. g., the so-called "cessation of prophecy" in Jewish antiquity).³⁵ But it should also be seen as Gunkel's unexamined adoption of a number of assumptions of his era—ideas that he unconsciously accepted even as he unwittingly provided evidence to undermine them.

The sentiment among scholars of spirits in the Hebrew Bible remained much the same throughout the twentieth century—though with significant exceptions.³⁶ Even as studies of Second Temple Jewish literature were flowering, the majority of scholars attempted to maintain the old stereotype of an anti-pneumatic early Judaism by characterizing Second Temple era spirit texts as reflecting only fringe Judaisms. Early scholars of the Dead Sea Scrolls, for example, argued that the scrolls displayed such prominent borrowing from Persian religion—not least in their conceptions of evil beings—that the influence of earlier biblical literature's portraits of spirits could have been only marginal.³⁷ Others blamed a process of Hellenization, arguing that spirit phenomena were not authentic to early Judaism.³⁸

In more recent years, the argument that Judaism was normatively anti-spirit in the Second Temple period has been compellingly refuted by several scholars,

---

perhaps the Greek period on, this graphic view of the Spirit altogether recedes in the writings of Judaism, although it is not totally absent." Gunkel, *The Influence of the Holy Spirit*, 46–48.

35 L. Stephen Cook, *On the Question of the "Cessation of Prophecy" in Ancient Judaism*, TSAJ 145 (Tübingen: Mohr Siebeck, 2011); John R. Levison, "Did the Spirit Withdraw from Israel? An Evaluation of the Earliest Jewish Data," *NTS* 43.1 (1997): 35–57; and Frederick E Greenspahn, "Why Prophecy Ceased," *JBL* 108.1 (1989): 37–49. See also Andrew T. Abernethy, "The Spirit of God in Haggai 2:5: Prophecy as a Sign of God's Spirit," *VT* 70.4–5 (2020): 511–20

36 See a list of examples in John R. Levison, *The Holy Spirit before Christianity* (Waco: Baylor University Press, 2019), 115–16. One significant corrective to Gunkel appeared in Paul Volz, *Der Geist Gottes und die verwandten Erscheinungen im Alten Testament und im anschliessenden Judentum* (Tübingen: Mohr, 1910). *Contra* Gunkel, Volz's study highlighted the vitality of spirit phenomena and the presence of "fruits of the spirit" not just in early Judaism but in his contemporary Judaism as well.

37 See for example, Karl G. Kuhn, "Die Sektenschrift und die Iranische Religion," *ZTK* 49.3 (1952): 296–316; Shaul Shaked, "Qumran and Iran: Further Considerations," *IOS* 2 (1972): 433–46. See critiques in James Barr, "The Question of Religious Influence: The Case of Zoroastrianism, Judaism, and Christianity," *JAAR* 53.2 (1985): 201–35.

38 Though this book does not wade into debates about notions of authenticity/inauthenticity in religious studies, its conclusions do problematize any interpretive method that attempts to map which elements of a given culture may be taken as authentic and which should be seen as foreign influence. See discussion in Simon Goldhill, "What Has Alexandria to Do with Jerusalem? Writing the History of the Jews in the Nineteenth Century," *HistJ* 59.1 (2016): 125–51.

perhaps most extensively by John R. Levison.[39] Yet even Levison, who has published prodigiously on the topic of spirits in biblical and early Jewish literature over the last twenty-five years, has framed one of his most recent monographs on the topic of pre-Christian spirit phenomena according to a Christian theological category, "pneumatology."[40] This approach risks setting up spirit phenomena in early Judaism as *stops along the way* for scholarly investigation rather than as *destinations* in and of themselves.

An important recent work defying this trend is *Der Geist Gottes im Alten Testament* by Mareike Verena Blischke.[41] In many ways, Blischke's book is a welcome complement to my own, since it engages so thoroughly in mapping possible chronological developments of the concept of *rûaḥ* (spirit) through the compositional history of the Hebrew Bible—a task with which my project does not engage. In the first comprehensive redaction-critical study on this topic, Blischke begins (as I do) in the Saul stories and moves through the Hebrew Bible into select Second Temple examples. Her study does conclude with a turn toward notions of spirits in the New Testament and early Christianity, but those ideas are framed as a continuation and expansion of earlier Jewish traditions, rather than as a completion.[42]

The mistakes I have critiqued in this section have been perpetrated most often by Christians writing about pre-Christian literature. Thus, I must acknowledge that I write as an ordained Christian minister myself. While I do believe that Christian theologians can and should read the Old Testament with particular pneumatological aims, I also believe that this can be done without mischaracterizing spirit phenomena in early Jewish texts as nonexistent, fringe, or halfbaked. Such characterizations are not only inaccurate with respect to the literature and to history; they are also dangerous. For too long, the biblical idiom for describing the development of Christian pneumatological traditions out of early Judaism has been that of the spirit of the LORD departing from Saul to David (1 Sam 16:13–14; cf. 18:12). I recommend instead that the Church look to the text preferred by Peter at Pentecost—God's spirit being poured out upon all flesh (Joel 3:1 [NRSV 2:28]; Acts 2:16–17).

---

39 See especially John R. Levison, *Filled with the Spirit* (Grand Rapids: Eerdmans, 2009), 114–17; *The Spirit in First Century Judaism*, AGJU 29 (Leiden: Brill, 1997).
40 Levison, *The Holy Spirit before Christianity*. See my critique in Reed Carlson, "Review of Levison, John R. *The Holy Spirit Before Christianity*," WW 40.1 (2020): 98–99.
41 Mareike Verena Blischke, *Der Geist Gottes im Alten Testament*, FAT2 112 (Tübingen: Mohr Siebeck, 2019).
42 Blischke, *Der Geist Gottes*, 300–01.

1.4.2 Religious Experience in Antiquity

A second methodological strategy employed in this book involves the use of the term *religious experience*. As Colleen Shantz has observed, "for many years, the possibility of accessing subjective experience has been considered a theoretical misstep at best and apologetics disguised as analysis at worst."[43] Indeed, both elements, "religious" and "experience" rightly came to be suspect toward the end of the twentieth century—especially when it came to studying ancient texts: the former because it is unclear what such a word could mean in a premodern context, the latter because of the inherent ambiguity of its meaning and the problem of normalizing any particular notion of what should count as *experience*.[44] Fortunately, the prospects for research on religious experience today are no longer quite so dire as Shantz described them in 2012—especially for those who, like Shantz, are working in biblical studies.

An increasing number of scholars working on religion in antiquity have begun exploring the possible utility of the concept of religious experience, while at the same time remaining cautious of its numerous pitfalls.[45] Indeed, as the study of religion has shifted its attention toward language, sources of power, embodiment, and materiality, some commentators see new opportunities

---

[43] Colleen Shantz, "Opening the Black Box: New Prospects for Analyzing Religious Experience," in *Experientia, Volume 2: Linking Text and Experience*, ed. Colleen Shantz and Rodney A. Werline (Atlanta: SBL Press 2012), 1–15. Though more than ten years old now, see the very helpful summary in Ann Taves, *Religious Experience Reconsidered: A Building-Block Approach to the Study of Religion and Other Special Things*, (Princeton: Princeton University Press, 2009), 1–11.

[44] See Robert H. Sharf, "Experience," in *Critical Terms for Religious Studies*, ed. Mark C. Taylor (Chicago: University of Chicago Press, 1998), 94–116; and Wayne Proudfoot, *Religious Experience* (Berkeley: University of California Press, 1987). See more recently Yvonne Sherwood, "Modern Trails and Tests of 'Experience': Plastic Commonplace and Managed Exception," in *Religious Experience Revisited: Expressing the Inexpressible?*, ed. Thomas Hardtke, Ulrich Schmiedel, and Tobias Tan (Leiden: Brill, 2016), 30–56.

[45] One set of examples is the *Ekstasis* series (in which the present volume appears). See also Shantz, *Paul in Ecstasy*; Frances Flannery, Colleen Shantz, and Rodney A. Werline, eds., *Experientia, Volume 1: Inquiry into Religious Experience in Early Judaism and Christianity*, SBLSS 40 (Atlanta: SBL Press, 2008); Colleen Shantz and Rodney Werline, eds., *Experientia, Volume 2, Linking Text and Experience*, EJL 35 (Atlanta: SBL Press, 2012); Rodney A. Werline, "Assessing the Prophetic Vision and Dream Texts for Insights into Religious Experience," in *"I Lifted My Eyes and Saw": Reading Dream and Vision Reports in the Hebrew Bible*, ed. Elizabeth R. Hayes and Lena-Sofia Tiemeyer, LHBOTS 584 (London: Bloomsbury, 2014), 1–15; Maxine L Grossman, "Religious Experience and the Disciple of Imagination: Tanya Luhrmann Meets Philo and the Dead Sea Scrolls," *DSD* 22.3 (2015): 308–24; and Bazzana, *Having the Spirit of Christ*.

for the category of experience.⁴⁶ In particular, they argue that a kind of empiricism is possible when analyzing how the presence and activity of gods and spirits become real in communities of people. Thus, analyzing the literary presentations of spirit phenomena brings spirit imagination "out of the recesses of unassailable interiority and situate[s] it soundly within material and social practices"—precisely in the domain where the study of religion at large now most comfortably dwells.⁴⁷

Following these cues, it is not my wish to set up religious experience as a *sui generis* category. This approach in the study of religion was especially popular in the mid-twentieth century and it involved casting various spirit phenomena as a fundamentally irrational and symbolic encounter with the superhuman (e.g., "the holy" or "the sacred").⁴⁸ Arguments of this type depend on the assumption that religious experience is a shared phenomenon spanning traditions and eras. Arguing from that perspective, we might claim that the ancient Dead Sea Scrolls poet, the premodern tantric mystic, and the contemporary West African Pentecostal all have essentially the same "experience," one that is simply contextualized accidentally according to various cultural expressions. Whether that foundational essence is called *religion*, *mysticism*, the *numinous*, *the Divine*, or some other generic term, the fault lies in treating each person's embodied and culturally defined experience not as the subject itself but as an obscured window into a larger pattern of ultimate reality that can be construed only through comparison with other "religious experiences." The suspicious utility of such a notion has been rightly recognized and criticized.⁴⁹ Not only does that approach lend itself to a certain kind of universalizing liberal Protestant theology; it also serves to protect the study of religion as an academic discipline from the perceived encroachment of other fields like sociology, psychology, and neurology.

---

46 David Chidester labeled this "New Materialism" in "Material Terms for the Study of Religion," *JAAR* 68.2 (2000): 367–79.
47 Stephen S. Bush, "Are Religious Experiences Too Private to Study?," *JR* 92.2 (2012): 215.
48 E.g., Rudolf Otto, *The Idea of the Holy: An Inquiry into the Non-Rational Factor in the Idea of the Divine and Its Relation to the Rational*, 2nd ed. (Oxford: Oxford University Press, 1958) and Mircea Eliade, *The Sacred and the Profane; the Nature of Religion* (New York: Harper & Row, 1961). See the summary in Frances Flannery, Colleen Shantz, and Rodney A. Werline, "Introduction: Religious Experience, Past and Present," in *Experientia, Volume 1: Inquiry into Religious Experience in Early Judaism and Christianity*, ed. Frances Flannery, Colleen Shantz, and Rodney A. Werline, SBLSS 40 (Atlanta: SBL Press, 2008), 1–10.
49 See Steven T. Katz, "The Conservative Character of Mystical Experience," in *Mysticism and Religious Traditions*, ed. Steven T. Katz (Oxford: Oxford University Press, 1983), 3–60.

My approach in this book is different: It is like a scholar who wishes to understand ancient eating practices using evidence derived from how meals are portrayed in certain ancient literature. The task is not merely to recover the ancient menu (though certainly that might be part of the project using archaeological or agricultural data). It is also to chart how meal rituals reflect social relationships and power structures, to trace how eating practices changed in response to historical events, and to pay attention to discrepancies between prescribed orders for meals and the realities of practice. This scholar might turn also to contemporary meal practices in diverse societies in order to become defamiliarized from their own culturally specific assumptions about food and meals. They might recognize that, with respect to consuming bodies, certain elements of our eating are universally biological (e. g., mastication, digestion, intoxication, satiation) but nevertheless construed variously and contextually across times and settings.[50] Crucially, this variance is present not only in how an ancient diner described what they ate but also in what they expected to eat in the first place.[51] Throughout the scholar's investigation, however, the focus of the study is less the food than it is the eater.

One further issue I discuss in this section is the challenge of assessing *ancient* religious experience. Biblical literature, of course, does not contain ethnographic reports or interview notes of the kind currently published by anthropologists and psychologists of religion. Even if we are certain spirit possession and similar phenomena were practiced among the communities that composed and interpreted the Hebrew Bible, what is there to be studied since we cannot have reliable access to the experiences that might lay behind such literature?

Yet, the textual nature of the primary evidence does not need to be a barrier. Indologist Frederick M. Smith has demonstrated the value of analyzing textual material using an expansive philological method in his study *The Self Possessed: Deity and Spirit Possession in South Asian Literature and Civilization*.[52] While charting spirit possession in a corpus both dramatically different and many

---

[50] A comparable study is Nathan MacDonald, *Not Bread Alone: The Uses of Food in the Old Testament* (Oxford: Oxford University Press, 2008).
[51] Analysis of human neurophysiology is another way forward in this vein. As different and distant as ancient religious communities are from modern ones, human biology delimits certain capacities for religious expression and experience. For a study of notions of the self and of moral agency in early Jewish literature informed by studies in neuroscience, see Carol A. Newsom, *The Spirit Within Me: Self and Agency in Ancient Israel and Second Temple Judaism* (New Haven: Yale University Press, 2021).
[52] Frederick M. Smith, *The Self Possessed: Deity and Spirit Possession in South Asian Literature and Civilization* (New York: Columbia University Press, 2006).

times larger than the Hebrew Bible, Smith nevertheless encountered barriers that may be familiar to biblical scholars. Smith needed, for instance, to identity the various vocabulary for spirit possession and trance across languages and dialects in different types of literature, as well as to grapple with the various conventions of those different literary forms. In an acknowledgment resonating with the current study, Smith allowed that spirit possession in classical Indian literature had previously been understudied—in large part because much of the secondary literature regarded it as absent from the primary literature.[53]

In this book, I adopt an approach similar to Smith's for studying spirit phenomena in the Hebrew Bible. Using a critical philological method informed by ethnographic studies, I attend to the literary presentation of spirit phenomena in biblical literature as well as to the earliest interpretive traditions that developed around such texts. A small modification of Ann Taves's designation "experiences deemed religious" is in order.[54] This endeavor is concerned with "phenomena deemed spiritual" in the Hebrew Bible; that is, biblical texts that utilize a related family of spirit language, descriptions of possession, and myths to indicate a particular kind of phenomenon in the tradition.

1.4.3 The Spirit and the Self

A third methodological emphasis of this book is an orientation toward subjectivity in the presentation of spirit phenomena in biblical literature. This emphasis is significant because discussions of spirit phenomena texts in the Hebrew Bible are usually subsumed under a different inquiry concerning conceptions of evil in Jewish and Christian antiquity. This trend has obscured the role that notions of the self and of communal identity played in shaping the presentation of spirit phenomena in biblical literature.

Since the turn of the millennium there has been increased investigation into the origins and development of the concept of evil in early Jewish literature and, in particular, its influence on rabbinic Judaism and early Christianity.[55] Recent

---

[53] Smith, *The Self Possessed*, 33. This was true both of later commentators from within the tradition and from Western scholars observing it from without.
[54] Taves, *Religious Experience Reconsidered*, 8–9.
[55] Many works varying in scope and approach could be listed here. Some representative examples include: Mark S. Smith, *The Genesis of Good and Evil: The Fall(out) and Original Sin in the Bible* (Louisville: Westminster John Knox, 2019); Chris Keith and Loren T. Stuckenbruck, eds., *Evil in Second Temple Judaism and Early Christianity*, WUNT2 417 (Tübingen: Mohr Siebeck, 2016); Archie T. Wright, *The Origin of Evil Spirits: The Reception of Genesis 6:1–4 in Early Jewish*

studies have included not only inquiry into so-called evil beings (e. g., Satan, Mastema, Belial, and *daimonia*) and the transformations of their respective myths but also attempts to find an origin for and to define early Jewish conceptions of evil itself.[56] Sometimes these treatments have attempted to discern the supposed intellectual system by which Israelites and early Jews comprehensively justified their own suffering. This latter effort is partly because of the modern focus on "theodicy," which frames the problem of suffering as one of "intelligibility."[57] Certainly some streams of biblical tradition did attempt to fit evil into the prevailing intellectual frameworks of their respective eras. Still, it would be difficult to find a biblical text that identifies the "unintelligibility" of evil as its distinguishing attribute, as many theorists do today.[58] Indeed, many mysteries were perceived as intrinsically unintelligible in antiquity. Biblical traditions instead tend to focus more on the prevention, announcement, lamentation, injustice, and ultimate defeat of evil (often with the deity as implied audience).[59] Thus, when spirit phenomena are studied primarily as they relate to those de-

---

Literature, 2nd ed. (Minneapolis: Fortress, 2015); Loren T. Stuckenbruck, *The Myth of Rebellious Angels: Studies in Second Temple Judaism and New Testament Texts*, WUNT 335 (Tübingen: Mohr Siebeck, 2014); Ishay Rosen-Zvi, *Demonic Desires: "Yetzer Hara" and the Problem of Evil in Late Antiquity* (Philadelphia: University of Pennsylvania Press, 2011); Annette Yoshiko Reed, *Demons, Angels, and Writing in Ancient Judaism* (Cambridge: Cambridge University Press, 2020); *Fallen Angels and the History of Judaism and Christianity: The Reception of Enochic Literature* (Cambridge: Cambridge University Press, 2005); and Esther Eshel, "Demonology in Palestine during the Second Temple Period (Hebrew)" (PhD. diss., Hebrew University, 1999). See also several older studies on similar themes: Elaine H. Pagels, *The Origin of Satan* (New York: Random House, 1995); and Jon D. Levenson, *Creation and the Persistence of Evil: The Jewish Drama of Divine Omnipotence*, 2nd ed. (Princeton: Princeton University Press, 1994).

56 I would include in this category studies on related concepts like sin and repentance, though some deal with evil more directly than do others. Examples include David A. Lambert, *How Repentance Became Biblical: Judaism, Christianity, and the Interpretation of Scripture* (Oxford: Oxford University Press, 2015); Miryam T. Brand, *Evil Within and Without: The Source of Sin and Its Nature as Portrayed in Second Temple Literature*, JAJSup 9 (Göttingen: Vandenhoeck & Ruprecht, 2013); and Gary A. Anderson, *Sin: A History* (New Haven: Yale University Press, 2009).

57 See Susan Neiman, *Evil in Modern Thought: An Alternative History of Philosophy* (Princeton: Princeton University Press, 2002).

58 On this, see the introduction to Terry Eagleton, *On Evil* (New Haven: Yale University Press, 2010).

59 See, for example, Loren T. Stuckenbruck, "Origins of Evil in Jewish Apocalyptic Tradition: The Interpretation of Genesis 6:1–4," in *The Myth of Rebellious Angels: Studies in Second Temple Judaism and New Testament Texts*, WUNT 335 (Tübingen: Mohr Siebeck, 2014), 1–33; Levenson, *Creation and the Persistence of Evil*; and John Day, *God's Conflict with the Dragon and the Sea: Echoes of a Canaanite Myth in the Old Testament*, UCOP 35 (Cambridge: Cambridge University Press, 1985).

bates, scholars can be forgiven for assuming that they occur only infrequently in the earliest biblical literature, and even then, only at the margins of the most significant texts.

Although I will address spirit phenomena within the context of this ongoing scholarly discussion of evil, I intend to frame the topic using a second recent conversation in biblical studies, one that heretofore has treated the subject of spirit phenomena relatively lightly. Focus on "the self" within the broader study of religion has spurred biblical scholars to take a greater interest in notions of "the self" in early Jewish literature.[60] Further, this interest has occasioned studies on biblical views of personhood, individual moral agency, religious experience, and embodiment. Many of the pertinent studies have focused on the relationship between ancient constructions of the self and modern ones.[61] As I will endeavor to show, spirit phenomena in biblical literature have been underexamined as they relate to these issues.

---

60 See, for example, Carol A. Newsom, *The Spirit Within Me*; *The Self as Symbolic Space: Constructing Identity and Community at Qumran*, STDJ 52 (Leiden: Brill, 2004); Hindy Najman, "Imitatio Dei and the Formation of the Subject in Ancient Judaism," *JBL* 140.2 (2021): 309–23; Angela Kim Harkins, *Reading with an "I" to the Heavens: Looking at the Qumran Hodayot through the Lens of Visionary Traditions*. Ekstasis 3 (Berlin: De Gruyter, 2012); Susan Niditch, *The Responsive Self: Personal Religion in Biblical Literature of the Neo-Babylonian and Persian Periods* (New Haven: Yale University Press, 2015); Shannon Burkes, *God, Self, and Death: The Shape of Religious Transformation in the Second Temple Period*, JSJSup 79 (Leiden: Brill, 2003); Jacqueline E. Lapsley, *Can These Bones Live?: The Problem of the Moral Self in the Book of Ezekiel*, BZAW 301 (Berlin: De Gruyter, 2000); and David E. Aune and John McCarthy, *The Whole and Divided Self: The Bible and Theological Anthropology* (New York: Crossroad, 1997). Of course, studies on conceptions of the self have concerned scholars of religion outside of biblical studies for several generations. See, for example, Janet Gyatso, *Apparitions of the Self: The Secret Autobiographies of a Tibetan Visionary* (Princeton: Princeton University Press, 1998); Michel Foucault, *Technologies of the Self: A Seminar with Michel Foucault*, ed. Luther H. Martin, Huck Gutman, and Patrick H. Hutton (Amherst: University of Massachusetts Press, 1988); and William James, "The Divided Self, and the Process of its Unification," in *Varieties of Religious Experience: A Study in Human Nature*, Centenary ed. (New York: Routledge, 2002), 132–49. 1st ed. (New York: Longmans, Green, and Co., 1902).
61 These issues are summarized in Carol A. Newsom, "Toward a Genealogy of the Introspective Self in Second Temple Judaism," in *Functions of Psalms and Prayers in the Late Second Temple Period*, ed. Mika S. Pajunen and Jeremy Penner, BZAW 486 (Berlin: De Gruyter, 2017), 63–79. See also David A Lambert, "Refreshing Philology: James Barr, Supersessionism, and the State of Biblical Words," *BI* 24.3 (2016): 332–56; Krister Stendahl, "The Apostle Paul and the Introspective Conscience of the West," *HTR* 56.3 (1963): 199–215.

1.4.4 Spirit Phenomena as Discourse

One final methodological emphasis requires mention: the use of anthropological literature that "reads" spirit-possession practices as a kind of "text" or discourse. One example is the work of cultural anthropologist Michael Lambek, who has written extensively about spirit-possession practicing communities in Madagascar and Mayotte over the last forty years.[62] Lambek, among others, treats possession not necessarily as a disorder or as a cry for help but as a *system of communication* complete with genre conventions, idioms, and endless opportunities for creativity. As Lambek elaborates:

> Trance behavior often strikes the inexperienced observer as wild, uncoordinated, incoherent, and unpredictable, and indeed, it is meant to. However, close observation and discussion with various mediums reveal an underlying "grammar" such that in a competent trancer most behavior can be interpreted as an expression of the identity or attitude of the spirit and the stage or immediate quality of its relationship with the host or interlocutor.[63]

Understanding possession as a system of communication enables observers to recognize a far wider range of functions for these practices in the context of a community. Possession thus becomes a kind of sandbox space for playing with ideas like Otherness, negotiating conceptions of the moral self, placing and replacing ethical boundary markers, interpreting communal history, and transgressing taboo safely.

Lambek's approach represents a departure from previous generations' anthropological treatment of spirit possession. For the better part of the twentieth century, it was customary to relegate ecstatic spirit practices to some other better-defined category of Western academic thought. That approach is notable in the immensely influential *Ecstatic Religion: A Study of Shamanism and Spirit Possession*, written by Ioan Lewis and first published in 1971, with a third edition published in 2003.[64] Lewis's structural-functionalist approach found explanations for spirit possession around the world primarily within the realm of sociological forces, especially along the lines of gender power dynamics. In this way, one might read the encouragement of ecstatic, spiritual experience in the dominant religion of a region as an

---

[62] See Michael Lambek, *Human Spirits: A Cultural Account of Trance in Mayotte*, CSCS 6 (Cambridge: Cambridge University Press, 1981); *Knowledge and Practice in Mayotte: Local Discourses of Islam, Sorcery, and Spirit Possession*, AnthHor 3 (Toronto: University of Toronto Press, 1993); *The Weight of the Past: Living with History in Mahajanga, Madagascar* (Basingstoke: Palgrave Macmillan, 2002); "On Being Present to History: Historicity and Brigand Spirits in Madagascar," *HAU* 6.1 (2016): 317–41.
[63] Lambek, "From Disease to Discourse," 42.
[64] Lewis, *Ecstatic Religion*.

attempt by the leadership class to strengthen and legitimate its authority. A similar practice present among women or a minority cult, however, might be expressed instead as a spiritual ailment and thus as a means to retaliate against a husband's mistreatment. One of Lewis's more controversial theories was the idea that possession often functioned as a kind of societal safety valve releasing pent up tension in a repressive social structure.[65]

Beginning in earnest in the 1990s, anthropologists criticized Lewis and others in his school on multiple fronts, suggesting that a merely "instrumental" understanding of possession (i.e., as a tool for accomplishing something else) was profoundly inadequate.[66] In a landmark article, Janice Boddy, summarizing the findings of others in her field, demonstrated that spirit possession rarely fits neatly into Western scholarly categories like "medicine," "psychology," or "religion"; thus, movement away from decontextualizing approaches is necessary if spirit-possession phenomena are to be recognized as being primarily about meaning.[67] Like Lambek, Boddy has characterized the theatrical, satirical, and historically perceptive aspects of spirit possession as "metacommentaries on the human world."[68]

Given the commentary-like nature of so much of the Hebrew Bible and Second Temple literature, Boddy's lens ought to be especially useful in biblical studies. For example, commentators have often noted the political implications of the story from the gospels of the demoniac among the tombs (Matt 8:28–34/Mark 5:1–20/ Luke 8:26–39). As early as the mid-twentieth century, commentators recognized the military significance of the name "Legion" in the story, as well as the conspicuous presence of tombs, pigs, and other elements suggesting ritual impurity.[69] Even without the benefit of comparison with ethnographic literature, it is not difficult to see the story as, at least in part, a kind of parable or performance about the debilitating state of life under the control of the Roman Empire. Frequently, however, the conclusion has followed that, with such an interpretation in hand, the story is simply too rife with political allusion for it to be anything other than a literary fiction.

---

[65] Lewis, *Ecstatic Religion*, 101. For an example of this approach in biblical studies, see J. Keir Howard, "New Testament Exorcism and Its Significance Today," *ExpTim* 96.4 (1985): 105–9.
[66] See, for example, Susan Starr Sered, *Priestess, Mother, Sacred Sister: Religions Dominated by Women* (Oxford: Oxford University Press, 1996).
[67] Janice Boddy, "Spirit Possession Revisited: Beyond Instrumentality," *ARAnth* 23 (1994): 407–34, 412.
[68] Boddy, "Spirit Possession Revisited: Beyond Instrumentality," 423.
[69] See J. Duncan M. Derrett, "Contributions to the Study of the Gerasene Demoniac," *JSNT* 2.3 (1979): 2–17. While their significance is clear, their meaning is still debated. See Warren Carter, "Cross-Gendered Romans and Mark's Jesus: Legion Enters the Pigs (Mark 5:1–20)," *JBL* 134.1 (2015): 139–55 and Joshua Garroway, "The Invasion of a Mustard Seed: A Reading of Mark 5.1–20," *JSNT* 32.1 (2009): 57–75.

Although engaging the historicity of a given biblical text is not a primary goal of this project, it should be noted that the mere presence of sophisticated political commentary in a biblical story is not itself evidence of fabrication—especially when that commentary is present in spirit-possession rituals, where such metacommentaries are common. Indeed, this is precisely what ethnographers and anthropologists have come to expect from spirit-possession episodes; that is, "an interpretation of the climate of affairs," where the medium or host is caught up socially, politically, or historically.[70]

1.5 The Organization of this Book

The remainder of this book is divided into four chapters.

Chapter 2, "Raising the Specter," demonstrates the effectiveness of the book's approach through an in-depth analysis of the figure of Saul in 1 Samuel. The investigation begins with a case study from Cuban *Espiritismo* drawn from the work of anthropologist Diana Espírito Santo. Based on her work with professional mediums (or *espiritistas*), Espírito Santo suggests that spirit mediumship is learned not through formal training but through everyday attention to the interplay between imagination and sensation in one's body. Consulting with the spirits of the dead is thus not spirit possession in the stereotypical, medieval exorcist mode but instead Espírito Santo suggests that mediums cultivate possession by learning to be affected bodily by the spirits around and inside them. I suggest that such frameworks for understanding spirit phenomena translate well into the Hebrew Bible and especially into the Saul stories. As one of the most profoundly spirit-affected figures in biblical literature, Saul's narrative presents spirit episodes that are both healthful and harmful, cultivated and involuntary. His spirit encounters are wrapped up in his conflicts, both in battle and in the royal court, and they resonate with current efforts by biblical scholars working in mental health and trauma studies—especially around Post-Traumatic Stress Disorder (PTSD) and moral injury (MI). Saul's spirit issues come to a climax in the account of his visit to a professional spirit medium at Endor in 1 Sam 28. I interpret this ritual as a consultation with an expert spirit-connected medium who calls up the dead prophet Samuel against his will and hosts him within her body in order to deliver an authentic oracle to King Saul.

Chapter 3, "Getting into the Spirit," presents an overview of different types of spirit phenomena in biblical literature. I begin with a description of varying modes

---

70 Lambek, "On Being Present to History," 318.

for "talking to the dead" among Gullah/Geechee women in the Lowcountry of the southeastern United States. Africana studies and religion scholar LeRhonda S. Manigault-Bryant demonstrates the myriad ways in which Gullah/Geechee women come to interact and "talk" to the dead, especially through music. Gullah/Geechee methods for noticing the presence and influence of spirits of the dead educate us in how to search for spirit phenomena outside of clearly demarcated spiritual settings or rituals. Translating this approach into biblical studies, I identify three overlapping and non-exhaustive literary types of spirit phenomena in the Hebrew Bible and in a few noncanonical Second Temple era examples: (1) spirit language, (2) descriptions of spirit possession, and (3) myths about spirits. First, in a philological and comparative analysis of the most conspicuous term, *rûaḥ* (רוח), and following the work of Ingrid Lilly, I detail how "spirit" is frequently portrayed as a part of the body, specifically *internal* moving air. Consistent with ancient Near Eastern conceptions of the movement of both inner and outer winds as being intimately connected to health, mood, and personality, spirit language in the Hebrew Bible becomes a productive tool for discussing the means by which humanity inhabits its world, emotionally, volitionally, and, at times, physically. Next, I argue that rooted in these conceptions are descriptions of spirit-possession episodes that describe spirits as both an aspect of the self and as "other." Finally, in an analysis of the third category of spirit phenomena, I suggest that myths about spirits have exercised undue influence on scholarly conclusions about conceptions of spirits in biblical literature and that a greater emphasis should be placed instead on the first two categories. I compare the story of Micaiah son of Imlah in 1 Kgs 22 with an account of a Sakalava spirit possession ritual as related by Michael Lambek, demonstrating how in both accounts, spirit possession hosts utilized myths about spirits in their performances of political and social commentaries on their respective contexts.

In chapter 4, "When a Spirit Moves," I distinguish two models of spirits in the Hebrew Bible that can be charted using the map that I developed in chapter 3. It begins with an account of an exorcism in sixteenth-century England, when Robert Brigges, a prominent law student, was possessed by none other than the devil while attending a theological lecture. Brigges went on to face a many-months-long possession ordeal, which casts his experiences as a microcosm of the Reformation-era conflicts then ravaging Europe. I use the story of Brigges, as told by historian Kathleen R. Sands, to highlight a conception of spirit possession as sudden, unwelcome, and disruptive. These attributes fit with the second of two models for spirits that I identify in this chapter: (1) abiding spirits (which rest and persist) and (2) migrating spirits (which are mobile and temporary). Previous scholarship has tended to distinguish spirits taxonomically, using markers like theological allegiance or the symptoms they cause in humans. In contrast, I derive my two categories using philological analysis, arguing that the other features are too varied and inconsistent. Over the course of this discussion, I criticize the hegemony of a model for human religious experience that contemporary scholars of religion have called the "self-cultivation" model. This paradigm, exemplified by Michel Foucault's notion of "technologies of the self," as applied to human religious activity, sees religious practices primarily as self-instigated actions designed to change aspects of the person (i.e., in soul, body, mind, or conduct). This paradigm is inadequate, however, when applied to those non-Western forms of religiosity that valorize being *acted upon* or that do not have a clear posture as either active or passive (e.g., dreaming). I demonstrate how self-cultivation is frequently an inaccurate paradigm when applied to spirit phenomena in biblical literature.

The fifth and final chapter, "In Good Spirits," amplifies the expansive use of medical idioms to describe spirit phenomena in the Hebrew Bible and Second Temple literature. Chapter 5 begins with a case study from an Umbandan possession ceremony, a Yoruba-descended religious tradition in Brazil. Anthropologist Diana DeGroat Brown describes the large, public ceremony in terms of a spirit triage center, where attendants dressed in nurses' uniforms help congregants find specialists who, empowered by their own respective spirit possessions, can diagnose and treat the spirit ailments of others. This setting underscores the widespread therapeutic function of spirit rituals in religious traditions around the world and invites us to consider this underemphasized aspect of spirit phenomena in early Jewish literature. I first do this by surveying select examples from the Dead Sea Scrolls and other Second Temple period literature which connect physical ailments to spirit troubles. Taking cues from disability studies, I explain how the therapies developed to treat spirit-based pathologies reflect how a spirit-afflicted body can nonetheless become empowered with alternative abilities. Next, I chart a network of interconnected biblical texts that expect an imminent moral transformation of God's people. In these texts, the prescription for treating Israel's chronic disobedience is described with surprisingly physical imagery (e.g., circumcising the foreskin of the heart, writing Torah on the heart, exchanging a heart of stone for a heart of flesh). A peak in this range is Ps 51, arguably the most sophisticated reflection on the therapeutic nature of spirit possession in the entire Hebrew Bible. Within the texts I survey in this chapter we find an overarching strategy of unfamiliarizing the self so that undesirable traits might be dealt with therapeutically or, alternatively, so that virtues might be accentuated. I conclude the book with a discussion of "holy spirit" in pre-Christian Jewish texts and suggest that fostering possession by God's holy spirit was perceived to be an effective counter against the detrimental effects of other kinds of harmful spirits.

2 Raising the Specter

2.1 Co-Creating with Spirits Among Cuban *Espiritistas*

Cuban *Espiritismo* (spiritism) in the twenty-first century is a complex religious phenomenon with several intermixed origins.[1] The initial articulation of spiritism as a distinct tradition is usually credited to Allan Kardec, the pen name of nineteenth-century French mystical writer Hippolyte Rivail. Over the course of five books and a recurring periodical, Kardec codified and expanded on several spiritual practices, such as séances and mediumship, that were popular as parlor entertainment across Europe and North America.[2] He called his system *spiritisme* (spiritism) and characterized it as a scientific approach to understanding the postmortem existence and interactions of the spirits of the dead. Due to its lack of hard dogmas and set rituals, spiritism (sometimes called Kardecism) was especially ripe for contextualization into existing religious traditions. As spiritism was exported to the Americas, it became popular in Latin America, where it was incorporated into existing cosmologies and practices—many of which were themselves descended from African Yoruba and Bakongo traditions.

In Cuba, the most popular form of *Espiritismo* is *Espiritismo Cruzado* (Crossed Spiritism). There are no formal initiation rites or training programs for practitioners of Espiritismo Cruzado but only a loose association of shared assumptions and discourses about the actions of spirits and their effect on the daily life of still-living human beings.[3] The dispersion of formal authority and expertise in the tradition has attracted the attention of cultural anthropologists, who have studied, in particular, how mediums develop in their religious profession in the absence of clear structures or organizing bodies.

In the world of Espiritismo Cruzado, each person is connected to their own collective of spirits, a *cordon espiritual* (spiritual cord), which is made up of various *muertos* (spirits of the dead). *Espiritistas* (mediums) have fostered their relationships with their cordon espiritual in such a way that they can interact and

---

[1] Due to the political circumstances of Cuba in the latter half of the twentieth century, non-Cuban anthropological work on *Espiritismo* was minimal until the twenty-first century. One of the leading recent scholars has been Diana Espírito Santo, "Spiritist Boundary-Work and the Morality of Materiality in Afro-Cuban Religion," *JMC* 15.1 (2010): 64–82; "Imagination, Sensation and the Education of Attention Among Cuban Spirit Mediums," *Ethnos* 77.2 (2012): 252–71; and *Developing the Dead: Mediumship and Selfhood in Cuban Espiritismo* (Gainesville: University Press of Florida, 2015).
[2] See Espírito Santo, *Developing the Dead*, 42–46.
[3] Espírito Santo, *Developing the Dead*, 4.

alternatively influence or be influenced by their muertos, who act as guides, informants, and healers. This is a carefully cultivated relationship in which common notions of possession, partnership, and the self are entangled:

> Spiritist ontology turns on a fundamental paradox. On the one hand, the protective *muertos* clearly exist. They come *with* the person at birth. On the other, their existence must also be achieved, somehow. The *cordon* must be awoken from an initial state of dormancy, activated, brought into being through the processes involved in becoming an *espiritista*.[4]

This "fundamental paradox," as characterized by anthropologist and ethnographer Diana Espírito Santo, intimates meanings more fluid and nuanced than is often admitted by theorists when discussing the presence and influence of spirits.

For example, Espírito Santo tells the story of Marcelina, an Afro-Cuban medium in her sixties who lived in Havana. Marcelina was a well-known espiritista in her community, and her small apartment often had a small line of people waiting outside to be seen. Marcelina's skill came from her partnership with the muerto Paloyansan, a Haitian healer who had lived more than 200 years earlier and who had passed on his skills and knowledge of medicinal plants to Marcelina.[5] Paloyansan first manifested his presence with Marcelina as epileptic attacks that afflicted her as a 12-year-old girl. Through decades of development and consultation, however, Marcelina had transformed this once debilitating relationship with her muerto into a partnership. The home they shared was as much his as it was hers, with trinkets and décor that reflected his tastes and biography. When consulting with those seeking her help, Marcelina incorporated the presence of Paloyansan fluidly, almost instantly, signaling his presence in her body through changed speech and the addition of a cigar. Espírito Santo described this process of transformation:

> Learning her trade, and refining her talent, had been for Marcelina not principally a matter of acquiring knowledge from *someone*—although she too had had her mentors—but of *learning a particular kind of body*, in this case a permeable, shifting body, tantamount to a particular kind of self.[6]

---

[4] Espírito Santo, "Imagination, Sensation and the Education of Attention," 259.
[5] Espírito Santo, *Developing the Dead*, 282–90; and Espírito Santo, "Imagination, Sensation and the Education of Attention," 257–58.
[6] Espírito Santo, "Imagination, Sensation and the Education of Attention," 258.

Spirits like Paloyansan are thus a quotidian presence in the lives of *espiritistas* who practice and develop spirit possession. More than this, despite the fact that the rituals and beliefs involved require a considerable degree of metaphysical assumption, in practice Espiritismo Cruzado is profoundly material and embodied. Marcelina and other espiritistas foster a refined sensibility to their world, which requires a body that is as much porous as it is attentive.[7]

This short account of Marcelina and Paloyansan demonstrates how notions about possession and other spirit phenomena in Espiritismo defy several of the conventions I discussed in chapter 1. For instance, within the cosmology and metaphysical expectations of spiritism, these practices are neither irrational nor erratic. They also do not require full suspension of a person's agency. In fact, "full" possession (where the presence of the host disappears completely and another being takes over completely) is often seen as a lesser form of mediumship among espiritistas because it downplays an understanding of spirits and mediums as "intentional and mutual co-creators."[8] Perhaps most indicative is Marcelina's daily sensitivity to her body and her environment as porous and spirit-filled spaces, which conveys certain assumptions about the materiality of such phenomena.

2.2 Chapter Overview

In this chapter I analyze two interconnected case studies from the book of 1 Samuel: (1) Saul's mysterious spirit malady (e.g., 1 Sam 16:15, 23; 18:10; 19:9) and (2) his visit to the medium at Endor (1 Sam 28). I showcase both as examples of spirit phenomena in the Hebrew Bible and complement my analysis through comparison with ethnographic and anthropological studies, like that of Espiritismo introduced above.

First, I demonstrate how the descriptions of Saul's spirit sickness map closely onto typical expressions of spirit possession in many contexts around the world. In particular, 1 Samuel presents the "harmful spirit of God" (רוח אלהים רעה) that repeatedly antagonizes Saul as a consequence of God's displeasure with Saul's rule as king. The narrative also depicts this spirit, however, as having a direct connection to Saul's trauma from battle, apart from his failures in the cult and at court. Saul's appeal to music therapy as well as treatment from spirit experts helps to mitigate the negative effects of his spirit illness for a time, but

---

[7] Espírito Santo, "Spiritist Boundary-Work."
[8] Espírito Santo, "Imagination, Sensation and the Education of Attention," 269.

they are not sufficient to heal his distress or to regain God's favor. My analysis of Saul's experiences resonates remarkably with contemporary discussions about the complex relationships between mental health and spirit phenomena. One promising avenue of integration between the two fields of inquiry emerges from recent work on moral injury (MI) in biblical studies.

Second, in my analysis of 1 Sam 28, I suggest that the woman with whom Saul meets at Endor is a professional spirit medium who hosts the "ghost" (אוב) of Samuel in her body. Utilizing techniques similar to those found in spirit-possession cults around the world today, the medium conjures Samuel's presence against his will and speaks his words—all of this likely by consequence of skills she has cultivated through a relationship with her own familiar spirit. Thus, the relationship that the medium at Endor has with the dead may not be so different phenomenologically from Marcelina's with Paloyansan.

My interpretation of Saul's spirit encounters offers an otherwise overlooked perspective and indicates how the field of biblical studies can benefit from comparative ethnographic evidence. This literature offers a glimpse of alternative models of what it means to be a human being, which may be operative in the biblical text but not in the mind of a modern biblical scholar.

2.3 Saul's Spirit Sickness

Many modern readers experience a foundational and recurring dissonance when reading biblical spirit phenomena in what philosopher Charles Taylor has called the distinction between the "porous" self and the "buffered" self.[9] Taylor suggests that in the modern conception of the "buffered" self, each human being is protected from outside influence by their own distinct individuality and moral will. A boundary might exist between *the inside* and *the outside* of a person, and each of us has the power of invitation and rejection regarding our own emotions, spirituality, and thoughts. In contrast, the premodern "porous" self

---

[9] Charles Taylor, *A Secular Age* (Cambridge, MA: Harvard University Press, 2007). For a discussion of Taylor's earlier work on the self in the context of biblical studies, see Robert A Di Vito, "Old Testament Anthropology and the Construction of Personal Identity," *CBQ* 61.2 (1999): 217–38. As Carol Newsom has recently demonstrated, such distinctions have been overstated, especially when it comes to making generalizations between "Western" and "Eastern" notions of the self. Here, I make no broader programmatic claims other than the fact that spirit "porousness" is not an aspect of biblical literature that modern scholars have typically taken seriously, though it was a common assumption in antiquity and exists in many places around the world today. Newsom, *The Spirit Within Me*, 2.

naturally assumed that the most powerful and important emotions originated outside of the mind—or better, that there was no boundary at all. Thus, according to Taylor, "the porous self is vulnerable, to spirits, demons, [and] cosmic forces."[10] This is not a sign of weakness or compromised human validity, but a simple fact, and it would seem, in some cultures, an aspect of the self-worth nurturing.

In 1 Samuel, figures like Samuel, Saul, David, and the Endor medium are presented as having porous spiritual borders. Thus, certain transgressions of those borders, which modern readers might expect to be explicitly stated, are instead left implied. Principal among these are the frequent backdrops of spirit-phenomena rituals, where spirits come and go and are influenced, conducted, and received by human hosts. Recognizing such settings while interpreting these texts is important because they add sense and context to the actions of these figures, who might otherwise appear erratic or irrational.

A failure to recognize the presence of spirit phenomena leads many contemporary interpreters to attribute Saul's malady to some form of unrecognized mental illness—either one from which the historical figure, Saul, actually suffered, or one that has been attributed to him for literary and theological effect. Diagnoses have varied, including neurosis, epilepsy, and Post Traumatic Stress Disorder (PTSD).[11] For some, however, this type of interpretation has a certain utility beyond simply providing a modern biomedical answer to an ancient question. Commentators with theological concerns have also used the "madness" argument to sidestep the uncomfortable idea that a good God would send an "evil" spirit against a person—especially someone like Saul, who was formerly spirit empowered. As I discuss below, however, this theological concern also reflects a misunderstanding of Saul's spirit sickness.

2.3.1 Saul's Early Spirit Encounters

Presentations of a porous self are especially evident in the narratives of King Saul, who is one of the most dynamically spirit-affected persons in the Hebrew

---

10 Taylor, *A Secular Age*, 38.
11 See, for example, Gillian Patricia Williams and Magdel Le Roux, "King Saul's Mysterious Malady," *HTS* 68.1 (2012); and Liubov Ben-Noun, "What Was the Mental Disease That Afflicted King Saul?," *CCS* 2.4 (2003): 270–82.

Bible.¹² Several elements of Saul's initial spirit encounter are suggestive of a possession-type episode.

> ⁵... "There, as you come to the town, you will meet a band of prophets coming down from the shrine with harp, tambourine, flute, and lyre playing in front of them; they will be playing the prophet (והמה מתנבאים).¹³ ⁶ Then a/the¹⁴ spirit of the LORD will seize you (וצלחה עליך)¹⁵, and you will play the prophet (והתנבית)¹⁶ along with them and be turned into a different person." (1 Sam 10:5b–6, cf. vv. 9–10)

These possession-type elements are treated in turn below.

In chapter 1, I suggested that contemporary spirit possession is frequently *corporate* and *cultivated*. Both elements are present here: a *group* of prophets practice possession together, *cultivating* the ritual with musical instruments. The presence of music is another significant clue, as it appears elsewhere in biblical spirit phenomena (e. g., 2 Kgs 3:15; 1 Sam 16:14–23). Further, the verb *ləhitnabbēʾ* (להתנבא, *hithpael* stem of the root נב״א, translated above as "to play the prophet") is one frequently related to spirit phenomena—and as often misunderstood. The NRSV translates the verb here as "be in a prophetic frenzy"; NJPS offers "speak in ecstasy." Gunkel understood what occurred to be "glossolalia."¹⁷ I treat this verb more completely in chapter 4. For now, it is enough to say that I understand it in this passage (and frequently elsewhere) to signify something like a spirit trance or ecstasy, though it does not always mean this in the Hebrew Bible.

Finally, Samuel himself names Saul's altered state by explaining to him that because of this possession experience, "You will be turned into a different per-

---

12 For a discussion contextualizing the Saul cycle literarily and historically, as well as a posited historical situation for the resurgence of Saul as a mythic/legendary figure, see Mark Leuchter, "The Rhetoric of Convention: The Foundational Saul Narratives (1 Samuel 9–11) Reconsidered," *JRH* 40.1 (2016): 3–19. For an alternative reconstruction of the compositional history of the Saul narratives in 1 Samuel, see Blischke, *Der Geist Gottes*, 10–24; and Reinhard G. Kratz, *The Composition of the Narrative Books of the Old Testament*, trans. John Bowden (New York: T & T Clark, 2005), 177–83.
13 NRSV: "they will be in a prophetic frenzy"
14 NRSV: "the spirit"; Usually, nouns that are in a construct relationship with a definite noun are also definite themselves but there are exceptions, including sometimes with names. Waltke and O'Connor list as one of these examples 1 Sam 18:10 "a (certain) evil spirit of God" (רוח אלהים רעה). *IBHS* 13.4c. I am inclined to read this recurring phrase in 1 Samuel as indefinite (i.e., "a spirit of" not "the spirit of), though this is not certain. See also the discussion in Levison, *Filled with the Spirit*, 36–41.
15 NRSV: "possess you"
16 NRSV: "you will be in a prophetic frenzy"
17 Gunkel, *The Influence of the Holy Spirit*, 31.

son" (v. 6). Three verses later, the narrator clarifies the purpose of this experience: "God gave him another heart" (ויהפך־לו אלהים לב אחר, v. 9), a phrase that can be interpreted as reflecting the kind of complex subjectivity expressed in spirit-possession episodes.

These words are said to Saul by the prophet Samuel, a figure who directs much of the main action in the book bearing his name. Of note is his title in 1 Sam 9:5–10, "seer" (ראה), which appears instead of the expected term, "prophet" (נביא).

> Formerly in Israel, anyone who went to inquire of God would say, "Come, let us go to the seer" (ראה); for the one who is now called a prophet (נביא) was formerly called a seer. (1 Sam 9:9)

More than a century ago, Julius Wellhausen argued that the appearance of the title "seer" here demonstrated that originally a "prophet" was an entirely different figure, one who practiced "prophetic trance" (להתנבא). According to Wellhausen, this distinction (and perhaps the practice itself) had all but disappeared by the time of Isaiah and Jeremiah, who used the term differently, to the extent that a later scribe could quite mistakenly equate the two words in a gloss (1 Sam 9:9). As Wellhausen explained, such a historical scheme had the advantage that "Samuel the Seer need not be degraded into one of the flagellants."[18]

I dispute Wellhausen's assumption that the connection between prophecy and ecstasy declined over time in ancient Israel as well as note the influence of his anti-ecstatic posture (see chapter 1). As Martti Nissinen has pointed out, mapping the nuances of how prophetic vocabulary varied and changed over the centuries in which biblical literature was composed is an incredibly difficult enterprise, one that is nearly impossible to verify.[19] A gloss like 1 Sam 9:9 only serves to verify that the biblical writers themselves struggled to chart such terms.[20] Nevertheless, there is merit in Wellhausen's initial insight that at some point in the compositional history of these texts, an editor coordinated existing traditions in order to position Samuel as the head of a group of ecstatic prophets.

---

18 Julius Wellhausen, *Prolegomena to the History of Israel: With a Reprint of the Article Israel from the "Encyclopaedia Britannica,"* trans. John Sutherland Black and Allan Menzies (Edinburgh: Adam & Charles Black, 1885), 268.
19 Nissinen, *Ancient Prophecy*, 31.
20 Jonathan Stökl, *Prophecy in the Ancient Near East: A Philological and Sociological Comparison* (Leiden: Brill, 2012), 198.

This conclusion is supported with evidence from ethnographic data. A common role in contemporary spirit possession is that of the experienced spirit host who directs others who are still developing their skills in the craft. Thus, one might expect an ancient scribe familiar with spirit-possession practices to depict such a group with an especially charismatic leader at its head. Compare, for example, the role of the *shaykha* (priestess) in the *zār* possession ceremonies in Muslim Sudan related by anthropologist Janice Boddy.[21] The shaykha is distinguished by her ability to cultivate relatively stable and controlled relationships with the spirits she hosts. Manipulating various props that indicate the presence of particular spirits, a village shaykha will direct a drumming circle of mediums and musicians in a possession ritual. An aspiring shaykha might apprentice with an established medium, usually a maternal kinswoman:

> The proclivity itself tends to be handed down in the maternal line: a woman whose mother or mother's sister is a *shaykha* is more likely than others to become one herself. During her apprenticeship she learns how to call the spirits, bargain with them, recognize their characteristics and demands. But having done, she does not proclaim herself a *shaykha*; others will attribute her this status as her reputation as a curer grows.[22]

The relationship is not unlike that of a master craftsperson who trains their apprentices on the job.

We may tentatively compare these dynamics to certain aspects of Samuel's biography; in particular, to the close ties that the narrative establishes between him and his mother (e. g., 1 Sam 1:22–28; 2:19). Although in contemporary conversations Hannah is not usually identified as a prophetic or spirit-empowered figure, she did have this reputation in Second Temple Jewish interpretation, and indeed, there are indications within her story in 1 Sam 1–2 that reinforce this identification.[23] With these parallels in mind, a portrait of Samuel as a spirit-empowered prophet directing a band of apprentices and incorporating the young Saul into his entourage as king-elect, thus becomes more plausible.

For his part, Saul is presented as a man with porous spiritual boundaries, not just in this passage but throughout 1 Samuel. In addition to his association with and selection by Samuel, his military victories are reminiscent of those of the spirit-empowered judges, especially Samson: "a/the spirit of God seized

---

[21] Janice Boddy, *Wombs and Alien Spirits: Women, Men, and the Zār Cult in Northern Sudan*, NDAW (Madison: University of Wisconsin Press, 1989).
[22] Boddy, *Wombs and Alien Spirits*, 154–55.
[23] Reed Carlson, "Hannah at Pentecost: On Recognizing Spirit Phenomena in Early Jewish Literature," *JPT* 27.2 (2018): 245–58.

Saul"[24] (ותצלח רוח אלהים על־שעול, 1 Sam 11:6; cf. Judg 14:6, 19; 15:14). I argue in chapter 4 that this construction—a/the "spirit seized" (תצלח רוח) with the preposition 'al (על)—signifies a spirit-possession episode, one where the host's personality is still present and where the host exercises limited agency. Like the judges before him, Saul is thus seen as collaborating with a/the spirit of God in accomplishing deliverance for Israel.

Despite this auspicious beginning, Saul's subsequent spirit encounters assume a more hostile tone. The turning point occurs in 1 Sam 15, when Saul is instructed to provide recompense for the Amalekite attack on the Israelites (Exod 17:8–16; Deut 25:17–19) by completely annihilating the Amalekites, "man and woman, child and infant, ox and sheep, camel and donkey" (1 Sam 15:3).[25] Although this command is likely to strike modern readers as ghastly, the "ban" (חרם) was a regular component of many sacrificial systems in the ancient Near East, a term that distinguished those possessions to be sacrificed to the deity (including human slaves and livestock) and not ransomed.[26]

In 1 Sam 15, Saul's victory against the Amalekites is total and the slaughter extensive, but he spares their king and the best of the livestock and other possessions. When confronted by Samuel, Saul explains that he preserved these only that they might be sacrificed at Gilgal (v. 21), presumably according to the parameters for allowable consumption (and perhaps also for ransom). Some have argued that Saul's mistake, then, was not disobedience *per se* but that of having a different interpretation of the "ban" (חרם) prerogative.[27] Regardless, for this transgression, Saul is rejected as king.

[22] And Samuel said,
"Has the LORD as great delight in burnt offerings and sacrifices,
as in obeying the voice of the LORD?
Surely, to obey is better than sacrifice,
and to heed than the fat of rams.
[23] For rebellion is no less a sin than divination,
and stubbornness is like iniquity and idolatry.
Because you have rejected the word of the LORD,
he has also rejected you from being king." (1 Sam 15:22–23)

---

[24] NRSV: "And the spirit of God came upon Saul."
[25] On the "legal blend" of these two Pentateuchal passages in 1 Sam 15, see Joshua A. Berman, "The Legal Blend in Biblical Narrative (Joshua 20:1–9), Judges 6:25–31, 1 Samuel 15:2, 28:3–25, 2 Kings 4:1–7, Jeremiah 34:12–17, Nehemiah 5:1–12)," *JBL* 134.1 (2015): 105–25.
[26] See the discussion in Susan Niditch, *War in the Hebrew Bible: A Study in the Ethics of Violence* (Oxford: Oxford University Press, 1993), esp. chps. 1–2.
[27] Annett Giercke-Ungermann, "Saul und der חרם: Beobachtungen zu den חרם-Konzepten in 1 Sam 15," *BN* 162 (2014): 47–65.

This oracle looks forward as well as back, naming not only the inadequacy of sacrifice without obedience but also Saul's impending paradigmatic transgression of divination, which he will commit through another spirit phenomenon, consultation with Samuel's antipathetic ghost.

Following Saul's failure, the narrative of the book and the fortunes of Israel shift focus to David. In the next chapter, Samuel clandestinely anoints David as king at home, despite the fear of deathly retribution from Saul (1 Sam 16:2). Once God's spirit seizes David, the narrator immediately reports that Saul's spiritual fortunes change:

> ¹³ Then Samuel took the horn of oil, and anointed [David] in the presence of his brothers; and a/the spirit of the LORD seized (תצלח)²⁸ David from that day forward. Samuel then set out and went to Ramah.
> ¹⁴ Now the spirit of the LORD departed from Saul, and a harmful spirit (רוח־רעה)²⁹ from the LORD tormented him. (1 Sam 16:13–14)

In the received form of 1 Samuel, these two verses belong to separate pericopes: verse 13 completes the story of David's anointing, whereas verse 14 introduces the first account in Samuel of how Saul and David meet. But this arrangement is likely an intentional juxtaposition.³⁰ Although the spirit(s) with which the judges collaborated to liberate Israel has found a new host in David, King Saul is still porous and his dealings with spirits have not ended.

Those following sequentially through the book of 1 Samuel will recognize the Amalekite episode as a climax in a cycle of missteps in Saul's reign.³¹ It is, in fact, the second time that Saul fails to follow through on a ban, the first being when he spared the life of his own son, Jonathan (1 Sam 14:24–45). Moreover, Saul has already run afoul of Samuel in cultic matters, having conducted a sacrifice without the prophet present (1 Sam 13:8–15a). Yet despite the content of Samuel's harsh critique, cited above, the portrait of Saul in these narratives is less that of a disobedient king than of a blundering one.

It is significant that Saul is characterized as tortured and traumatized even before the arrival of God's harmful spirit. Saul is a perpetually embattled king, facing conflict with the Philistines throughout the entirety of his reign (1 Sam

---

28 NRSV: "the spirit of the LORD came mightily upon"
29 NRSV: "an evil spirit"
30 See David M. Howard Jr., "The Transfer of Power from Saul to David in 1 Sam 16:13–14," *JETS* 32.4 (1989): 473–83.
31 Dawn Maria Sellars, "An Obedient Servant?: The Reign of King Saul (1 Samuel 13–15) Reassessed," *JSOT* 35.3 (2011): 317–38; and Stephen M. Wilson, "Fear, Love, and Leadership: Posing a Machiavellian Question to the Hebrew Bible," *JBL* 139.2 (2020): 247–49.

14:52). He rules under the threat of constant deposition and is told as much by Samuel even before his failure with the Amalekites (1 Sam 13:13–14). Saul's mistakes, though fatal, are presented sympathetically.[32] The king dutifully waits the planned seven days for Samuel's arrival before conducting the ill-fated sacrifice, but the prophet does not come (1 Sam 13:8). As a result, Saul rushes the offering only because his soldiers are beginning to desert him, and the enemy is regrouping (1 Sam 13:12). Further, a rash oath, not a divine command, puts him in the position of being obliged to execute his son (1 Sam 14:24; 43–44). Even so, he would not have known of the obligation had God not been silent after Saul's inquiry through a priest (1 Sam 14:37). In the end, it is not a father's mercy but the intervention of Saul's own soldiers that spares Jonathan's life (vv. 45–46).

In these ways, Saul's story in 1 Samuel follows the path of a classic tragedy.[33] Though he is regularly victorious in combat (at least at first, 1 Sam 14:47–48) and eager to please both prophet and people, Saul's frequent cultic missteps are his undoing. His kingdom is lost, then, not on the battlefield but at the altar—this despite his attention to issues of ritual purity (1 Sam 14:31–35). When we recognize that spirit possession today is often practiced in cultic and sacrificial contexts, we are better positioned to understand how Saul's spirit malady compromises his ability to rule effectively. Further, the failures of his reign only to serve to heighten his mental trauma.

2.3.2 Spirit Phenomena and Mental Illness

Questions of madness have never been far from discussions of spirit phenomena, even in antiquity, but in modern times the pathologization of spirit phenomena has become a hallmark.[34] Sigmund Freud, analyzing a famous seventeenth century case of exorcism, concluded that demonic possession was the result of re-

---

32 Sellars argues that Saul's mistakes are not so much disobedience as they are repeatedly acquiescing to the will of the people, precisely the opposite of the portrait of the oppressor king that Samuel presents in chapter 8; "An Obedient Servant?," 318–19.

33 W. Lee Humphreys, "From Tragic Hero to Villain: A Study of the Figure of Saul and the Development of 1 Samuel," *JSOT* 7.22 (1982): 95–117; and Yairah Amit, "The Delicate Balance in the Image of Saul and Its Place in the Deuteronomistic History," in *Saul in Story and Tradition*, ed. Carl S. Ehrlich, FAT 47 (Tübingen: Mohr Siebeck, 2006), 71–79.

34 Michel Foucault, *History of Madness*, ed. Jean Khalfa, trans. Jonathan Murphy and Jean Khalfa (London: Routledge, 2006).

pressed instinctual and harmful impulses—the outbursts of the unconscious.[35] Carl Jung, operating with a different understanding of the unconscious, characterized mental ailments as the contemporary equivalents of ancient spirit possession:

> We are still as much possessed by autonomous psychic contents as if they were Olympians. Today they are called phobias, obsessions, and so forth; in a word, neurotic symptoms. The gods have become diseases...[36]

Efforts to classify possession behavior within an overarching medical framework still persist. But most modern medical specialists on spirit possession have come to recognize a greater complexity in the relationship between spirit phenomena and mental health than these early theories would suggest.

In contemporary parlance, spirit-possession and trance episodes are more often discussed in the context of "dissociation."[37] Dissociative disorders "are characterized by a disruption of and/or discontinuity in the normal integration of consciousness, memory, identity, emotion, perception, body representation, motor control, and behavior."[38] Since many forms of dissociation are the natural processes of a well-functioning mind (e.g., a reader's ability to dissociate from their environment in order to focus on a written text), considerable debate exists over which dissociative behaviors are healthy and which should be characterized as disorders. For instance, some evidence suggests that religious adherence is as-

---

[35] Sigmund Freud, "A Seventeenth-Century Demonological Neurosis (1923 [1922])," in *The Ego and the Id and Other Works*, trans. James Strachey, vol. 19 of *The Standard Edition of the Complete Psychological Works of Sigmund Freud* (London: Hogarth, 1961), 72–105.
[36] Carl G. Jung, "Commentary on 'The Secret of the Golden Flower,'" in *Alchemical Studies*, trans. R. F. C. Hull, vol. 13 of *The Collected Works of C. G. Jung* (Princeton: Princeton University Press, 1967), 37. On these passages from Freud and Jung, see Lucy Huskinson, "Analytical Psychology and Spirit Possession: Towards a Non-Pathological Diagnosis of Spirit Possession," in *Spirit Possession and Trance: New Interdisciplinary Perspectives*, ed. Bettina E. Schmidt and Lucy Huskinson (New York: Continuum, 2011), 85.
[37] Etzel Cardeña, "Trance and Possession as Dissociative Disorders," *TPRR* 29.4 (1992): 287–300; Kate M. Loewenthal, *Religion, Culture, and Mental Health* (Cambridge: Cambridge University Press, 2007); and Stanley Krippner, "Learning from the Spirits: Candomble, Umbanda, and Kardecismo in Recife, Brazil," *AnthCon* 19.1 (2008): 1–32.
[38] American Psychiatric Association, *Diagnostic and Statistical Manual of Mental Disorders: DSM-5*, 5th ed. (Arlington: American Psychiatric Publishing, 2013), 291–307, 291.

sociated with slightly higher rates of certain types of dissociative behavior and that these practices can have positive effects on mental health.[39]

Consequently, many theorists view some forms of dissociative disorders as therapeutic. For example, dissociative disorders can often develop as a means to avoid past or present pain.[40] Psychologists and anthropologists alike have come to wonder whether this perspective may be extended to some extent to spirit possession and trance—particularly in non-Western settings.[41] As psychologist Kate Lowenthal argues:

> Trance and spirit possession states can be understood in terms of dissociation, though there may be culture-specific features which may make these states better categorised as culture-specific. Trance and spirit possession may be unwanted, uncontrolled and malign, or be culturally and religiously channelled responses to stress with some beneficial side-effects, or be deliberately fostered as therapeutic.[42]

This point should not be overstated, however, as spirit possession is often harmful and is regularly recognized as such by both practitioners and theorists alike.

The challenge of classifying dissociation as harmful or healthy often emerges along the blurred lines of cultural specificity. The most recent edition of the *Diagnostic and Statistical Manual of Mental Disorders* (DSM-5) responded to this issue by clarifying that:

> Possession form dissociative identity disorder can be distinguished from culturally accepted possession states in that the former is involuntary, distressing, uncontrollable, and often recurrent or persistent; involves conflict between the individual and his or her surrounding family, social, or work milieu; and is manifested at times and in places that violate the norms of the culture or religion.[43]

Despite this caveat, many anthropologists are uncomfortable with the inclusion of spirit possession and trance under the category of "dissociation," seeing it as

---

39 Many forms of contemplative prayer or meditation, for example, can be categorized as positive, non-pathological forms of religious dissociation. Loewenthal, *Religion, Culture, and Mental Health*, 107–10.
40 Loewenthal, *Religion, Culture, and Mental Health*, 106.
41 E.g., Colleen A. Ward and Michael H. Beaubrun, "The Psychodynamics of Demon Possession," *JSSR* 19.2 (1980): 201–7; Tapio Nisula, *Everyday Spirits and Medical Interventions: Ethnographic and Historical Notes on Therapeutic Conventions in Zanzibar Town*, SAST 43 (Helsinki: Finnish Anthropological Society, 1999); and Eli Somer, "Culture-Bound Dissociation: A Comparative Analysis," *PCNA* 29.1 (2006): 213–26.
42 Loewenthal, *Religion, Culture, and Mental Health*, 124.
43 American Psychiatric Association, *DSM-5*, 295.

a strategy for using the "madness" diagnosis to avoid answering the question.[44] Further, anthropologists will sometimes point to the frequent inadequacy of psychiatric methods in treating non-Western spirit-possessed persons who are seeking relief, particularly when compared to indigenous methods like exorcism, deliverance, or spirit healing, which can be more effective.[45]

All of this is not to say that contemporary studies in mental health cannot be profitably applied to biblical literature. To the contrary, in recent years scholars utilizing critical lenses related to mental health (including disability and trauma studies) have made significant contributions to biblical studies.[46] These approaches have drawn attention to how bodies and minds were conceptualized differently in antiquity, as well as to how corporate experiences of trauma could have contributed to the composition and early interpretation of biblical literature.

One promising mental health lens that theorists have applied recently to spirit phenomena is moral injury (MI).[47] MI is generally defined as resulting from "exposure to events that involve either perpetrating or witnessing actions that

---

[44] E.g., "The use of terms like *dissociation* and *dissociative state* without further analysis ineluctably implies that altered states of consciousness reflect some degree of psychopathology: used this way, dissociation runs the danger of becoming merely an anthropological euphemism for the older and supposedly discarded answer ('They are crazy!') to the question of 'what is really happening?'" *Emphasis original.* Morton Klass, *Mind Over Mind: The Anthropology and Psychology of Spirit Possession* (Lanham: Rowman & Littlefield, 2003), 69. Quoted in Huskinson, "Analytical Psychology and Spirit Possession," 73–74.

[45] E.g., Lesley A. Sharp, "Exorcists, Psychiatrists, and the Problems of Possession in Northwest Madagascar," *SSM* 38.4 (1994): 525–42; Jean Mercer, "Deliverance, Demonic Possession, and Mental Illness: Some Considerations for Mental Health Professionals," *MHRC* 16.6 (2013): 595–611; and Krippner, "Learning from the Spirits."

[46] See, for example, Elizabeth Boase and Christopher G. Frechette, eds., *Bible through the Lens of Trauma*, SemeiaSt 86 (Atlanta: SBL Press, 2016); Candida R. Moss and Jeremy Schipper, *Disability Studies and Biblical Literature* (New York: Palgrave Macmillan, 2011); Eve-Marie Becker, Jan Dochhorn, and Else Kragelund Holt, eds., *Trauma and Traumatization in Individual and Collective Dimensions: Insights from Biblical Studies and Beyond*, SAN 2 (Göttingen: Vandenhoeck & Ruprecht, 2014); and Saul M. Olyan, *Disability in the Hebrew Bible: Interpreting Mental and Physical Differences* (Cambridge: Cambridge University Press, 2008).

[47] See, for example, Brad E. Kelle, *The Bible and Moral Injury: Reading Scripture alongside War's Unseen Wounds* (Nashville: Abingdon, 2020); Jan Grimell, "Contemporary Insights from Biblical Combat Veterans through the Lenses of Moral Injury and Post-Traumatic Stress Disorder," *JPCC* 72.4 (2018): 241–50; and Joseph McDonald, ed., *Exploring Moral Injury in Sacred Texts* (Philadelphia: Jessica Kingsley, 2017). More broadly, see Brandon J. Griffin et al., "Moral Injury: An Integrative Review," *JTrauSt* 32.3 (2019): 350–62; Jonathan Shay, *Odysseus in America: Combat Trauma and the Trials of Homecoming* (New York: Scribner, 2002); and Rita Nakashima Brock, *Soul Repair: Recovering from Moral Injury after War* (Boston: Beacon Press, 2012).

violate one's core beliefs or betrayal by a leader or trusted authority."[48] MI, then, is identified as a distinct phenomenon from PTSD, though the two often occur together, especially in veterans.

In a biblical context, Brad Kelle has identified Saul's early confrontations with the Philistines and Amalekites (1 Sam 13–15) as depicting precisely the kinds of moral and ethical ambiguities that can result in MI.[49] Such experiences can be understood as contributing to Saul's later distressing encounters with spirits. Kelle notes, for example, that combat veterans have described feeling as if a "monster" or "evil" has taken up residence within them and that these intruders at times exert efforts to control them.[50] It is notable that even within societies where spirit possession is practiced regularly, researchers have documented higher rates of possession among soldiers, who were in turn associated with higher rates of PTSD, depression, and attempted suicide.[51] In certain war-torn countries where varieties of possession are more common, there is evidence that pathological forms of spirit possession can function as an explanatory framework for subjectively unexplainable mental health conditions—especially trauma.[52]

Informed, then, by advances on the relationship between spirit phenomena in biblical literature and current conceptions of mental health, I can make two suggestions. First, attempts to diagnose biblical figures like Saul with specific modern mental illnesses are best rejected as overly optimistic, even if we recognize that mental state and health remain real factors in matters of spirit phenomena. Cultural expectation, literary convention, and the uncertainty of biblical authorship each provide their own barriers to such an examination. Second, the oversimplifying and patronizing conclusion that depictions of spirit phenomena in biblical literature were simply the ignorant way that ancient peoples conceived of what we now call mental illness must be rejected.[53]

---

[48] Griffin et al., "Moral Injury," 350–51.
[49] Kelle, *The Bible and Moral Injury*, 43–67.
[50] Kelle, *The Bible and Moral Injury*, 57.
[51] Frank Neuner et al., "Haunted by Ghosts: Prevalence, Predictors and Outcomes of Spirit Possession Experiences among Former Child Soldiers and War-Affected Civilians in Northern Uganda," *SSM* 75.3 (2012): 548–54.
[52] Tobias Hecker et al., "Pathological Spirit Possession as a Cultural Interpretation of Trauma-Related Symptoms," *PsyT* 8.4 (2016): 468–76.
[53] In addition to those psychological studies of Saul cited above, see other examples: George Stein, "The Voices That Ezekiel Hears," *BrJPsych* 196.2 (2010): 101; and Paul M. Joyce, "The Prophets and Psychological Interpretation," in *Prophecy and Prophets in Ancient Israel: Proceedings of the Oxford Old Testament Seminar*, ed. John Day (New York: T & T Clark, 2010), 133–48. See also the range of psychological ailments theorized to lay behind Paul's "thorn in the flesh"

This latter point is especially important since it is apparent that many early Jewish texts operate with implicit distinctions between spirit possession and mental disability. One frequently discussed New Testament example occurs in Mark 3:21–22, where some in the crowd accuse Jesus of being "out of his mind" (ἐξίστημι) but the scribes counter that he "has Beelzebul," a conclusion that, in context, suggests spirit possession.[54] The fact that these accusations are presented as two alternatives and not identical phenomena suggests that, at least in the final redaction of Mark, there is some distinction between a person being mentally ill and demonized.

We can turn also to an example closer to the figure of Saul. In 1 Sam 21, David mimics the behavior of someone who is mentally ill in order to disguise his identity:

> [11] David rose and fled that day from Saul; he went to King Achish of Gath. [12] The servants of Achish said to him, "Is this not David the king of the land? Did they not sing to one another of him in dances, 'Saul has killed his thousands, and David his ten thousands'?" [13] David took these words to heart and was very much afraid of King Achish of Gath. [14] So he changed his behavior (וישנו את־טעמו) before them; he pretended to be insane (ויתהלל)[55] when in their presence. He scratched marks on the doors of the gate, and let his spittle run down his beard. [15] Achish said to his servants, "Look, you see the man is mad (משתגע); why then have you brought him to me? [16] Do I lack madmen (משגעים), that you have brought this fellow to play the madman (להשתגע) in my presence? Shall this fellow come into my house?" (1 Sam 21:11–16 [NRSV vv. 10–15])[56]

The passage is revealing, since it utilizes not only a specific vocabulary for "madness" (*hithpael* form of הל"ל in v. 14 [NRSV v. 13] and forms of שג"ע in vv. 15–16 [NRSV vv. 14–15]) but also an example of what is stereotypically understood as "mad" behavior (i.e., drooling on one's beard). Whatever ailment David is feigning, it is likely something similar to what we might call a mental illness or disability (cf. Ps 34:1). Moreover, it does not seem to be connected to a spirit phenomenon in any way. Clearly, then, there is some operative distinction in 1

(2 Cor 12:7) that are surveyed in Adela Yarbro Collins, "Paul's Disability: The Thorn in His Flesh," in *Disability Studies and Biblical Literature*, ed. Candida R. Moss and Jeremy Schipper (New York: Palgrave Macmillan, 2011), 172–73. One especially extreme example is Juan B. Cortés and Florence M. Gatti, *The Case Against Possessions and Exorcisms: A Historical, Biblical, and Psychological Analysis of Demons, Devils, and Demoniacs* (New York: Vantage, 1975). This is by no means a new approach, e. g., Edwin Cornelius Broome, "Ezekiel's Abnormal Personality," *JBL* 65.3 (1946): 277–92.

54 See Bazzana, *Having the Spirit of Christ*, 33.
55 NRSV: "mad"
56 See the discussion of this passage in Olyan, *Disability in the Hebrew Bible*, 66–70.

Samuel between mental illness and spirit possession, though the boundary does not necessarily match contemporary descriptions.

This conclusion becomes more apparent when we consider Saul's spirit sickness in the same book. Conspicuously, none of the vocabulary for "madness" that was used in the David episode appears in connection to Saul. Instead, Saul's sickness is constructed theologically (i.e., as God-sent). He is said to be antagonized by a harmful spirit of God (רוח אלהים רעה), whose presence is manifest through Saul's unstable, aggressive, and violent behavior (e.g., 1 Sam 16:14–15; 23; 18:10; 19:9; cf. 20:33). Here, the translation of רעה as "harmful" is preferable to the more conventional rendering, "evil." This spirit of God is not categorically "evil" in a modern sense, but rather, is harmful or detrimental from the perspective of Saul. (From God's perspective, we might say it is a *good* spirit, since it is carrying out the divine will).[57]

There are, of course, many precedents in antiquity for understanding prophets and poets as stricken "mad" by the gods, in contexts both close to ancient Israel and Judaism and farther afield.[58] Some ancient writers saw madness as a side effect of receiving insight from the gods, or perhaps as a necessary precursor. What Saul suffers from, however, is not a necessary component of his being elected by God as king. Rather, it is an ailment that afflicts him only after the mantle has passed to another who is more (spiritually) fit.

Anthropologists and ethnographers have long noted how spirit possession often manifests first as a type of ailment. In some Somali cultures, for example, the word *sar* refers to both the possessing spirits and the various maladies they can cause.[59] In the *bori* possession cults of Niger, spirits choose their hosts by first afflicting their health. The afflicted hosts can attempt to resist the spirits' influence, but by their own account it is almost always better to "give in to the spirit's demands and seek a balanced and equitable relationship from which both

---

57 See Anne Marie Kitz, "Demons in the Hebrew Bible and the Ancient Near East," *JBL* 135.3 (2016): 447–64; and McCarter Jr., "Evil Spirit of God."
58 See, for example, the classic study by Abraham J. Heschel, *The Prophets* (New York: Harper Collins, 1962), 498–523. See also John R. Levison, "Prophecy in Ancient Israel: The Case of the Ecstatic Elders," *CBQ* 65.4 (2003): 503–21; Martti Nissinen, "Prophetic Madness: Prophecy and Ecstasy in the Ancient Near East and in Greece," in *Raising Up a Faithful Exegete: Essays in Honor of Richard D. Nelson*, ed. Kurt L. Noll and Brooks Schramm (University Park: Penn State University Press, 2010), 3–29; Thomas Pola, "Ekstase im Alten Testament," in *Gott fürchten und lieben: Studien zur Gotteserfahrung im Alten Testament*, BthSt 59 (Neukirchen-Vluyn: Neukirchener, 2007), 1–77; Wilson, "Prophecy and Ecstasy"; and Laura S. Nasrallah, *An Ecstasy of Folly: Prophecy and Authority in Early Christianity*, HTS 52 (Cambridge, MA: Harvard University Press, 2003).
59 Lewis, *Ecstatic Religion*, 66–67.

parties can benefit."⁶⁰ Those afflicted by spirits can seek help from the wider cult, where other mediums who have learned to live as hosts can act as mentors.

Comparison with *sar* and *bori* spirit ailments illuminate certain aspects of Saul's malady. In the longest exposition on his condition, Saul receives spirit therapy:

> ¹⁵ And Saul's servants said to him, "See now, a harmful⁶¹ spirit from God is tormenting you. ¹⁶ Let our lord now command the servants who attend you to look for someone who is skillful in playing the lyre; and when the harmful⁶² spirit from God is upon you, he will play it, and you will feel better." ¹⁷ So Saul said to his servants, "Provide for me someone who can play well, and bring him to me." ¹⁸ One of the young men answered, "I have seen a son of Jesse the Bethlehemite who is skillful in playing, a man of valor, a warrior, prudent in speech, and a man of good presence; and the LORD is with him." ¹⁹ So Saul sent messengers to Jesse, and said, "Send me your son David who is with the sheep. […]." ²³ And whenever the [harmful] spirit from God came upon Saul, David took the lyre and played it with his hand, and Saul would be relieved and feel better, and the harmful⁶³ spirit would depart from him. (1 Sam 16:15–19, 23)

Here, as in 1 Sam 10 and in 2 Kgs 3:15, music is a key tool for influencing spirits, a trend reflected throughout ethnographic literature. In 1 Sam 10, however, a neophyte Saul joins a band of experienced prophets. The circumstance in 1 Sam 16 seemingly reverses what might have been the anticipated practice inasmuch as a younger David provides spirit therapy for the older Saul. David at this point is already spirit influenced himself, having been anointed by Samuel, the first spirit influencer of the book. Further, as I discussed above, an editor has juxtaposed 1 Sam 16 verses 13 and 14, thereby suggesting that Saul's empowering spirit has passed on to David. Now David is able to use Saul's former spirit to calm his new harmful one.

Returning to the context of Cuban Espiritismo offers a contemporary comparison. Espírito Santo tells another story of a spirit-influenced young man dubbed H, who sought to develop his skills as a medium.⁶⁴ H attended a small assembly of mediums (about twelve) gathered at a home in Havana as part of an *investigación*, a process by which more experienced mediums help an acolyte determine the identities, characteristics, and wills of their attendant spirits. As Espírito Santo reports, the session began with prayers, including an Our Father

---

60 Adeline Masquelier, "From Hostage to Host: Confessions of a Spirit Medium in Niger," *Ethos* 30.1/2 (2002): 54.
61 NRSV: "an evil"
62 NRSV: "the evil"
63 NRSV: "the evil"
64 Espírito Santo, *Developing the Dead*, 150–52.

and a reading from Kardec. H was brought to the center of the room and told to relax as he began to host the spirit that was to be investigated. H began humming, while the other mediums sang along. Eventually H collapsed onto the floor, and those in attendance recognized that a spirit was now fully present within him. Senior mediums, two brothers named Antonio and Servando, interrogated the spirit. The spirit (speaking through H) explained that it was "ashamed." The questions continued, but the spirit was reluctant to speak, explaining that it did not "want to face life." The more experienced mediums discussed this testimony among themselves, tentatively concluding that the spirit attached to H had experienced cerebral development issues while alive (Antonio and Servando were also medical doctors, a cardiologist and pediatrician) and that these problems had been affecting H's own brain as well. They suggested that the spirit was jealous of H. "You can let go of this anguish, this anxiety you carry," they said to the spirit. "You must stop causing H harm."

This event, captured by an anthropologist who was present, was just one episode in a series of sessions that someone like H might have. The aim for such sessions is that over time and through the support of a wider network of mediums, a person like H and the spirits comprising his *cordon* might come to better understandings of one another and develop less antagonistic and more collaborative relationships. Further, by learning attentiveness, a beginning medium like H might better come to recognize the presence and messages of his spirits, making it possible for them to communicate without the full suspension of H's personality. Although exorcisms of harmful spirits are also an aspect of Espiritismo, the goal of such rituals is not the complete erasure of all spirit experiences and thus a return to "normal," but the cultivation of a particular kind of spiritual relationship and a particular kind of self.[65]

Although the portraits of Saul's and H's spirit-filled worlds are undeniably different in cultural particulars, their broader brush strokes are suggestively similar. In each of the two instances, it is not only the suffering figure who is conceived as spiritually porous but also the experts whose advice he seeks. Further, Saul's and H's respective conditions are pathologized but their diagnoses are not limited by that perspective; rather, the existence of spirits affecting the two is still recognized. The underlying spirit phenomena are arguably framed according to quite expansive theological and ideological frameworks. In H's case, the diagnosis is articulated in Spiritist (Kardecist) language. The doctor brothers, Antonio and Servando, are as comfortable discussing the cordon espiritual as they are discussing "metabolism," "somatization," "corpuscular theory" and other tech-

---

[65] Espírito Santo, *Developing the Dead*, 163–65.

nical terminology.⁶⁶ Likewise, within the theological framework of 1 Samuel and the wider Hebrew Bible, Saul's malady has been contextualized into the broader narrative of God's people, Israel, and the fortunes of their pre-exilic monarchies. Nowhere is this more apparent than in the final spirit consultation of Saul's life, his meeting with the medium at Endor.

2.4 The Spirit Medium of Endor

There is no shortage of creative approaches to interpreting the enigmatic story in 1 Sam 28 of Saul's visit to the medium at Endor. Previous strategies have made comparisons with cognate literature or with other scholarly disciplines. Interpreters have brought to bear Hittite incantation formulas, Sumerian-Akkadian necromancer texts, Babylonian Wisdom poetry, classical Greek texts, Ugaritic materials, traditional South African ancestor cults, contemporary studies on mental illness, and preliminary insights from developments in neuroscience.⁶⁷ Although some scholars have discussed 1 Sam 28 in connection with contemporary divination practices in various parts of the world, few have looked at the theoretical work that has been done on spirit-possession phenomena in cultural anthropology and ethnography.⁶⁸ My current effort engages this literature, by suggesting new answers to old questions. Most essential is one question that recurs throughout the secondary literature: How is the prophet Samuel's presence manifest?

The profusion of approaches to understanding this episode stems, in part, from disagreement about the provenance of the pericope. Many commentators

---

66 Espírito Santo, *Developing the Dead*, 152.
67 Representative examples include Manfred Hutter, "Religionsgeschichtliche Erwägungen zu 'elohîm in 1 Sam 28:13," *BN* 21 (1983): 32–36; Josef Tropper, *Nekromantie: Totenbefragung im Alten Orient und im Alten Testament*, AOAT 223 (Neukirchen-Vluyn: Neukirchener, 1989), 205–27; Mordechai Cogan, "The Road to En-Dor," in *Pomegranates and Golden Bells: Studies in Biblical, Jewish, and Near Eastern Ritual, Law, and Literature in Honor of Jacob Milgrom*, ed. David P. Wright, David Noel Freedman, and Avi Hurvitz (Winona Lake, IN: Eisenbrauns, 1995), 319–26; Theodore J. Lewis, *Cults of the Dead in Ancient Israel and Ugarit*, HSM 39 (Atlanta: Scholars Press, 1989); Stefan Fischer, "1 Samuel 28: The Woman of Endor – Who Is She and What Does Saul See?," *OTE* 14.1 (2001): 26–46; Williams and Le Roux, "King Saul's Mysterious Malady"; and Bill T. Arnold, "Soul-Searching Questions About 1 Samuel 28: Samuel's Appearance at Endor and Anthropology," in *What about the Soul?: Neuroscience and Christian Anthropology*, ed. Joel B. Green (Nashville: Abingdon, 2004), 75–83.
68 But see J. Kabamba Kiboko, *Divining the Woman of Endor: African Culture, Postcolonial Hermeneutics, and the Politics of Biblical Translation*, LHBOTS 644 (New York: T & T Clark, 2017).

seek to reconstruct a plausible historical setting for the ritual and typically date the text relatively early. For this task, the most influential perspective among English-speaking scholars was introduced by P. Kyle McCarter Jr. in his 1980 commentary on 1 Samuel.[69] McCarter argued for an older, pre-deuteronomistic kernel in 1 Sam 28 that originally did not specify Samuel as the ghost (אוֹב) raised by the medium.[70] If one accepts McCarter's reconstruction (or another, similar theory) it becomes much easier to see a hypothetical, historical kernel involving a king named Saul and a medium behind this story, however fragmentary and obscured by tradition it may be.

There are compelling textual reasons, however, to be suspicious that 1 Sam 28 is really this old. Swiss scholar Christophe Nihan, for example, has noted how 1 Sam 28 is conspicuously aware of other parts of the Bible—most prominently Samuel's robe and curse in 1 Sam 15, as well as Deut 18 and 2 Kgs 23.[71] Likewise, Joshua Berman has recognized the tight intertextual structuring of 1 Sam 28 (as well as that of 1 Sam 15).[72] Berman highlights a sophisticated strategy of "legal blending" at work in these chapters, demonstrating that they know not only the general prohibitions about divination in Pentateuchal passages like Lev 19–20 and Deut 18 but the specific texts themselves. With such "blending," even a small narrative detail like Saul prostrating himself before Samuel (1 Sam 28:14) could be a subtle scribal nod to another text (in this case, Lev 19:32).[73] Since 1 Sam 28 seems to be aware of and in fact playing off these other biblical texts, it is unlikely that any part of it could be pre-deuteronomistic.[74]

---

69 P. Kyle McCarter Jr., *I Samuel: A New Translation with Introduction, Notes, and Commentary*, AB 8 (Garden City, NY: Doubleday, 1980).
70 McCarter suggests that the episode was later removed by a conscientious redactor who did not care for Israel's king engaging in a form of divination explicitly prohibited by Deuteronomy. The story was then reinserted, with the figure of Samuel added as part of the "prophetic layer" in the Deuteronomistic History. However, it may have been put in the wrong place. Scholars at least as far back as Wellhausen have recognized that 1 Sam 28:1–2 reads very neatly into 29:1 and, when paying attention to geographic signifiers, the story of Saul and the medium could very well fit after 1 Sam 30. McCarter Jr., *I Samuel*, 417–23.
71 Christophe Nihan, "1 Samuel 28 and the Condemnation of Necromancy in Persian Yehud," in *Magic in the Biblical World: From the Rod of Aaron to the Ring of Solomon*, ed. Todd Klutz, JSNTSup 245 (New York: T & T Clark, 2003), 23–54, 34–35.
72 Berman, "The Legal Blend in Biblical Narrative"; *Inconsistency in the Torah: Ancient Literary Convention and the Limits of Source Criticism* (Oxford: Oxford University Press, 2017), 160–65.
73 Berman, "The Legal Blend in Biblical Narrative," 121.
74 Nihan offers a number of examples in 1 Sam 28 of typical Deuteronomistic language and references. Nihan, "1 Samuel 28," 34–35. These elements, Nihan argues, are too integral to the chapter to be insertions, and so he sees no need to posit an earlier tradition that has been reworked. He suggests instead a Persian date for 1 Sam 28, noting that the divination practices

Since my chief concern in this book is the literary presentation of spirit phenomena in the Hebrew Bible, my analysis of 1 Sam 28 is not dependent on whether we read it exclusively within any particular historical context. The brief commentary just provided demonstrates, however, that a literary approach must grapple with the intertextual nature of biblical literature. Though parallels with anthropological literature can be drawn, especially in relatively clean narrative accounts like 1 Sam 28, it should be obvious that they are not the same type of literature. Biblical texts are not ethnographic reports but instead are traditions that have been contextualized as parts of broader theological agendas.

2.4.1 The Setting for a Spirit-Possession Ritual

The beginning of the story (1 Sam 28:3) predates Charles Dickens's *A Christmas Carol* by several millennia, but its first words accomplish a goal similar to those that begin the nineteenth century novella: "Marley was dead: to begin with."[75] Even Dickens's elaboration fits here as well: "There is no doubt that Marley was dead. This must be distinctly understood, or nothing wonderful can come of the story I am going to relate."[76] To compare:

> Now Samuel had died, and all Israel had mourned for him and buried him in Ramah, his own city. Saul had expelled the mediums (אבות) and the wizards (ידענים) from the land. (1 Sam 28:3)

By reiterating Samuel's death (which was already similarly narrated in chapter 25), the narrative emphasizes the truly marvelous nature of what follows. Samuel is dead, and moreover his body is buried in Ramah. Further, Saul has turned away the אבות and ידענים from the land. Various English translations have been put forward for these terms, including *witches*, *wizards*, *diviners*, and *mediums*, but cognates in other Semitic languages as well as occurrences in other parts of the Hebrew Bible determine that they refer to specific types of spirit beings (cf. Lev 19:31; 20:6; Isa 8:19; 19:3). As indicated by the OG versions, the terms

---

depicted in the chapter have more in common with mid-first millennium Mesopotamian divination practices than with older Levantine, Egyptian, or Anatolian practices. See also Brian B. Schmidt, "The 'Witch' of En-Dor, 1 Samuel 28, and Ancient Near Eastern Necromancy," in *Ancient Magic and Ritual Power*, ed. Marvin W. Meyer and Paul Allan Mirecki, RGRW 129 (Leiden: Brill, 1995).

75 Charles Dickens, *A Christmas Carol*, ed. Richard Kelly (Peterborough: Broadview, 2003), 39.
76 Dickens, *A Christmas Carol*, 39.

were understood by some as referring both to the spirits and to the hosts that possess them.⁷⁷

When modern readers interpret this passage through the lens of the dominant stereotypes for spirit possession (exemplified in the story of Arne Johnson from chapter 1), it is easy to characterize the episode as a marginal practice or one prevalent only at the level of popular religion. Esther Hamori rightly criticizes this stream of interpretation for operating with false dichotomies, such as those between "official" and "folk" religion.⁷⁸ Although the episode is certainly enigmatic within the corpus of the Hebrew Bible, there is nothing explicit in the passage to suggest that practices like this are especially "marginal," other than the fact that Saul has perhaps recently made them so.

In possession studies as well, anthropologists repeatedly observe how often possession rituals are treated as normal and expected—even among those who do not regularly participate in them. Referring to Swahili possession cults in coastal Kenya and Tanzania, anthropologist Linda Giles explained how many of the most avid participants in spirit possession were from wealthy, upper-class, and cosmopolitan families. Several were well-educated, professional, and very involved in public Muslim life—some were even teachers of Qur'an.⁷⁹ In short, none of the participants were marginal to Islam.⁸⁰

Thus, when attempting to situate the ritual described in 1 Sam 28 within the context of the diverse religious practices of ancient Israel, we should recognize that there is nothing a priori unusual, rare, or unsavory about the ritual or this woman other than the king's recent ban.⁸¹ Some commentators make too much of the fact that Saul must go in disguise or by night, but these factors are best understood as an effort by the king to hide what he is doing, or perhaps as necessary parts of the ritual.

Next, we see the full extent of Saul's failure and the ironic tragedy that his life has become:

---

77 ἐγγαστριμύθους and γνώστας respectively. See Josef Tropper, "Spirit of the Dead," *DDD*, 806–9; and "Wizard," *DDD*, 907–8.
78 Esther J. Hamori, *Women's Divination in Biblical Literature: Prophecy, Necromancy, and Other Arts of Knowledge* (New Haven: Yale University Press, 2015), 19–40.
79 Linda L. Giles, "Possession Cults on the Swahili Coast: A Re-Examination of Theories of Marginality," *Africa* 57.2 (1987): 241–47.
80 Giles, "Possession Cults on the Swahili Coast," 243.
81 This being said, it would be difficult to show (particularly in its later redactions) any place in the Hebrew Bible that would approve of this form of divination. This is because biblical literature itself offers its own (sometimes contradictory) criteria for distinguishing between illegitimate and legitimate forms of spirit phenomena. See my discussion on this in the next chapter.

> [4] The Philistines assembled, and came and encamped at Shunem. Saul gathered all Israel, and they encamped at Gilboa. [5] When Saul saw the army of the Philistines, he was afraid, and his heart trembled greatly. [6] When Saul inquired of the LORD, the LORD did not answer him, not by dreams, or by Urim, or by prophets. [7] Then Saul said to his servants, "Seek out for me a woman who is a medium of a ghost[82] (אשת בעלת־אוב), so that I may go to her and inquire through her." His servants said to him, "There is a woman who is the medium of a ghost at Endor."[83] (1 Sam 28:4–7)

King Saul, on the eve of a climactic battle with Philistines, seeks guidance from God, who refuses to answer. Though he began his desperate inquiry piously—seeking knowledge from the approved forms of divination (1 Sam 28:6)—each has failed him.[84]

It is possible that Saul perceives his task at Endor to be permissible, or at least in a gray area. After all, Samuel is a recognized prophet and thus an allowable source of divine knowledge; it is just that he also happens to be dead. The narrative of 1 Samuel has previously identified Saul as a spiritually porous person susceptible to the influences of outside powers, and he has already sought spirit consultations from experienced experts and found relief. Why would he not do the same when God refuses to answer him (cf. 1 Sam 14:37)? Like his previous cultic missteps, it is in the borderlines where Saul has tread and, as in the past, Saul is chastised for his infractions.

Despite clear literary evidence to the contrary, many commentators of this text have been reluctant to recognize the medium as a professional. For example, despite the popular appellation for this story, the word "witch" (מכשפה) does not appear here (cf. Exod 22:18; Deut 18:10). Rather, the term that does appear, אשת בעלת־אוב (v. 7), seems to be, as Joseph Blenkinsopp argued, a kind of job title.[85] The word translated above as "ghost" (אוב) occurs sixteen times in the Hebrew

---

82 NRSV: "a woman who is a medium"
83 NRSV: "There is a medium at Endor"
84 E. g., *Urim* [and *thummim*] (e. g., 1 Sam 14:41), dreams (e. g., 1 Kgs 3:5–15), and prophets (e. g., 1 Sam 22:5). See Frederick H. Cryer, *Divination in Ancient Israel and Its Near Eastern Environment: A Socio-Historical Investigation*, JSOTSup 142 (Sheffield: Sheffield Academic, 1994), esp. chp. 5. To the list of approved forms of divination we might also add the ephod (1 Sam 23:9) and lots (Num 26:55). See Yeḥezkel Kaufmann, *The Religion of Israel: From its Beginnings to the Babylonian Exile*, trans. Moshe Greenberg (Chicago: University of Chicago Press, 1960), 88.
85 Joseph Blenkinsopp, "Saul and the Mistress of the Spirits," in *Sense and Sensitivity: Essays on Reading the Bible in Memory of Robert Carroll*, ed. Alastair G. Hunter and Philip R. Davies, JSOTSup 348 (London: Sheffield, 2002), 53. As Hamori demonstrates, the construction has precedents in Sumerian-Akkadian lists of professionals. Hamori, *Women's Divination in Biblical Literature*, 105–10.

Bible, and most often it designates the spirit of a dead person.⁸⁶ Thus, "a woman who consults ghosts," as the NJPS has it, or "a woman who is a medium," according to the NRSV, are defensible translations.

One other intriguing option for translating the medium's title exists. P. Kyle McCarter Jr. also suggests a translation of "spirit-" or "ghost-wife."⁸⁷ Hamori rejects this translation because she believes it downplays the woman's skill and mastery over "ghosts" (אובות) in favor of the marital imagery.⁸⁸ In my opinion, however, one need not preclude the other. Titles along the lines of "spirit-spouse" are prevalent in possession-practicing communities across the world without implying less status or spirit power. In a *Saora* Hindu possession cult in India, for example, both men and women can acquire not only spouses who are spirits but spirit-children as well.⁸⁹ In Haiti, as recently as the mid-twentieth century, voodoo marriage announcements between a woman and her spirit husband could be found in local newspapers.⁹⁰ Because the complicated relationships between hosts and the dead are conceptualized differently across cultures, one ought not rule out this translation (or at least some element of its meaning) in interpreting of the medium at Endor.

It may also be significant that the woman's title indicates she is the medium of a particular "ghost" (אוב singular) and not "ghosts" in general (אובות plural). In many spirit-possession cults, it is customary for mediums first to establish a special relationship with one spirit in particular, who then enables the medium to consult other spirits of the dead.⁹¹

As the story continues, Saul and his two servants make their way to Endor, where Saul engages the medium.

⁸ So Saul disguised himself and put on other clothes (ויתחפש שאול וילבש בגדים אחרים) and went there, he and two men with him. They came to the woman by night. And he said, "Consult a spirit for me, and bring up for me the one whom I name to you." ⁹ The woman said to him, "Surely you know what Saul has done, how he has cut off the mediums and wizards from the land. Why then are you laying a snare for my life to bring about my death?" (1 Sam 28:8–9)

---

86 Hamori, *Women's Divination in Biblical Literature*, 106–07. For a discussion of אוב and other Semitic cognates, see Harry A. Hoffner Jr., "Second Millennium Antecedents to the Hebrew 'ôb," *JBL* 86.4 (1967): 385–401.
87 McCarter Jr., "Evil Spirit of God," 420.
88 Hamori, *Women's Divination in Biblical Literature*, 106.
89 Lewis, *Ecstatic Religion*, 53–54.
90 See Lewis, *Ecstatic Religion*, 55. See also Karen McCarthy Brown, *Mama Lola: A Vodou Priestess in Brooklyn*, Rev. ed., CSRS 4 (Berkeley: University of California Press, 2001).
91 See, for example, the discussion of Cuban *Espiritismo Cruzado* at the start of this chapter.

The precise location of Endor is disputed, but it would seem to be a place within Saul's kingdom.[92] Otherwise, why would the medium express fear at being found out? Similarly, any effort to portray the medium as a foreigner who has imported some obscure and out of place practice into ancient Israel overlooks Saul's closest aids knowing precisely where to find just such a person when asked (v.7). Although there is much we are not told about this medium, we can be certain that she is one of Saul's own subjects.

The actual narrative of the meeting is incredibly sparse, making it the most disputed section of the entire story. The first portion of the encounter reads:

> [10] But Saul swore to her by the LORD, "As the LORD lives, no punishment shall come upon you for this thing." [11] Then the woman said, "Whom shall I bring up for you?" He answered, "Bring up Samuel for me." [12] When the woman saw Samuel, she cried out with a loud voice; and the woman said to Saul, "Why have you deceived me? You are Saul!" [13] The king said to her, "Have no fear; what do you see?" The woman said to Saul, "I see divine beings[93] coming up out of the ground" (אלהים ראיתי עלים מן־הארץ). [14] He said to her, "What is his appearance?" She said, "An old man is coming up; he is wrapped in a robe." So Saul knew that it was Samuel, and he bowed with his face to the ground, and did obeisance. [15] Then Samuel said to Saul, "Why have you disturbed me by bringing me up?" Saul answered, "I am in great distress, for the Philistines are warring against me, and God has turned away from me and answers me no more, either by prophets or by dreams; so I have summoned you to tell me what I should do." (1 Sam 28:10–15)

Though only five verses long, this section contains a multitude of possible interpretations. In what follows, I offer one possible scenario, which I suggest in light of comparative evidence from ethnographic descriptions of similar spirit-possession rituals from around the world.

2.4.2 The Possession Ritual at Endor: Three Answered Questions

Numerous ambiguities exist in this ritual scene. The most pressing question for many readers is likely the matter of identity: Is this actually Samuel? Although it may be troubling for some, it seems clear to me that, from the point of view of the text, it is indeed Samuel whom the medium raises up, and his prophecy is every bit as authentic as any other found in the Hebrew Bible. Further, in recog-

---

92 Cogan, "The Road to En-Dor," 319.
93 NRSV: "divine being"

nizing the authenticity of the possession, 1 Sam 28 does not represent a significant departure from other perspectives on divination in the Hebrew Bible.[94]

Beyond the matter of identity, three slightly more procedural questions have habitually vexed commentators:
1) When does the ritual start?
2) What is it about seeing Samuel that causes the woman to recognize Saul in verse 12?
3) How does Samuel appear?

These questions are treated in order below.

1. When Does the Ritual Start?
Many commentators regard the ritual as starting between verses 11 and 12, assuming that the medium must know whom she is raising before she can begin. I propose that the ritual might actually begin between verses 10 and 11—that is, after the medium has received a promise that her life will be saved.[95] Although the depiction is succinct, possession rituals today are usually neither short nor simple but can take hours and might also involve consultation with several different spirits. Lên đồng rituals in Vietnam, for example, may take weeks of preparation and last for hours, wherein dozens of spirits are consulted, each requiring a costume change.[96] When the medium in our text is ready to make the final possession, Saul (who is perhaps also participating in the ritual) speaks the name, "Samuel."

2. Why Does the Medium Recognize Saul?
The reaction of the woman in verse 12 is sudden and surprising. If she is a professional, why does she cry out? What is it about seeing *Samuel* that causes the woman to recognize *Saul*? Some have argued that the woman is a fraud and did not expect anything to happen, while others have suggested that simply seeing Samuel and Saul together helped her recognize the latter. A few scholars have

---

[94] Among the handful of mentions of divination by means of ghosts of the dead, the veracity of such practices is not usually disputed (e.g., Lev 19:31; Deut 18:11; 2 Kgs 21:6; 23:24; Isa 8:19; 29:4; 1 Chr 10:13). Rather they are prohibited *because* they are effective and yet not of God (Lev 20:6, 27).
[95] Another possibility is suggested by Hamori that the raising does not occur until between verses 12 and 13. This possibility, however, requires some emendation of the text (see discussion below). Hamori, *Women's Divination in Biblical Literature*, 121.
[96] Karen Fjelstad and Nguyễn Thị Hiền, *Spirits without Borders: Vietnamese Spirit Mediums in a Transnational Age* (New York: Palgrave Macmillan, 2011), 56–67.

argued that verses 11–12 are an insertion. While this suggestion may make a hypothetical original kernel of text run more smoothly, it does not explain why a later scribe would opt to confuse an otherwise orderly account.[97] One old argument has been to emend the text, changing Samuel's name in verse 12 to "Saul."[98] In this vein, ותרא "she saw" would need to be understood in the sense of "seeing through a disguise," but that meaning is unattested. Another solution, offered by Hamori and others, emends וַתֵּרֶא to וַתִּרָא, thereby changing the root (from רא״ה to יר״א) and the meaning to "she *feared* Samuel." That change would pair nicely with Saul's command for her not to be afraid in verse 13;[99] however, there is no manuscript evidence to support that reading, and, in any case, it still does not answer the question: Why should the woman be afraid of Samuel when calling him up was precisely what she was trying to do? Moreover, how does seeing Samuel help her recognize Saul?

Rejecting these partial solutions, I believe that we can accept the Masoretic Text as is and without insertion and understand the medium as beginning to host the spirit of Samuel in verse 12. The possession gives her special insight by which she recognizes Saul through his disguise.[100] She cries out, then, not because she is afraid of Samuel or because something has gone wrong in her ritual, but rather because she recognizes her oppressor, King Saul, standing right in front of her.[101]

The ensuing verses, then, can be read as the expected performance of a possession ritual. Contrary to popular portrayals of spirit possession as violent, sudden, and uncontrollable, possession in most cults occurs in highly ritualized settings and according to a familiar script (with room for acceptable variations—not unlike musicians riffing on a theme or playing a solo). Even though the ritual has started in verse 12, it is clear that the medium's personality has not departed entirely (i.e., she continues to speak as herself in vv. 12–14). Again, personality retention is not unusual within the context of contemporary spirit cults, where a spirit's presence may come and go, where the host's personality may or may not also be present simultaneously, and where multiple spirits may be present. This last point is especially pertinent when we consider use of the word אלהים in verse 13. It is best understood not as a reference to Israel's deity, but as a rarer (though well-enough attested) title for Israel's departed dead (cf. 2 Sam 14:16, Isa

---

97 See the survey of scholarship in Blenkinsopp, "Saul and the Mistress of the Spirits," 54.
98 See Karl Budde, *Die Bücher Samuel*, (Tübingen: Mohr Siebeck, 1902), 180–81.
99 Hamori, *Women's Divination in Biblical Literature*, 121.
100 Fischer also argues for this, Fischer, *Gotteskünderinnen*, 139.
101 Pamela Tamarkin Reis, "Eating the Blood: Saul and the Witch of Endor," *JSOT* 73 (1997): 10.

8:19).¹⁰² Reading אלהים as a plural not only dovetails with ethnographic accounts of spirit rituals where multiple non-fleshly presences are active, it also makes the most sense grammatically, since the participle "rising" (עלים) is also plural.¹⁰³ The medium is thus aware of the presence of several spirits, and eventually one emerges fully—Samuel.

3. How Does Samuel Appear?

Most of the commentators I surveyed believe that Samuel appears as some kind of visual apparition. This perspective is certainly the dominant one when we look at how this episode has been portrayed in Western art.¹⁰⁴ Others, including Blenkinsopp, follow the cues of the OG, suggesting that the woman is utilizing some kind of visual trick and then throwing her voice.¹⁰⁵ Admittedly, the appearance of a visible ghost may initially seem to be the answer, not least because the narrative uses the verb for *seeing* so frequently. However, on closer inspection, we notice that Saul is never the subject of any verbs of seeing. In fact, in verses 13–14, he must ask the medium what *she* sees, and it is only after she gives a physical description that he recognizes the ghost as Samuel. Further, Samuel's monologue is clustered together in verses 15–19, and within this section the woman does not speak.

> ¹⁶ Samuel said, "Why then do you ask me, since the LORD has turned from you and become your enemy? ¹⁷ The LORD has done to you just as he spoke by me; for the LORD has torn the kingdom out of your hand, and given it to your neighbor, David. ¹⁸ Because you did not obey the voice of the LORD, and did not carry out his fierce wrath against Amalek, therefore the LORD has done this thing to you today. ¹⁹ Moreover the LORD will give Israel along with you into the hands of the Philistines; and tomorrow you and your sons shall be with me; the LORD will also give the army of Israel into the hands of the Philistines." (1 Sam 28:16–19)

Given the other indications of spirit possession already discussed above, I think it most likely that the medium is depicted here as hosting the spirit of Samuel

---

102 Blenkinsopp, "Saul and the Mistress of the Spirits," 53–54; and Hutter, "Religionsgeschichtliche Erwägungen Zu 'elohîm in 1 Sam 28."
103 This is how the OG reads it as well: καὶ εἶπεν αὐτῷ Θεοὺς ἑόρακα ἀναβαίνοντας ἐκ τῆς γῆς.
104 See, for example, the neoclassicist painting by Benjamin West, which features a ghostly Samuel draped in white and emerging from a cloud of smoke: Benjamin West, *Saul and the Witch of Endor*, Oil on Canvas, 1777, London, Victoria and Albert Museum, http://collections.vam.ac.uk/item/O134041/saul-and-the-witch-of-oil-painting-west-benjamin/.
105 This perspective is informed by the OG, ἐγγαστριμύθους, "ventriloquist" (1 Sam 28:3, 7–9). Blenkinsopp, "Saul and the Mistress of the Spirits," 56. While this may or may not be the intended sense in the OG, the case is considerably weaker in Hebrew and goes against the plain sense that the medium is not a fraud but simply doing what she is known to be able to do.

within her body and speaking all of Samuel's words as his host. There is no visible apparition or ghostly figure. Like the ethnographic report of Marcelina discussed at the outset of this chapter, the medium at Endor is possessed by (or better *possesses*) the spirit of Samuel within herself. Indeed, in instances of possession, we might be tempted to think of the host as *being* possessed passively by spirit(s), but it seems clear to me that the Endor medium is, in fact, calling up Samuel against his will (e. g., v. 15). Although this interpretation of the narrative is not the most popular interpretation, it is not unprecedented.[106]

Even without considering the prevalence of deceased ancestor-consultation rituals in the ethnographic literature reviewed so far, several indications within the text of 1 Samuel suggest just such a situation. To begin, it is notable that Samuel addresses Saul in the second person singular in verse 15, "Why have you [masc. sg.; *you*, and not the medium] disturbed me ...?" Perhaps the medium is effectively no longer present. As Pamela Tamarkin Reis has incisively pointed out, it is conspicuous that the medium does not speak again until verse 21, where she is reintroduced (the woman "came" to Saul), even though we have not been told that she ever left:[107]

> [20] Immediately Saul fell full length on the ground, filled with fear because of the words of Samuel; and there was no strength in him, for he had eaten nothing all day and all night. [21] The woman came to Saul (ותבוא האשה אל־שאול), and when she saw that he was terrified, she said to him, "Your servant has listened to you; I have taken my life in my hand, and have listened to what you have said to me. [22] Now therefore, you also listen to your servant; let me set a morsel of bread before you. Eat, that you may have strength when you go on your way." [23] He refused, and said, "I will not eat." But his servants, together with the woman, urged him; and he listened to their words. So he got up from the ground and sat on the bed. [24] Now the woman had a fatted calf in the house. She quickly slaughtered it (ותזבחהו), and she took flour, kneaded it, and baked unleavened cakes. [25] She put them before Saul and his servants, and they ate. Then they rose and went away that night. (1 Sam 28:20–25)

According to Reis, the beginning of verse 21 (ותבוא האשה אל־שאול) indicates that the woman offers herself sexually to Saul out of fear he might punish her for committing this act of divination. Upon noticing his terror, Reis continues, the medium changes her strategy, providing instead the fattened calf as a blood sacrifice to ap-

---

[106] See, for example, Tikva Frymer-Kensky, *Reading the Women of the Bible* (New York: Schocken, 2002), 312. See also Kaufmann, *The Religion of Israel*, 87–88. For an ancient parallel, see the survey of the Theban Magical Library in Jacco Dieleman, "The Greco-Egyptian Magical Papyri," in *Guide to the Study of Ancient Magic*, ed. David Frankfurter, RGRW 189 (Leiden: Brill, 2019), 297–98.
[107] Reis, "Eating the Blood," 13.

pease the spirits and spare her life from Saul's retribution.¹⁰⁸ There is little else in the story, however, to suggest a sexual invitation. More likely in my mind is that verse 21 is simply explaining that the ghost of Samuel has departed and that the medium is now fully present once again. She has "come [back]" to Saul fully and so is able to appreciate how the spirit-possession ritual is affecting him.

Along these lines, it is more significant than is usually recognized that Saul fasts before visiting the medium (v. 20).¹⁰⁹ Within 1 Samuel, Saul has already shown himself overeager to fast in connection to battle (1 Sam 14:24).¹¹⁰ More broadly, in biblical literature fasting is most readily associated with mourning and repentance.¹¹¹ However, commentators have also noted that visionary figures frequently fast before embarking on heavenly journeys—especially in later Second Temple literature (cf. Dan 9:3, 10:2–3; 2 Bar 9:2; 4 Ezra 5:13). This may be because fasting makes one more like the angels, who do not eat.¹¹² In many other spirit-possession practices as well, fasting is often undertaken as one aspect of preparation before a ritual.¹¹³ Although there is little enough detail provided about the rationale behind Saul's fasting, it is possible that spiritual preparation prior to his meeting with this professional medium is one factor.

Further, Reis's suggestion that the meal has ritual significance beyond mere sustenance is, I think, similarly possible but inconclusive. Saul's changing of clothes and his fasting are common behaviors among possession practices described in ethnographic literature; these practices also frequently feature ritual meals and slaughters. One especially graphic example is captured in the influential and frequently criticized 1955 ethnographic film, *Les Maîtres fous* (*The Mad Masters*), directed by Jean Rouch.¹¹⁴ The film depicts the *hauka* cults of Nigerian expatriates in Ghana (then Gold Coast) engaged in a spirit-possession pageant wherein

---

108 Reis, "Eating the Blood," 13–19.
109 I am grateful to Angela Harkins and Meredith Warren for encouraging me to explore this point in their comments at my presentation to the Religious Experience in Antiquity section of the 2017 SBL Annual Meeting in Denver.
110 I am grateful to Carol Wise for alerting me to this parallel.
111 Lambert, *How Repentance Became Biblical*, 13–31.
112 See Ithamar Gruenwald, *Apocalyptic and Merkavah Mysticism*, 2nd ed., AJEC 90 (Leiden: Brill, 2014); Carla Sulzbach, "When Going on a Heavenly Journey, Travel Light and Dress Appropriately," *JSP* 19.3 (2010): 163–93; and Tobias Nicklas, "'Food of Angels' (Wis 16:20)," in *Studies in the Book of Wisdom*, ed. Géza G. Xeravits and József Zsengellér, JSJSup 142 (Leiden: Brill, 2010), 83–100.
113 See, for example, the role of fasting in many examples of middle age exorcisms, Caciola, *Discerning Spirits*.
114 Jean Rouch, *Les Maîtres Fous (The Mad Masters)* (France, Les Films de la Pléiade, 1955).

they are possessed by French and British colonizing spirits.[115] The participants utilize props (e.g., mock military paraphernalia, cigars, and brandy) to indicate their possession and engage in striking behavior that often violates social taboos, notably slaughtering a dog and eating its meat half-cooked. Despite this brutality, there is an element of parody and even comedy to the portrayal of these displacing colonizers, as the filmmaker and later commentators have noted. Rouch himself interpreted the pageant as a depiction of the violence imposed upon African cultures by Europeans, akin to the "safety valve" approach described by Lewis in chapter 1.[116] Returning then to 1 Samuel, the constellation of parallel spirit-possession elements that we find in the episode (i.e., fasting, changing clothes, and ritual meal), each coincidental and dismissible on its own, may suggest the presence of a much more elaborate and detailed possession ritual than is usually supposed.

This point is provocative, in fact, when we contemplate the ways in which spirit-possession rituals frequently play with and at times redefine the borders around taboo behavior.[117] Spirit hosts under spirit influence may acquire new prohibitions (compare the restrictions on Nazirites in Num 6:1–21), or alternatively, may engage in disrespectful, taboo, or licentious behavior while under the influence of a spirit.[118]

These factors might be at work in Samuel's response to Saul (as mediated through the medium) in verses 16–19. The intermixing of Saul's many opponents in this prophecy makes the agency behind it complicated. First, there is the voice of the medium, whose profession Saul has outlawed; second, there is the presence of Samuel, whom Saul has grieved and called up against his will (1 Sam 15:35); and, finally, there is the judgment of God, who has rejected Saul as king. The source of such unequivocal condemnation of the king could be any

---

[115] See discussion in Bazzana, *Having the Spirit of Christ*, 88–91.
[116] More recent theorists have interpreted this ritual as being more culturally productive than a mere unhealthy and ultimately ineffective form of resistance. Ethnographic filmmaker and visual anthropologist Paul Henley, for example, has argued that the participants in this *hauka* ritual are not just making observations about the foreign colonizers but actively attempting to harness their power by mimicking and appropriating their culture. *The Adventure of the Real: Jean Rouch and the Craft of Ethnographic Cinema* (Chicago: University of Chicago Press, 2009).
[117] See, for example, Michael Lambek, "Taboo as Cultural Practice Among Malagasy Speakers," *Man* 27.2 (1992): 245–66.
[118] Lewis cites the example of the Swahili-speaking Pokomo of Mafia island, near Tanzania, a tribe usually excluded from the public life of more dominant tribes. These practitioners nonetheless exercise a degree of power and influence in wider society through their skills in treating spiritual ailments, despite the fact that their "flamboyant rites" violate various taboos of the predominantly Muslim culture. Lewis, *Ecstatic Religion*, 97–98.

one of these figures. The spirit-possession ritual, however, succeeds in dispersing it among the three.

In assessing the episode at Endor, a lingering question remains: If setting the narrative within the context of spirit possession is as straightforward as I have made it out to be, why have so many interpreters before me missed it? Although a variety of answers might be suggested here, one seems especially pertinent. I believe that many readers—particularly modern interpreters—have missed the cues for spirit possession in this story because their assumptions about such phenomena were shaped by the anachronistic portraits I have been critiquing, especially in chapter 1. A reader operating with a modern conception of the self as "buffered," for example, would expect such breaches of Saul's and the medium's boundaried interiorities to be noted explicitly by the text. But, if we grant that the communities behind this literature lived in a world with much more porous borders between the "inside" and the "outside" of a person, it would be perfectly natural, for instance, for all of the spirit's dialogue in 1 Sam 28:15–19 to be narrated with Samuel as the subject of all the verbs, even though it is the medium's voice that is speaking. We would expect this, in fact, since we have already been told explicitly that she is a professional medium and that through her expertise, Samuel really is present and communicating with Saul.

2.5 Conclusions

Chapter 2 has investigated two interconnected case studies from the book of 1 Samuel: Saul's spirit sickness and his visit to the medium at Endor. Both examples are better understood when read in comparison with contemporary ethnographic and anthropological studies of spirit possession. Saul's various encounters with spirits reflect the dynamic relationships with spirits that many possessed individuals experience in cultures that embrace spirit possession. I have suggested that mental health—especially issues of PTSD and moral injury—is a likely factor in Saul's spirit encounters but that these phenomena alone cannot account completely for the literary presentation of Saul's spirit experiences. Saul's visit to the medium at Endor maps closely onto the kinds of consultations that spirit-affected persons may have with various experts in their respective settings. In particular, Cuban Espiritismo Cruzado serves as a productive milieu for comparison. I have argued that the medium at Endor is a spirit professional who summons the ghost of Samuel against his will and hosts his presence within her body, speaking his dialogue with her voice. The case studies discussed in this chapter demonstrate not only how spirit phenomena may be functioning in these particular biblical passages but also the interpretive possibilities that this overall approach can yield.

3 Getting into the Spirit

3.1 The Myriad Modes of Talking to the Dead Among Gullah/Geechee Women

Today, Gullah/Geechee refers to a distinct cultural group of African Americans who are associated historically with the Sea Islands and the Lowcountry of the southeastern United States, particularly South Carolina. Due to their relative geographic isolation, Gullah/Geechee culture developed somewhat independently from other communities in the American South, retaining many African elements and innovating novel aspects of religion, language, food, art, and music. For these reasons and more, in recent years Gullah/Geechee culture has come under increasing interest from both scholars and the wider culture.[1] Of particular interest to this project is the well-known practice of "talking to the dead," widely associated with Gullah/Geechee women in particular, though not exclusively. In her book discussing this aspect of Gullah/Geechee religion, LeRhonda S. Manigault-Bryant categorizes it in this way:

> Talking to the dead most often occurs in two types of practices. The first are customs traditionally interpreted as religious, which include prayer, seekin' (a process of gaining church membership), shouting or experiencing ecstatic spiritual moments, and sacred music traditions. The second category includes cultural activities that may not be typically understood as religious: storytelling, sweetgrass basketry, dreaming, and the concept of remembering.[2]

The dead interlocutors are deceased family members and close friends, usually those that the Gullah/Geechee practitioners knew intimately. "Talking" to the

---

[1] While the terminology is recognized as inconsistently applied, the term "Gullah" has been used to describe African Americans who speak in the unique dialect of the Sea Island and the Lowcountry, including many who lived further inland. "Gullah" itself can be traced back to a combination of the abbreviated form of Angola and the Gola people of the West African coast. Various etymologies have been suggested for "Geechee," but there is no consensus. LeRhonda S. Manigault-Bryant, *Talking to the Dead: Religion, Music, and Lived Memory among Gullah-Geechee Women* (Durham: Duke University Press, 2014), 2. See also Jason R. Young, *Rituals of Resistance: African Atlantic Religion in Kongo and the Lowcountry South in the Era of Slavery* (Baton Rouge: Louisiana State University Press, 2007); Yvonne P. Chireau, *Black Magic: Religion and the African American Conjuring Tradition* (Berkeley: University of California Press, 2003); and Michael C. Wolfe, *The Abundant Life Prevails: Religious Traditions of Saint Helena Island* (Waco: Baylor University Press, 2000).

[2] Manigault-Bryant, *Talking to the Dead*, 104–05.

dead does not usually require speech, but is accomplished inaudibly, through acknowledging the presence of a spirit and then listening for what they might be "saying."

> Usually, these women do not literally see the dead. Rather, they feel the dead physically, which gives the women a distinct sense of peace. Talking to the dead, though related in the sense that it is a connection with spirits, should not be interpreted as the expression of a haunting or the presence of evil spirits such as the hag; rather, it has a positive connotation and is not characterized by fear or dread.[3]

In this way, the spirits of dead parents, grandfathers, siblings (who died as children or as adults), spouses, and childhood friends provide comfort, advice, and correction. Sometimes the dead have nothing to "say" at all, but simply abide as a comforting, invisible presence, for minutes or hours.

Gullah/Geechee religious practices like talking to the dead have conventionally existed harmoniously with Christian religion and church membership—this despite the fact that some may wish to characterize such traditions as unorthodox or unusual. For example, all seven women whose interviews shape Manigault-Bryant's *Talking to the Dead* are highly involved church members in what might be called mainstream or mainline Protestant traditions, and they see these practices that they have inherited as a native component of their faith. In this regard, they are not unique. Yvonne Chireau points to the semi-legendary figure of "Dr. Buzzard," a popular antebellum "root worker" or "conjure man" who was said to have financed the construction of the largest church on St. Helena Island in the early 1900s.[4] From such seamless synthesis, it is clear that Gullah/Geechee spirit practices should not be dismissed as misguided lay fancies or syncretistic appendages to Christian practice in the region.

These practices among the Gullah/Geechee of talking to the dead demonstrate how consultation and interaction with spirits occur in a myriad of modes beyond what might be expected. The blend includes both passive and active postures toward spirits in individual as well as corporate settings. Frequently, spirit phenomena accompany other practices that might be characterized as "creative" (e.g., basket weaving, storytelling, and making music), though not explicitly "possession." It is not enough then for contemporary ethnographers and anthropologists to look only at the clearly demarcated spirit rituals when studying such phenomena. They must also attend to the ways that spirits are conceived as penetrating other parts of life—even an episode as "uncharismatic"

---

[3] Manigault-Bryant, *Talking to the Dead*, 106.
[4] Chireau, *Black Magic*, 27.

as sitting quietly on a front porch in the evening. Similarly, the conspicuous spirit episodes of Saul's life discussed in chapter 2 are enlightening, but it would be a mistake to view such parade examples as telling the whole story.

3.2 Chapter Overview

This chapter takes on the task of recognizing some of the plurality of spirit phenomena found in the Hebrew Bible. To do this, I have organized my discussion into three heuristic and overlapping categories: (1) spirit language, (2) descriptions of spirit possession, and (3) myths about spirits. Each category contains discussions of texts that are frequently identified as spirit phenomena by interpreters, as well as some less obvious examples that emerge as relevant only after comparison with ethnographic literature. An overarching argument guides all of this taxonomy, however. Informed by recent studies by Bernd Janowski and Carol Newsom, I seek to demonstrate how notions of spirits and spirit phenomena in the Hebrew Bible and Second Temple Literature were shaped more by assumptions about theological anthropology than by mythological pneumatology.[5] Put differently, mapping ancient ideas about human beings and the inner workings of our bodies can be more revealing about spirit texts in the Hebrew Bible than can deciphering ancient mythological accounts of demons, angels, spirits, and other divine entities. In the final section of the chapter, I analyze the relationship between spirit rituals and spirit myths through analysis of an ethnographic case study of Sakalava spirit possession in comparison with the story of Micaiah son of Imlah in 1 Kgs 22 as well as the myth of fallen angels in Second Temple Judaism. I argue that myths should not only be read by modern interpreters as etiological *descriptions*, designed to explain why a certain (usually odd) practice existed in antiquity, but also as rival *prescriptions* for what a practice ought to have meant against the backdrop of the socio-political issues of its setting.

3.3 Spirit Language

The word most commonly rendered from Hebrew into English as "spirit" is *rûaḥ* (רוח), a term that has long been a starting point for studies of spirits in biblical

---

[5] Bernd Janowski, *Anthropologie Des Alten Testaments: Grundfragen – Kontexte – Themenfelder* (Tübingen: Mohr Siebeck, 2019); and Newsom, *The Spirit Within Me*.

literature by theologians and Hebraists alike.[6] As many have recognized, *rûaḥ* in a general sense refers to air in motion, allowing for other translations, including "wind" and "breath."[7] Like many words in Hebrew that strike modern readers as having a wide semantic range, there is no indication that *rûaḥ* is a *homograph*. That is, it is not like the English words *bat*, *down*, or *fine*, each of which has more than one semantically unrelated meaning. Instead, it would seem that certain modern languages operate with distinctions between "wind," "breath," and "spirit" that did not exist in early Jewish literature.

This point is poignantly illustrated in Ezek 37:1–14, the prophet's vision of the valley of dry bones. In the span of these fourteen verses, *rûaḥ* appears ten times, and a range of meanings for the term is obviously at work.

> [1] The hand of the LORD came upon me, and he brought me out by the *rûaḥ*[8] of the LORD and set me down in the middle of a valley; it was full of bones. [2] He led me all around them; there were very many lying in the valley, and they were very dry. [3] He said to me, "Mortal, can these bones live?" I answered, "O Lord GOD, you know." [4] Then he said to me, "Prophesy to these bones, and say to them: O dry bones, hear the word of the LORD. [5] Thus says the Lord GOD to these bones: I will cause *rûaḥ*[9] to enter you, and you shall live. [6] I will lay sinews on you, and will cause flesh to come upon you, and cover you with skin, and put *rûaḥ*[10] in you, and you shall live; and you shall know that I am the LORD." [7] So I prophesied as I had been commanded; and as I prophesied, suddenly there was a noise, a rattling, and the bones came together, bone to its bone. [8] I looked, and there were sinews on them, and flesh had come upon them, and skin had covered them; but there was no *rûaḥ*[11] in them. [9] Then he said to me, "Prophesy to the *rûaḥ*[12], prophesy, mortal, and say to the *rûaḥ*[13]: Thus says

---

[6] Several early studies include: Charles A. Briggs, "The Use of רוח in the Old Testament," *JBL* 19.2 (1900): 132–45; William Ross Schoemaker, "The Use of רוּחַ in the Old Testament, and of Πνεῦμα in the New Testament: A Lexicographical Study," *JBL* 23.1 (1904): 13–67; Johannes H. Scheepers, *Die Gees van God En Die Gees van Die Mens in Die Ou Testament* (Kampen: Kok, 1960); and Daniel Lys, *"Rûach": Le Souffle Dans l'Ancien Testament*, EHPI 56 (Paris: Presses universitaires de France, 1962). See also Aubrey R. Johnson, *The Vitality of the Individual in the Thought of Ancient Israel*, 2nd ed. (Cardiff: University of Wales Press, 1964), 23–37; and Hans Walter Wolff, *Anthropology of the Old Testament*, trans. Margaret Kohl (Philadelphia: Fortress, 1974). Most recently, see Blischke, *Der Geist Gottes*, 1–5.

[7] In this, the word parallels other conceptions of winds and spirits in ancient Near Eastern cognate literature. See lexical discussions in Claus Westermann, "Geist im Alten Testament," *EvT* 41.3 (1981): 223–30; Sven Tengström and Heinz-Josef Fabry, "רוח," *TDOT* 13:365–402; and "רוח," *HALOT* 3:1195–1201.

[8] NRSV: "spirit"
[9] NRSV: "breath"
[10] NRSV: "breath"
[11] NRSV: "breath"
[12] NRSV: "breath"
[13] NRSV: "breath"

the Lord God: Come from the four *rûḥôt*[14], O *rûaḥ*[15], and breathe upon these slain, that they may live." ¹⁰ I prophesied as he commanded me, and the *rûaḥ*[16] came into them, and they lived, and stood on their feet, a vast multitude. ¹¹ Then he said to me, "Mortal, these bones are the whole house of Israel. They say, 'Our bones are dried up, and our hope is lost; we are cut off completely.' ¹² Therefore prophesy, and say to them, Thus says the Lord God: I am going to open your graves, and bring you up from your graves, O my people; and I will bring you back to the land of Israel. ¹³ And you shall know that I am the Lord, when I open your graves, and bring you up from your graves, O my people. ¹⁴ I will put my *rûaḥ*[17] within you, and you shall live, and I will place you on your own soil; then you shall know that I, the Lord, have spoken and will act," says the Lord. (Ezek 37:1–14)

In a few instances of the word *rûaḥ* in this passage, one particular valence of the term dominates. The four *rûḥôt* (רוחות) in verse 9b, for instance, most readily refer to "winds," corresponding to the four points on a compass. Additionally, when there are references to bones, sinews, and flesh, it makes sense that it would be "breath" that God is putting inside of these reconstituting bodies (vv. 4–6). Meanwhile, the introduction of the vision in verse 1 (ויצאני ברוח [ה']) is familiar from other parts of the book, a phrase that most have interpreted as indicating that God brings the prophet out "by a/the *spirit* of the Lord."

Still, in other instances, identifying a single intention behind *rûaḥ* is less easily accomplished. For instance, in verse 9a, which is the prophet instructed to prophesy to—a "spirit," a "breath," or a "wind"? Indeed, this ambiguity at times seems intentional. Over the course of these several verses, God instructs Ezekiel to prophesy by means of a *rûaḥ*, to a *rûaḥ*, concerning a *rûaḥ*, which comes from the four *rûḥôt*! Given this abundance of what would otherwise feel like tiring tautology, it would be unusually dim of us not to realize that in these instances, more than just one of these meanings is intended. This multiplicity of meaning is especially pertinent when reading verse 14, "I will put my *rûaḥ* in you (all) and you (all) shall live." This is, of course, not only poetic wordplay on the part of the prophet but an expression of Ezekiel's hopeful theological anthropology.[18] The liberating, life-giving *rûaḥ* of God is as intimate as

---

14 NRSV: "winds"
15 NRSV: "breath"
16 NRSV: "breath"
17 NRSV: "spirit"
18 See Daniel I. Block, "The Prophet of the Spirit: The Use of רוּחַ in the Book of Ezekiel," in *By the River Chebar: Historical, Literary, and Theological Studies in the Book of Ezekiel*, ed. Daniel I. Block (Cambridge, UK: James Clarke Company, 2014); Jon D. Levenson, *Resurrection and the Restoration of Israel: The Ultimate Victory of the God of Life* (New Haven: Yale University Press, 2006), 156–65; and Levison, *Filled with the Spirit*, 205–08.

your breath, as dynamic as the winds, and as immanent as this prophecy, he seems to say.

Allowing for this semantic elasticity is essential. Word-study focused approaches can too easily boil down to isolating particular occurrences of *rûaḥ* in the Bible and then debating how the instance should be translated. *Does a certain occurrence represent a reference to a "spirit," or is it something apparently less metaphysical like "wind" or "breath"?* These either/or fallacies not only introduce anachronistic distinctions into the literature; they also fail to address the broader theological and anthropological frameworks that allowed for phenomena as disparate as *wind, breath,* and *spirit* to share a label in the first place.

More promising, then, for my goals in this project are interpretive methods that investigate the cultural models and conceptual metaphors that might lie behind the range of this word's depictions in biblical literature.[19] Examples of this approach can be seen in several recent articles by Ingrid Lilly, who compares the function of winds in ancient Mesopotamian medicinal literature with that of *rûḥôt* in Job and Ezekiel.[20] Using this comparative evidence, Lilly demonstrates how *rûaḥ* can be understood in these biblical texts as a term for a *guided* wind, either on the inside or outside of a person, that affects health, mood, and personality. When the maladies of biblical *rûaḥ* are compared to ghost-induced illnesses in Mesopotamian literature, there turns out to be considerable overlap.[21] Indeed, to the extent that ghosts and winds often work together, the two can become almost indistinguishable.[22]

Thus, even when the context makes clear that *rûaḥ* means "wind" or "breath," we cannot be sure that "spirit" to some extent is not also implicit. This fuller aspect of spirit language is particularly pronounced in those instances where a passage may not have originally foregrounded the meaning of "spirit," but it nevertheless came to be interpreted that way in later tradition.

---

19 See Newsom, *The Spirit Within Me*, chp. 2.
20 Lilly, "Rûaḥ Embodied"; and "Conceptualizing Spirit."
21 Lilly, "Rûaḥ Embodied," 328. See also Jo Ann Scurlock, *Magico-Medical Means of Treating Ghost-Induced Illnesses in Ancient Mesopotamia*, AMD 3 (Leiden: Brill, 2006).
22 In a similar fashion, scholars have long recognized a precedent in Egyptian literature for describing human breath as originally the property of the gods. See Johannes Hehn, "Zum Problem des Geistes im Alten Orient und im Alten Testament," *ZAW* 43 (1925): 210–25. See also Admiel Kosman, "Breath, Kiss, and Speech as the Source of the Animation of Life: Ancient Foundations of Rabbinic Homilies on the Giving of the Torah as the Kiss of God," in *Self, Soul, and Body in Religious Experience*, ed. Albert I. Baumgarten, Jan Assmann, and Guy G. Stroumsa, SHR 78 (Leiden: Brill, 1998), 96–124; and Jan Assmann, *Death and Salvation in Ancient Egypt* (Ithaca: Cornell University Press, 2005), 26–38.

With this perspective, then, *rûaḥ* language in biblical literature becomes a productive tool for discussing the means by which humanity inhabits and relates to its world, emotionally, volitionally, and, at times, physically. Modes of spirit language in biblical literature can be further broken down into two non-exhaustive and overlapping modes: (1) Spirit as a part of the body and (2) Spirit as other.

3.3.1 Spirit as a Part of the Body

As scholars have long pointed out, the Hebrew Bible often expresses emotion by portraying the physical symptoms of that state.[23] Specifically, biblical literature frequently describes parts of the body, rather than merely labeling feelings. Thus, for example, eyes run with tears (e.g., Jer 9:17; Ps 116:8), bones shake in fright (e.g., Isa 66:14; Ps 6:2), arms are encouraged with strength (e.g., Exod 30:24; Hos 7:15), and flesh yearns (e.g., Ps 63:2). To some degree, this can be construed as an intentional literary strategy. When Joseph meets his brothers in Pharaoh's court, the hearer is rarely told explicitly that he is sad, angry, or conflicted. Rather, the narrator "shows" us instead of "tells" us. We observe Joseph weeping and watch his erratic activity (Gen 42:24; 45:2; 45:14; 46:29; but cf. 43:30). We can thus infer his feelings because we "observe" his behavior.

Yet more broadly, narrating parts of the body in order to communicate emotion seems also to be a natural consequence of human biology. It is reflective of a mode of speech that cognitive linguists have sometimes called "metonymy."[24] When a person is angry, their body temperature may rise, and depending on skin tone and other factors, their face may flush. Thus, in English, one may say things like, "I'm fuming" and "Don't be a hothead."[25] Comparable expressions exist also in Hebrew (e.g., noses kindling with anger, Gen 30:2; Exod 32:22; Num 24:10). When such expressions are similar across languages, they usually strike us as unremarkable. Indeed, modern translations will often substitute one expression for the other, ignoring the literal idiom. When Potiphar's wife

---

[23] See, for example, Wolff, *Anthropology of the Old Testament*; and Mark S Smith, "The Heart and Innards in Israelite Emotional Expressions: Notes from Anthropology and Psychobiology," *JBL* 117.3 (1998): 427–36. More recently see Janowski, *Anthropologie Des Alten Testaments*, 142–45.

[24] For an introduction, see Jeannette Littlemore, *Metonymy: Hidden Shortcuts in Language, Thought and Communication* (Cambridge: Cambridge University Press, 2015).

[25] George Lakoff and Zoltán Kövecses, "The Cognitive Model of Anger Inherent in American English," in *Cultural Models in Language and Thought*, ed. Dorothy C. Holland and Naomi Quinn (Cambridge: Cambridge University Press, 1987), 195–221.

falsely accuses Joseph, for example, the slave master's "nose kindles" (ויחר אפו, Gen 39:19). Yet, the NRSV explains simply that "he became enraged," while too, the NJPS has "he was incensed with anger."

On the other hand, *dissimilar* metonymy can reveal contrasting, specifically enculturated ideas for conceiving of how human beings function biologically, emotionally, self-consciously, or otherwise.[26] Naomi Quinn and Dorothy Holland call these specifically enculturated ideas "cultural models," which are:

> presupposed, taken-for-granted models of the world that are widely shared (although not necessarily to the exclusion of other, alternative models) by the members of a society and that play an enormous role in their understanding of that world and their behavior in it.[27]

Accordingly, to locate the potential cultural model behind a biblical idiom like "nose kindling," we might try to expand the frame of reference by posing questions and testing answers, like: What is conceived as causing the raised body heat and flushed skin? Might it be an imbalance in the fluid humors? A passing spirit that has penetrated the body? The lingering effects of an unresolved moral or cultic transgression?[28]

How, then, can we reconstruct the Bible's cultural model for spirits and bodies? One way is to assess how *rûaḥ* functions to communicate emotion. We find that one's *rûaḥ* can be "troubled" (להפעם, Gen 41:8) and "broken" (נכאה, Prov 15:13), but also "stirred" (להעיר, Jer 51:11) and "revived" (להחיות, Isa 57:15).[29] In this way, *rûaḥ* is comparable to other body-part words like "heart" (לבב), "liver" (כבד), "kidneys" (כליה), "face" (פנה), and "throat" (נפש), all of which

---

[26] See Dorothy C. Holland and Naomi Quinn, "Culture and Cognition," in *Cultural Models in Language and Thought*, ed. Dorothy C. Holland and Naomi Quinn (Cambridge: Cambridge University Press, 1987), 3–40 and Benjamin Blount, "Situating Cultural Models in History and Cognition," in *Approaches to Language, Culture, and Cognition: The Intersection of Cognitive Linguistics and Linguistic Anthropology*, ed. Masataka Yamaguchi, Dennis Tay, and Benjamin Blount (London: Palgrave Macmillan, 2014), 271–98.
[27] Holland and Quinn, "Culture and Cognition," 4.
[28] See some explorations of these and related questions: Jack R. Lundbom, "Burning Anger in the Old Testament: Hebrew *Ḥrh*, *Yṣt*, and *Yqd*," in *Theology in Language, Rhetoric, and Beyond: Essays in Old and New Testament* (Cambridge, UK: Lutterworth, 2014); Ellen van Wolde, "Sentiments as Culturally Constructed Emotions: Anger and Love in the Hebrew Bible," *BI* 16 (2008): 1–24; and Zacharias Kotzé, "A Cognitive Linguistic Approach to the Emotion of Anger in the Old Testament," *HTS* 60.3 (2004): 843–63.
[29] Emotive phrases utilizing רוח in the Hebrew Bible are often treated as metaphor in English translation, obscuring this term's meaning as a part of the body. See, for example, Job 7:7 and 1 Sam 1:15.

can indicate emotion in similar ways.³⁰ These words and others are part of a family of terms that frequently express conceptions of the self in biblical literature. Yet despite its nearly identical usage, *rûaḥ* is sometimes treated differently from these other words by modern interpreters.³¹ It could be that *rûaḥ* receives special treatment by scholars because it does not readily correspond to a part of the modern anatomy the way that "heart" or "liver" does (even if we are aware that ancient writers did not use these words in the same way as a medical textbook today).

Consequently, I contend that in many biblical texts *rûaḥ* is simply another component of the body—"an *internal* wind," as Ingrid Lilly would have it.³² Although it is true that a creature's body would not function without a *rûaḥ*, this alone does not make it a different category of organ, since a body would not function without a heart or a throat either. Additionally, it would seem that one chief function of the *rûaḥ* organ is as a seat of will. One's *rûaḥ* can be "hardened" when it is obstinate (לקשה, Deut 2:30), it can "seek" for another (לשחר, Isa 26:9), and it can contain deceit (רמיה, Ps 32:2). In this usage too, *rûaḥ* overlaps considerably with the functions of one's heart or throat, which can communicate similar intentions.³³

What distinguishes *rûaḥ*, then, is not its nature or function but its potential for movement. Of all these words for communicating aspects of the self in Hebrew, *rûaḥ* is the only "organ" that can also exist most readily external to the body. It is breathed in and out and shared with others around oneself. It can blow fiercely in a storm or subtly infiltrate through a pleasant or offensive scent. Remarkably, it is a substance that can even be shared with God. It should come as no surprise, then, that in biblical literature, some of the most powerful human feelings, compulsions, and "passions" often originate from outside of a person.³⁴ In such scenarios, it is frequently spirit language that is used to describe the interaction.

---

30 E.g., Deut 15:10; Judg 19:6; Isa 1:14; Ps 13:2; 73:21; Lam 2:11.
31 For example, Wolff, in his term-by-term study of body-part words, distinguishes רוח alone as a "theo-anthropological term," because, more often than the others, it is used to describe aspects and actions of God. *Anthropology of the Old Testament*, 32. Janowski does not include רוח in his list of inner organs and body parts *Anthropologie Des Alten Testaments*, 139.
32 Lilly, "Rûaḥ Embodied."
33 E.g., Ezek 3:7; Ps 63:2; Prov 19:15
34 See Philip Fisher, *The Vehement Passions* (Princeton: Princeton University Press, 2002).

3.3.2 Spirit as Other

When spirit language is used to describe an aspect of the self that is nonetheless to some degree distinct, I have called it a "spirit as other." In Proverbs, for example, the human spirit is often unpredictable and thus requires regulation. Proverbs 16:32 valorizes one who "rules his spirit" (מֹשֵׁל בְּרוּחוֹ), explaining that he is better than one who captures a city. The NRSV renders this as "one whose temper is controlled," and similarly the NJPS has "self-control." Although these translations might be technically correct in capturing the message of the proverb, they also obscure the repeated warning in the collection that one's spirit is a dangerous liability: "Like a city breached, without walls / is a man without constraint of his spirit" (אִישׁ אֲשֶׁר אֵין מַעְצָר לְרוּחוֹ, Prov 25:28).[35] In these examples, the *rûaḥ* is described with a degree of independent agency, having a limited ability to cause a person to do what they might otherwise not wish to do.

Interpreting metonymic language, however, can be challenging. How do we discern when a text is intentionally evoking a cultural model as opposed to when it is simply utilizing a common figure of speech? For instance, not every English-speaking parent who uses the phrase, "What has gotten into you?" believes that a foreign entity has taken some measure of control over their child's behavior. They might not even believe that such a thing is even possible. Similarly, in many biblical texts, metonymic language does not necessarily indicate a robustly functioning mythological conviction. This ambiguity can be seen, for example, in the use of the phrase "spirit of whoredom" (רוּחַ זְנוּנִים) in Hosea (Hos 4:12; 5:4). The prophet identifies this spirit as leading Israel into improper forms of worship and does so using strong sexual language. This has led some scholars to speculate about whether Hosea is condemning the practice of temple prostitution in ancient Israel and/or referencing a literal misleading spirit.[36] Yet, with such little evidence to go on, we may wonder if such a reading is too literal. Perhaps the "spirit" identified here by the prophet is just that aspect of the self (in this case the corporate self of Israel) that can be led astray. The language of harlotry, then, might be a metaphorical extension of the term's sexual connotation into a cultic context.[37]

---

[35] NRSV: "one who lacks self-control"; cf. Prov 16:2; 17:27; 29:11.
[36] See, for example, Karin Adams, "Metaphor and Dissonance: A Reinterpretation of Hosea 4:13–14," *JBL* 127 (2008): 291–305. See also a critique, James E. Miller, "A Critical Response to Karin Adams's Reinterpretation of Hosea 4:13–14," *JBL* 128.3 (2009): 503–6.
[37] Esther Hamori connects the "spirit of fornication" here to other traditions in the Hebrew Bible concerning the "spirit of falsehood." "The Spirit of Falsehood," *CBQ* 72.1 (2010): 15–30.

In contrast, when we find richer descriptions of cultural models, we can be more confident in concluding that they are operative. We can compare the Damascus Document to the example from Proverbs given above.³⁸ In column 12, the Damascus Document utilizes the same idiom of "ruling" a spirit but adds some detail:

> ²... Any man whom the spirits of Belial take sway of ³ and who speaks waywardly as the mediums and wizards do shall be condemned (to death). (CD 12:2b–3a)³⁹

Although it is not impossible that the Damascus Document is speaking idiomatically of troublesome desires, it is more likely that a foreign entity, called Belial, is conceived as being capable of causing mischief within and through a person or community.⁴⁰ Certainly the connection that the Damascus Document establishes with mediums and diviners suggests that being ruled by Belial is a parallel transgression to that of associating voluntarily with spirits that are not of God.

One of the most poignant examples of a rich description of a "spirit as other" in the Hebrew Bible is the "spirit of jealousy" (רוח־קנאה) in Num 5, which affects the husband who suspects his wife of unfaithfulness.

> if a spirit of jealousy (רוח־קנאה) comes on him, and he is jealous of his wife who has defiled herself; or if a spirit of jealousy comes on him, and he is jealous of his wife, though she has not defiled herself... (Num 5:14; cf. v. 30)

---

38 The Damascus Document or Rule was first discovered in the Cairo Genizah and its manuscripts were dated to the tenth and twelfth centuries CE. The antiquity of its original composition in the third–second centuries BCE was confirmed when portions were found among the Dead Sea Scrolls, some of which contained sections not attested in the Genizah. Scholars believe that the Damascus Document was one of the foundational documents for the sectarian community. On provenance, see Ben Zion Wacholder, *The New Damascus Document: The Midrash on the Eschatological Torah of the Dead Sea Scrolls: Reconstruction, Translation and Commentary*, STDJ 56 (Leiden: Brill, 2007), 3–4.
39 Text and translations of the Damascus Document are from Wacholder, *The New Damascus Document*.
40 S. David Sperling, "Belial," *DDD*, 169–71; Rosen-Zvi, *Demonic Desires*, chp. 3; and Devorah Dimant, "Between Qumran Sectarian and Non-Sectarian Texts: The Case of Belial and Mastema," in *The Dead Sea Scrolls and Contemporary Culture: Proceedings of the International Conference Held at the Israel Museum, Jerusalem (July 6–8, 2008)*, ed. Adolfo D. Roitman, Lawrence H. Schiffman, and Shani Tzoref, STDJ 93 (Leiden: Brill, 2011), 235–56.

The association of jealousy with spirits or demons is widespread in both ethnographic literature and studies of antiquity.[41] Although the nature of this ritual continues to be debated, in my reading, the problem portrayed as needing a solution in this text is at least as much the husband's overwhelming and potentially violent jealousy as it is the wife's supposed infidelity.[42] Various explanations for the ensuing ritual of drinking bitter water have been suggested, ranging from the practical (e.g., ending an illegitimate pregnancy) to the cultic (e.g., cleansing the community of ritual impurity). It may also be the case that the ritual is designed to appease the jealous spirit and deter any violent reprisal from the husband that the jealous spirit provokes.

In reviewing these examples of the spirit as other, we are much closer to spirit-possession-type episodes than we were with those texts that portray the spirit functioning as a part of the body. However, even when spirit language occurs in a biblical text that does not suggest possession or trance, its articulations and themes are nevertheless liable to be taken up and expanded that way in new contexts. Hence, spirit language in biblical literature is frequently used as a building block for descriptions of spirit-possession–type episodes.

---

41 See, as a few selective examples: The chart comparing medieval demonological traditions with the practices of contemporary charismatic Catholics in Thomas J. Csordas, *The Sacred Self: A Cultural Phenomenology of Charismatic Healing* (Berkeley: University of California Press, 1997), 181–85; Pliny the Elder who identified an amulet of Fascinus as defending against jealousy, Magali Bailliot, "Rome and the Roman Empire," in *Guide to the Study of Ancient Magic*, ed. David Frankfurter, RGRW 189 (Leiden: Brill, 2019), 182; the lyrics of a popular Pentecostal gospel singer in Anglophone Cameroon in which jealousy is said to spread where the Holy Ghost is absent, David Ngong, "African Pentecostal Pneumatology," in *Pentecostal Theology in Africa*, ed. Clifton Clarke, ACSS 6 (Eugene: Pickwick, 2014), 82; and the early Kabbalist Rabbi Isaac ben Jacob ha-Kohen who identified a list of "princes of jealousy and hatred," Joseph Dan, "Samael, Lilith, and the Concept of Evil in Early Kabbalah," *AJSR* 5.5 (1980): 18.

42 The literature on the *Sotah* ritual is vast. See, the survey in Lisa Grushcow, *Writing the Wayward Wife: Rabbinic Interpretations of Sotah* (Leiden: Brill, 2006), 1–31. See also some studies related to my discussion here: Anne Katrine de Hemmer Gudme, "A Kind of Magic? The Law of Jealousy in Numbers 5:11–31 as Magical Ritual and as Ritual Text," in *Studies on Magic and Divination in the Biblical World*, ed. Anne Katrine de Hemmer Gudme, Helen R. Jacobus, and Philippe Guillaume (Piscataway: Gorgias, 2013), 149–68; Eve Levavi Feinstein, *Sexual Pollution in the Hebrew Bible* (Oxford: Oxford University Press, 2014), 43–50; and Richard S. Briggs, "Reading the Sotah Text (Numbers 5:11–31): Holiness and a Hermeneutic Fit for Suspicion," *BI* 17.3 (2009): 288–319.

3.4 Descriptions of Spirit Possession

Criteria developed in cultural anthropology are vital for identifying biblical texts that may qualify as descriptions of spirit possession. A good place to start is Janice Boddy's landmark 1994 essay, which gathered several dozen studies from a variety of cultures and surveyed a nearly overwhelming array of modes in which possession has occurred. Boddy consistently rejected overly reductive models linking the diverse possession practices of the world by a few "master narratives" usually articulated primarily in medical terms. In contrast, Boddy explained that

> [...] possession widens out from the body and self into other domains of knowledge and experience—other lives, societies, historical moments, levels of cosmos, and religions—catching these up and embodying them. Their direction ensures that possession cults are flexible and continuously transformative. It enables adherents to explore multiple refractions of order and morality; to distill the lessons of history; to sift, evaluate and situate external influences; and to respond. Phenomena we bundle loosely as possession are part of daily experience, not just dramatic ritual.[43]

The "we" in the last sentence refers to anthropologists studying possession phenomena, but it might as well refer to any academic who would assume spirit possession to be both universally explicable and subsumable into culturally familiar intellectual categories. At the conclusion of her article, Boddy turned the microscope around on these scholars and suggested that the question in possession studies had shifted from, "'How is it that other peoples believe the self to be permeable by forces from without?' to 'How is it that Western models have repeatedly denied such permeability?'"[44]

Taking Boddy's insightful challenge to heart, we should adjust our expectations regarding what constitutes a spirit-possession event or practice. Rather than putting the burden of proof on spirit possession to reveal itself according to an expected paradigm (e.g., the models of exorcism stories familiar from the gospels), we might instead assume that spirit-possession practices (more broadly defined) almost certainly existed at most levels of development in the composition and interpretive traditions of biblical literature. (More self-consciously, we might also recognize that it is, in fact, modern Western cultures that conspicuously lack popular spirit-possession and trance practices.)

---

[43] Boddy, "Spirit Possession Revisited: Beyond Instrumentality," 414.
[44] Boddy, "Spirit Possession Revisited: Beyond Instrumentality," 427.

3.4 Descriptions of Spirit Possession — 73

So, how might these phenomena have been represented in biblical literature? Michael Lambek provided a helpful suggestion by shifting the scholarly gaze away from determining the physiological, psychological, social, or external factors that supposedly causes possession and trance and instead focusing on their expression. In a discussion on the difficulties of categorizing these diverse practices, Lambek observed that taxonomic theories that are clear enough to analysts rarely map well onto the observable phenomena in practice. This is because so many theoretical models use a phenomenon's imagined cause as the determining variable. He explained:

> While trance, like sex, eating, or vocalization, is "natural" in the sense that, under the right stimuli, it is a condition or activity (or range of conditions or activities) of which the human species at large is capable, the form or manifestation of trance in any specific context is no more "natural" (necessary, unmediated, given) than the model that guides it. Trance may include certain universal features or attributes from which each culture selects points of emphasis (much as a language, viewed phonemically, selects from the range of possible human vocalizations). Yet the institutionalized appearance of trance—its form, meaning, incidence, etc.—is cultural.[45]

Within Lambek's explanation, then, spirit possession is not a problem to be solved so much as a language to be translated. It may indeed be communicating an exceptional environmental or personal condition, such as an illness, a form of institutional oppression, or any of the other "natural" explanations posited by other scholars. But it may (also) be communicating celebration, devotion, satire, lament—or any other part of human experience. This aspect of possession is what makes it a "system of communication" and translatable into a text.

With these criteria in mind, I have detailed three types of descriptions of spirit possession in the Hebrew Bible: (1) Third-Person Narrative Descriptions of Spirit-Possession Events or Rituals, (2) First-Person Accounts of Spirit Possession, and (3) Apotropaic/Exorcistic Intercessions and Liturgies. As with the examples of spirit language provided above, it is rare that any particular text would function in just one mode.

3.4.1 Third-Person Narrative Descriptions of Spirit-Possession Events or Rituals

Third person narrative texts are perhaps the easiest to identify. I have already discussed in chapter 2 several conspicuous examples; namely, Saul's spirit-phe-

---

[45] Lambek, "From Disease to Discourse," 38.

nomena episodes in 1 Samuel. Other narrative descriptions of spirit possession include the seventy(-two) prophesying elders in Num 11:16–30 and the ritual for testing a potentially unfaithful wife in Num 5:11–31. Instances of spirit empowerment also qualify here (especially in the book of Judges; e.g., Judg 3:10; 6:34; 11:29; 14:6; see also the selection of Joshua in Num 27:16–23),[46] as do episodes of spirit confusion or frustration (e.g., Isa 19:14; 29:9–10). In several cases, the decisions of leaders both foreign and domestic are the result of subtle spirit tampering/possession (e.g., Jer 51:11; Isa 37:7/2 Kgs 19:7; Hag 1:14). The description of Bezalel the craftsmen also fits the category, though this particular instance may be of a less charismatic nature than is sometimes assumed.[47] Narratives about prophetic sign acts or performances of prophecy belong as well.[48] For example, Ezekiel is compelled by a spirit to be restrained in his house, bound and speechless as a sign act (Ezek 3:22–27; cf. 24:25–27; 33:21–22). Actually, the prophet engages so often in this kind of formulaic yet odd behavior that we may include his other sign acts in the category—even if key examples of spirit language (e.g., רוח) are missing in that particular instance (e.g., Ezek 6:11–12; 12:1–16; 21:23–29 [NRSV vv. 18–24]).

In addition to prophetic oracles *initiated* by some mode of spirit possession, instances of oracles *about* spirit possession abound—particularly a future possession that will be both corporate and positive. Isa 32:15–18 is an apt example:

> [15] Until a spirit from on high is poured out on us,
> and the wilderness becomes a fruitful field,
> and the fruitful field is deemed a forest.
> [16] Then justice will dwell in the wilderness,
> and righteousness abide in the fruitful field.
> [17] The effect of righteousness will be peace,
> and the result of righteousness, quietness and trust forever.
> [18] My people will abide in a peaceful habitation,
> in secure dwellings, and in quiet resting places. (Isa 32:15–18)

The fact that the spirit effects described by the prophet are abiding and tranquil rather than momentary and delirious does not disqualify the prophecy as a spirit

---

[46] Several verbal constructions are used in these cases ranging from a spirit merely "being upon" (ותהי עליו, e.g., Num 24:2; Judg 3:10; cf. 2 Chr 15:1) to "clothing" (לבשה, e.g., Judg 6:34; 1 Chr 12:19) and even "seizing" (ותצלח עליו, e.g., Judg 14:6; 1 Sam 10:6) (my translations). See the discussion in chapter 4.

[47] Levison, *Filled with the Spirit*, 36–41.

[48] See Kelvin G. Friebel, *Jeremiah's and Ezekiel's Sign-Acts: Rhetorical Nonverbal Communication*, JSOTSup 283 (Sheffield: Sheffield Academic, 1999), esp. chapter 1.

phenomenon.[49] Indeed, the permanent quality of the abiding peace is all the more reason to appreciate the potency of this spirit emptied out from above. Similar examples include Isa 11:1–5; 59:21; Joel 3:1–2 [NRSV 2:28–29]; and Zech 12:10.

Of course, theological shaping lies behind all biblical texts and complicates our ability to discern the nature of the third-person narrative descriptions of spirit phenomena. Indeed, biblical literature frequently provides its own categories for spirit phenomena; that is, those that are approved by Israel's God and those that are not. As a means to chart such distinctions, David Frankfurter has recently recommended searching for "vocabularies of illegitimate or ambiguous ritual action" in primary texts and employing more carefully terms like "magic."[50] The problem with "magic" as a category is that it very often uncritically merges scholarly analysis with distinctions developed by the observed culture.[51] Thus, from an anthropological comparative perspective, the distinction between Saul's inquiry of the medium in 1 Sam 28 and his inquiry of the *urim* and *thummim* in 1 Sam 14:41 is not one of "magic" versus "religion." Rather, it is that the latter is a divination ritual approved throughout the Hebrew Bible and the former is not.

3.4.2 First-Person Accounts of Spirit Possession

Substantial overlap exists between this category and the previous, but one important distinction should be recognized; namely, the possibility that spirit possession is implied in some texts but obscured to a degree by a first-person point of view.[52] To compare first- and third-person perspectives: We have little insight

---

49 Though in such instances, the conventional term "possession" is especially inadequate. See my methodological comments in chapter 1.
50 David Frankfurter, "Ancient Magic in a New Key: Refining an Exotic Discipline in the History of Religions," in *Guide to the Study of Ancient Magic*, ed. David Frankfurter, RGRW 189 (Leiden: Brill, 2019), 3–20.
51 Frankfurter recommends instead that the term "magic" be used by scholars, not as an etic or emic descriptor at all, but as a heuristic term to highlight qualities of ancient practices and materials that we might not otherwise appreciate Frankfurter, "Ancient Magic in a New Key," 13–14.
52 A broad consensus exists among historians, anthropologists, and biblical scholars that prophetic performance in the ancient Near East was usually associated with a particular state of mind, variously called ecstasy, trance, or more recently ASC (see chapter 1). Marti Nissinen has written widely on this. See *Ancient Prophecy*; "Prophetic Madness: Prophecy and Ecstasy in the Ancient Near East and in Greece"; and "Biblical Prophecy from a Near Eastern Perspective: The Cases of Kingship and Divine Possession," in *Congress Volume Ljubljana 2007*, ed.

as to what it is like "on the inside," so to speak, when it is narrated to us in the third-person that Saul is seized by a spirit of the LORD, engaged in prophetic frenzy, and "turned into a different person" in 1 Sam 10:6. Are we meant to understand that Saul is still conscious? Or has his person been replaced by another presence? Is it a pleasurable experience? Euphoric? Does Saul have rational thoughts, or does he lose coherence? So too, we know little of what it is like "from the outside" when Ezekiel relates in the first-person voice how he prophesies to the *rûaḥ* in Ezek 37:10 (see the discussion above). Had someone "been there," what are we meant to conclude they would have seen? Was the prophet babbling incoherently to himself? Sitting quietly? Asleep and dreaming? Was he walking through an actual valley but sensing things that others present would not have, à la Gullah/Geechee practices of talking to the dead?

These questions are not avoided if we prefer to read prophetic accounts of spirit possession as primarily the products of scribal innovation. Even if Ezekiel's visions are "only" a literary invention forged in the minds of creative scribes, this would not disqualify such texts as spirit phenomena. The description of spirit possession still exists as a literary construct, comparable with other forms in biblical literature. Further, it is possible that the scribes responsible for these accounts based their literary creations on spirit-possession practices from their own community and era. Perhaps even the process of scribal writing itself was perceived as a kind of spirit possession.[53] If it was conventional (if not in history, then at least in literary tradition) for the utterances of prophets to coincide with possession rituals (as it seems they often were; e.g., 1 Sam 10:5; 19:20; 1 Kgs 18:29; 22:10), then even stray references to spirit-empowered prophecy should be considered (e.g., Isa 61:1–4; Mic 3:8).

3.4.3 Apotropaic Intercessions and Liturgies

Apotropaic texts are used themselves as a means to manage or deflect the threats from spirits. Prayers falling into this category usually feature supplications to a

---

André Lemaire, VTSup 133 (Leiden: Brill, 2010), 441–68. See also Peter Michaelsen, "Ecstasy and Possession in Ancient Israel: A Review of Some Recent Contributions," *SJOT* 3.2 (1989): 28–54; and David L. Petersen, "Ecstasy and Role Enactment," in *"The Place Is Too Small for Us": The Israelite Prophets in Recent Scholarship*, ed. R. P. Gordon, SBTS 5 (Winona Lake, IN: Eisenbrauns, 1995), 279–88.
53 Dobroruka, *Second Temple Pseudepigraphy*.

deity or sympathetic spirit for help in discernment and protection.⁵⁴ Often they utilize language in the mode of "spirit as other" (outlined above), though this is not a requirement. See for example, Psalm 91.

> ³ For he will deliver you from the snare of the fowler
> and from the deadly pestilence;
> ⁴ he will cover you with his pinions,
> and under his wings you will find refuge;
> his faithfulness is a shield and buckler.
> ⁵ You will not fear the terror of the night,
> or the arrow that flies by day,
> ⁶ or the pestilence that stalks in darkness,
> or the destruction that wastes at noonday. (Ps 91:3–6)

It is possible that the various threats mentioned in this Psalm are hypostasized or demonized figures.⁵⁵ Already in its early reception history, Psalm 91 served as a model for more elaborate apotropaic prayers in later Jewish tradition, as in the Qumran text 11Q11.⁵⁶ Additionally, several prayers of appeasement to Israel's God in the Hebrew Bible seem to follow convention for apotropaic prayers in the ancient Near East.⁵⁷

---

54 In this sense, these prayers and rituals may be seen as "speech acts." On the long history of speech act theory in biblical studies, see Andreas Wagner, "Speech Acts: Biblical Hebrew," *EHLL*, 605–10; and Brevard S. Childs, "Speech-Act Theory and Biblical Interpretation," *SJT* 58.4 (2005): 375–92. For a recent treatment, see Michael J. Morris, *Warding Off Evil: Apotropaic Tradition in the Dead Sea Scrolls and Synoptic Gospels*, WUNT2 451 (Tübingen: Mohr Siebeck, 2017).
55 E.g., "pestilence" (דבר) in vv. 3, 6 and "destruction" (קטב) in v. 6. See Esther Eshel, "Apotropaic Prayers in the Second Temple Period," in *Liturgical Perspectives: Prayer and Poetry in Light of the Dead Sea Scrolls: Proceedings of the Fifth International Symposium of the Orion Center for the Study of the Dead Sea Scrolls and Associated Literature, 19–23 January, 2000*, ed. Esther G. Chazon, STDJ 48 (Leiden: Brill, 2003), 70–74; Morris, *Warding Off Evil*, 74–76; and Gerrit C. Vreugdenhil, *Psalm 91 and Demonic Menace*, OtSt 77 (Leiden: Brill, 2020)
56 The priestly blessing, Num 6:24–26, was also used in this way. See Eshel, "Apotropaic Prayers in the Second Temple Period," 85–86; Brand, *Evil Within and Without*, 206; and Morris, *Warding Off Evil*, 92–94. See also the persistence of Psalm 91 in apotropaic formulae beyond the Second Temple period, Lawrence H. Schiffman and Michael D. Swartz, *Hebrew and Aramaic Incantation Texts from the Cairo Genizah: Selected Texts from Taylor-Schechter Box K1*, STS 1 (Sheffield: JSOT Press, 1992).
57 Marian W. Broida, *Forestalling Doom: "Apotropaic Intercession" in the Hebrew Bible and the Ancient Near East*, AOAT 417 (Münster: Ugarit-Verlag, 2014); and "Apotropaic Intercession in the Hebrew Bible and the Ancient Near East," in *Studies on Magic and Divination in the Biblical World*, ed. Helen R. Jacobus, Anne Katrine de Hemmer Gudme, and Philippe Guillaume, BibInters 11 (Piscataway: Gorgias, 2013), 19–38.

With reference to spirit possession, one especially notable example of an apotropaic text in early Judaism appears in the second century BCE book of Jubilees. The composition is a heavily edited and expanded retelling of select narratives from the book of Genesis and the first twelve chapters of Exodus. The bulk of the text is a first-person narration addressed to Moses on Sinai by a figure called "the angel of the presence," who witnessed and at times participated at key moments in the story. In his account of how Abram came to recognize God as lord and creator, the angel relates a prayer that was then offered by the patriarch (though not included in Genesis itself). Although it is now set within a narrative context, many commentators suspect that Abram's prayer for protection against spirits is borrowed from an existing apotropaic prayer.[58]

> [19] That night [Abram] prayed and said:
> "My God, my God, God most High,
> You alone are my God.
> You have created everything;
> Everything that was and has been is the product of your hands.
> You and your lordship I have chosen.
> [20] Save me from the power of the evil spirits who rule the thoughts of people's minds.
> May they not mislead me from following you, my God.
> Do establish me and my posterity forever.
> May we not go astray from now until eternity." (Jub. 12:19–20)[59]

Abram's prayer reflects a worldview extensively narrated in Jubilees in which evil is "an essentially defeated power whose activity has already been subjected to a preliminary judgment."[60] Yet even so, the prayer reflects the very warranted concern that even those whose worship and devotion is oriented toward God are still liable to spirit invasion and affliction. In taking this perspective, the prayer is not terribly different from a wide range of other Second Temple era spirit-phenomena texts.

This example from Jubilees is especially noteworthy since, according to the narrative, Abram's apotropaic prayer is followed by a type of possession experience—in this case, an empowering one. In Jubilees 12, the angel of the presence

---

[58] See discussions in James L. Kugel, *A Walk through Jubilees: Studies in the Book of Jubilees and the World of Its Creation* (Leiden: Brill, 2012), 89–90; and Michael Segal, *The Book of Jubilees: Rewritten Bible, Redaction, Ideology and Theology*, JSJSup 117 (Leiden: Brill, 2007), 259–61.

[59] Translations of Jubilees from James C. VanderKam, *The Book of Jubilees*, CSCO 511 (Louwain: Peeters, 1989).

[60] Loren T. Stuckenbruck, "The Need for Protection from the Evil One and John's Gospel," in *The Myth of Rebellious Angels: Studies in Second Temple Judaism and New Testament Texts*, WUNT 335 (Tübingen: Mohr Siebeck, 2014), 207.

explains how he told Abram of God's promises, using language that is reminiscent of Gen 12 and the second angelic address of the *Aqedah* (Gen 22:15–18). Here in Jubilees, as in Gen 15:5, Abram is gazing at the stars (Jub. 12:16). Whereas in Genesis the stars function to signify the overwhelming number of Abram's eventual descendants, in Jubilees the posture has an added significance as Abram rejects the astrological divinatory practices of his Mesopotamian roots and embraces instead the one God who controls the very stars he was taught to read (Jub. 12:17–18). The angel goes on to explain to Moses:

> [25] Then the Lord God said to me: "Open [Abram's] mouth and his ears to hear and speak with his tongue in the revealed language." For from the day of the collapse it had disappeared from the mouth(s) of all mankind. [26] I opened his mouth, ears, and lips and began to speak Hebrew with him—in the language of the creation. [27] He took his fathers' books (they were written in Hebrew) and copied them. From that time he began to stud[y] them, while I was telling him everything that he was unable (to understand). He studied them throughout the six rainy months. (Jub. 12:25–27)

Abram has recognized God's mastery of the heavens and prayed for protection from the deleterious incursions of evil spirits. God thus grants him instead the beneficial incursion of the angel of the presence.[61] As Kugel suggested, the miraculous gift of language may be, in part, triggered by a curious title in Gen 14:13, "Abram the Hebrew."[62] Yet, the possibility of an exegetical motive makes the portrayal of Abram's experience no less intense. Indeed, alteration of speech is a well-known motif associated with spirit phenomena. Abram's body is also transformed through his encounter with the angel: "I opened his mouth, ears, and lips and began to speak Hebrew with him" (Jub. 16:26).[63] Although this is not quite equal to the miraculous speech of Pentecost in Acts 2, the reference to "the day of the collapse" introduces an intriguing connection. According to Jubi-

---

[61] The fact that this spirit experience is caused by an "angel" rather than by a "spirit" is not as significant as it may initially appear. Categories for intermediary figures such as spirits, angels, and demons were considerably more fluid in the Second Temple period than they would eventually become in later traditions. Additionally, conceptions of angels varied radically. See Tobias Nicklas, Karin Schöpflin, and Friedrich V. Reiterer, *Angels: The Concept of Celestial Beings: Origins, Development and Reception*, DCLY (Berlin: De Gruyter, 2007); Dale B. Martin, "When Did Angels Become Demons?," *JBL* 129.4 (2010): 657–77; Andy M. Reimer, "Rescuing the Fallen Angels: The Case of the Disappearing Angels at Qumran," *DSD* 7.3 (2000): 334–53; and James C. VanderKam, "The Angel of the Presence in the Book of Jubilees," *DSD* 7.3 (2000): 378–93.
[62] Kugel, *A Walk through Jubilees*, 91.
[63] On the topic of Hebrew-speaking angels and early Jewish and Christians debates over the language of heaven, see John C. Poirier, *The Tongues of Angels: The Concept of Angelic Languages in Classical Jewish and Christian Texts*, WUNT2 287 (Tübingen: Mohr Siebeck, 2010).

lees, the Hebrew language had been lost since the "collapse" of the tower of Babel (Jub. 10:22–26; 16:25; cf. Gen 11:1–9). Abram's experience therefore restores to humanity not only the language of Hebrew but also the meaning of the ancient writings that had been illegible. Strikingly, the day of Pentecost in Acts 2 has long been read in Christian tradition as an undoing or overcoming of the curse of Babel.[64] In both instances, God grants language miraculously by means of a spirit-phenomenon experience.

This example from the book of Jubilees also demonstrates why, for the purpose of analysis, it is necessary to separate a description of a spirit possession event from the myth(s) that might accompany it. What Abram undergoes bodily according to Jubilees is not drastically different from other religious experiences that ethnographers have catalogued among spirit possession practitioners around the world. The mythic world narrated by the angel of the presence and the biblical allusions used to describe it, however, are particular to early Jewish tradition. Thus, the mythic explanation for what a particular spirit practice means, changes, or accomplishes in the world is variable and changes over time depending on context and participants.

3.5 Myths About Spirits

Myths about spirits can be defined for our purposes as any stories or accounts in biblical literature that purport to explain or narrate the otherwise unobservable activities of spirits and/or other divine figures. For many readers, spirit myths are all they may think of when hearing about spirit phenomena in biblical literature. Yet, as I have demonstrated above, myths about spirits are neither the most frequent type of spirit phenomena in biblical literature, nor the most revealing of the underlying cultural models for thinking about spirits and the self in the societies behind the literature. One reason, then, why spirit myths may be especially prevalent in our imagination today is that the myths about divine intermediary and/or oppositional figures in the Hebrew Bible (e.g., Gen 6:1–4; Job 1–2; 26:12; Pss 74:10–22; Isa 27:1; 51:9–11) often provided exegetical fuel for the more expansive and arresting myths about spirits and other divine beings found in

---

[64] The earliest explicit occurrences I have found for this interpretation date to the fourth century CE (e.g., Cyril of Jerusalem [*Catechetical Lectures* 17.17]; and Augustine *Enarrat.* [*Ps. 55*]). However, it is possible that the interpretation is older—perhaps even as an intertextual allusion in Acts 2. See Heidi J. Hornik and Mikeal C. Parsons, *The Acts of the Apostles Through the Centuries*, WBBC (Chichester, UK: Wiley-Blackwell, 2016), 39–50.

later Second Temple Jewish literature (e.g., 1 En. 1–36; Jub. 17:15–18:16; Rev 12:1–12).

Our confidence in these myths may also be the result of our taking biblical spirit myth too readily at its word as being a uniquely revealing genre when it comes to origins. As folklorists and scholars of ancient sagas have often explained, myths by their very nature usually present themselves as etiological and as giving a full account of some contemporary situation or metaphysical reality.[65] In the history of theology as well as in the study of religion, scholars have sometimes mistakenly assumed that the exposition or decoding of a myth could (by itself) explain either the fullness or the essence of a certain ritual or tradition.[66] We find compelling examples of this presupposition at work among early Enlightenment Protestant scholars, for example, who, through analysis of the myths of the Old Testament, sought a window into the "primitive" religious mind of ancient Israel.[67] More recently, this has sometimes been the case in discussions of the so-called myth of fallen angels, which some have read as providing an origin for the concept of evil in early Jewish tradition.[68]

In the next section, I delve into the relationship between spirit myths and spirit rituals in biblical literature. I suggest that myths should not be read as etiological *descriptions*, designed to explain why a certain (usually odd) practice existed in antiquity, but rather as rival *prescriptions* for what a practice should mean and how it should be performed. I demonstrate this point through analysis of a Sakalava spirit-possession ritual in Madagascar with comparison to the story of Micaiah son of Imlah in 1 Kgs 22. Then, in the subsequent section, I analyze how the interpretive history of the myth of fallen angels has shaped scholarly thinking about the relationship between spirit myths and spirit practices in Second Temple Judaism

---

[65] See, for example, Paul Ricoeur: Myth is "[...] a traditional narration which relates to events that happened at the beginning of time and which has the purpose of providing grounds for the ritual actions of men of today and, in a general manner, establish all the forms of action and thought by which man understands himself in his world." Paul Ricoeur, *The Symbolism of Evil*, trans. Emerson Buchanan (Boston: Beacon, 1967), 5.
[66] "For a critical understanding of the myth, it is first necessary that the myth be entirely divorced from the 'etiological' function with which it appears to be identified." Ricoeur, *Symbolism of Evil*, 164.
[67] See, for example, Johann Gottfried Eichhorn and others from the Göttingen School. Henning Graf Reventlow, *History of Biblical Interpretation, Volume 4: From the Enlightenment to the Twentieth Century*, trans. Leo G. Perdue, RBS 63 (Atlanta: SBL Press, 2009), 211–29.
[68] See, for example, Wright, *The Origin of Evil Spirits* and my discussion in chapter 1.

3.5.1 Rival Spirits in Sakalava Possession

For several generations, Western ethnographers and cultural anthropologists have taken a special interest in Malagasy spirit-possession practices, including those of the Sakalava people, an ethnic minority who live on the northern and western coasts of Madagascar.[69] Sakalava spirit possession is notable for its commonality across various sectors of society and the ways in which it continues to play a significant role in the daily life of many people into the post-colonial era. Spirits called *tromba*—which are mostly (but not entirely) those of deceased ancestors—habitually possess appointed mediums who come from all walks of life, religions, and clans. Their presence is not usually announced explicitly but is expected in certain ritual settings and, even outside of them, is signaled by well-known cues, such as clothing, conspicuous behavior, and certain greetings.

One story, as relayed by Michael Lambek, offers a parallel to the episode of Micaiah son of Imlah discussed below. The ritual on that occasion concerned a gathering of several spirits (who were embodied in mediums) at a shrine on the occasion of an especially senior *tromba* spirit receiving new clothes—a very important occasion.[70] The spirits present at the celebration came from a three-hundred-year span of Sakalava history, and they were joined by living members of the community. In these types of gatherings, it is traditional for the most senior spirits to be seated, while others stand. (This is maintained irrespective of the ages of the particular mediums who host the spirits.) However, at this event, there were only two chairs. One was occupied by Ndramandaming, a former regional governor who is always portrayed as immobile due to paralysis. In the other sat his father, Ndramanefa. When more senior spirits arrived at the event, Ndramanefa gave up his chair according to custom but refused to allow the assembly to take the chair from his son, due to the younger's disability. When the other *tromba* persisted, removing Ndramandaming from his seat, Ndramanefa left the shrine, and later, after his medium regained consciousness, she did not rejoin the gathering.

---

[69] Most of the pertinent ethnographic data for this section come from Michael Lambek, "The Sakalava Poiesis of History: Realizing the Past Through Spirit Possession in Madagascar," *AmEthno* 25.2 (1998): 106–27; *The Weight of the Past*; "On Being Present to History". See also Lesley A. Sharp, *The Possessed and the Dispossessed: Spirits, Identity, and Power in a Madagascar Migrant Town*, CSHSMC 37 (Berkeley: University of California Press, 1993); "Playboy Princely Spirits of Madagascar: Possession as Youthful Commentary and Social Critique," *AQ* 68.2 (1995): 75–88; and "Royal Difficulties: A Question of Succession in an Urbanized Sakalava Kingdom," *JRAf* 27.1–4 (1997): 270–307.

[70] Lambek, "The Sakalava Poiesis of History," 119–21.

The incident was much discussed by the mediums later, revealing some of the subtext of the event. It was widely observed that Ndramanefa had not shown proper respect to his ancestors, who, crucially, had been leaders during the precolonial period in Madagascar. It was especially significant, then, that in life, Ndramanefa had been only half Sakalava, *his* father being a member of the Merina, the dominant ethnic group in Madagascar. Thus, whenever Ndramanefa and Ndramandaming become manifest, their mediums wear the traditional garb of the Merina and not of the Sakalava (costumes being a kind of shorthand that can be used to identify the various spirits). In popular Sakalava memory, both figures—the upset father and the paralyzed son—are seen as representatives of a group who made certain concessions to the French occupiers in order to maintain their power. As interpreted by Lambek, one issue being communicated in the episode at the shrine

> is that of who carries more authority and should be granted greater respect: the earlier rulers, who manifest Sakalava autonomy and power, or the later rulers who were incorporated into the Merina and colonial states and who here also represent the westernized sector.[71]

According to Lambek, the drama concerning the chair was as much political commentary as it was performance art. Was the spirit-possession ritual a platform for postcolonial critique? A refusal to allow those that would accommodate colonizing powers to rebuff Sakalava traditions? While asking these questions, one final layer of complexity is also worth mentioning: while the father *tromba*, Ndramanefa, in this episode was a Protestant Christian, his medium—at least at this gathering—was a Muslim woman.

This account of a Sakalava spirit possession event reveals how the unseen mythic backdrop of a story can invest even seemingly minor ritual actions with profound significance. We can compare this coordination of ritual and myth to that of an analogue account of spirit possession in the Hebrew Bible.

3.5.2 Micaiah son of Imlah's Spirit Myth Gambit

1 Kings 22 is one of those rare examples in the Hebrew Bible where a spirit myth is framed explicitly by a description of an attendant spirit-possession event. Moreover, two rival camps exist within the story and both employ spirit myth to articulate their version of the truth over against one another. A large portion of the text is reproduced below:

---

[71] Lambek, "The Sakalava Poiesis of History," 120.

⁶ Then the king of Israel gathered the prophets together, about four hundred of them, and said to them, "Shall I go to battle against Ramoth-gilead, or shall I refrain?" They said, "Go up; for the Lord will give it into the hand of the king." ⁷ But Jehoshaphat said, "Is there no other prophet of the Lord here of whom we may inquire?" ⁸ The king of Israel said to Jehoshaphat, "There is still one other by whom we may inquire of the Lord, Micaiah son of Imlah; but I hate him, for he never prophesies anything favorable about me, but only disaster." Jehoshaphat said, "Let the king not say such a thing." ⁹ Then the king of Israel summoned an officer and said, "Bring quickly Micaiah son of Imlah."

¹⁰ Now the king of Israel and King Jehoshaphat of Judah were sitting on their thrones, arrayed in their robes, at the threshing floor at the entrance of the gate of Samaria; and all the prophets were prophesying before them. ¹¹ Zedekiah son of Chenaanah made for himself horns of iron, and he said, "Thus says the Lord: With these you shall gore the Arameans until they are destroyed." ¹² All the prophets were prophesying the same and saying, "Go up to Ramoth-gilead and triumph; the Lord will give it into the hand of the king."

¹³ The messenger who had gone to summon Micaiah said to him, "Look, the words of the prophets with one accord are favorable to the king; let your word be like the word of one of them, and speak favorably." ¹⁴ But Micaiah said, "As the Lord lives, whatever the Lord says to me, that I will speak." ¹⁵ When he had come to the king, the king said to him, "Micaiah, shall we go to Ramoth-gilead to battle, or shall we refrain?" He answered him, "Go up and triumph; the Lord will give it into the hand of the king." ¹⁶ But the king said to him, "How many times must I make you swear to tell me nothing but the truth in the name of the Lord?" ¹⁷ Then Micaiah said, "I saw all Israel scattered on the mountains, like sheep that have no shepherd; and the Lord said, 'These have no master; let each one go home in peace.'" ¹⁸ The king of Israel said to Jehoshaphat, "Did I not tell you that he would not prophesy anything favorable about me, but only disaster?"

¹⁹ Then Micaiah said, "Therefore hear the word of the Lord: I saw the Lord sitting on his throne, with all the host of heaven standing beside him to the right and to the left of him. ²⁰ And the Lord said, 'Who will entice Ahab, so that he may go up and fall at Ramoth-gilead?' Then one said one thing, and another said another, ²¹ until a spirit came forward and stood before the Lord, saying, 'I will entice him.' ²² 'How?' the Lord asked him. He replied, 'I will go out and be a lying spirit in the mouth of all his prophets.' Then the Lord said, 'You are to entice him, and you shall succeed; go out and do it.' ²³ So you see, the Lord has put a lying spirit in the mouth of all these your prophets; the Lord has decreed disaster for you."

²⁴ Then Zedekiah son of Chenaanah came up to Micaiah, slapped him on the cheek, and said, "Which way did the spirit of the Lord pass from me to speak to you?" ²⁵ Micaiah replied, "You will find out on that day when you go in to hide in an inner chamber." ²⁶ The king of Israel then ordered, "Take Micaiah, and return him to Amon the governor of the city and to Joash the king's son, ²⁷ and say, 'Thus says the king: Put this fellow in prison, and feed him on reduced rations of bread and water until I come in peace.'" ²⁸ Micaiah said, "If you return in peace, the Lord has not spoken by me." And he said, "Hear, you peoples, all of you!" (1 Kgs 22:6–28)⁷²

---

⁷² The story also appears in 2 Chr 18 with minor textual differences. See comparison of the two texts in the MT and OG in Simon J. De Vries, *Prophet against Prophet: The Role of the Micaiah*

It has been customary among interpreters of a certain theological persuasion to read this peculiar episode of Micaiah son of Imlah as an especially savage and "primitive prophetic tale."[73] More recently, however, scholars have countered that it is a late addition—though perhaps it contains older materials.[74] Regardless of its vintage, the text is informative for the way it interweaves a description of a spirit-possession ritual with an explanatory myth.

The possession ritual may be implied in verse 6b, but at least one aspect of it is explicitly demonstrated in verses 10–12.[75] Here, among the four hundred other prophets, Zedekiah son of Chenaanah emerges as an especially charismatic figure, engaging in a sign-act (utilizing a prop set of iron horns) and performing his prophecy in a manner not dissimilar from how Jeremiah or Ezekiel might have. Although the word "spirit" (רוח) does not appear, we know that the prophetic activity in this passage is understood as spirit-empowered due to Zedekiah's later accusation of Micaiah in verse 24: "Which way did the spirit (רוח) of the LORD pass from me to speak to you?" (cf. 1 Sam 16:13–14).

Commentators have offered varying views as to what readers are meant to make of Micaiah's character as a prophet in verses 13–18, but what concerns us here is Micaiah's subsequent account of God's court and how it serves to undermine the possession ritual of Zedekiah and the other prophets (vv. 19–23).[76] Micaiah describes a vision wherein God seeks to deceive the king of Israel (likely Ahab, though perhaps not always in the transmission of the text) into engaging

---

Narrative (I Kings 22) in the Development of Early Prophetic Tradition (Grand Rapids: Eerdmans, 1978), 11–24.

73 E.g., Walter Brueggemann, *Theology of the Old Testament: Testimony, Dispute, Advocacy* (Minneapolis: Fortress, 1997), 360–61.

74 Kratz, *The Composition of the Narrative Books of the Old Testament*, 166–67; and R. W. L. Moberly, "Micaiah Ben Imlah: The Costs of Authenticity and Discernment," in *Prophecy and Discernment*, CSCD 14 (Cambridge: Cambridge University Press, 2006), 100–129.

75 The motif of one prophet in the right against hundreds in the wrong has already been established in the narrative by Elijah against the four hundred and fifty prophets of Baal and four hundred of Asherah (1 Kgs 18:17–46).

76 One recurring question regards the characterization of Micaiah as either a true or false prophet according to Deut 18:12. Commentators have also speculated as to the function that his conspicuous dissenting voice may have played in the presumed scribal community behind the episode. See, for example, K. L. Noll, "The Deconstruction of Deuteronomism in the Former Prophets: Micaiah Ben Imlah as Example," in *Far from Minimal: Celebrating the Work and Influence of Philip R. Davies*, ed. Duncan Burns and John W. Rogerson, LHBOTS 484 (New York: T & T Clark, 2014), 325–34; and Ehud Ben Zvi, "A Contribution to the Intellectual History of Yehud: The Story of Micaiah and its Function within the Discourse of Persian-Period Literati," in *Sense and Sensitivity: Essays on Reading the Bible in Memory of Robert Carroll*, ed. Alastair G. Hunter and Philip R. Davies, JSOTSup 348 (London: Sheffield, 2002), 89–102.

in a military attack that will see him killed. Uncharacteristically, however, the specifics of the plan are not firm, and God consults the lesser beings of the divine council, looking for a volunteer. The council mulls over the plan and eventually a certain "spirit" (רוח) volunteers to entice the king by means of lying to his prophets (v. 21). God consents to the plan and promises the deceiving spirit success.[77]

The vision is enigmatic for several reasons. First, it is one of only a handful of places in the Hebrew Bible where God's divine council is described in any detail (cf. Isa 6; Ps 82; Job 1–2). Further, God's relationship to the voluntary spirit and his actions may strike us as unusually loose. Readers are left wondering how much freedom this spirit-agent of God might have. We also know nothing of the spirit's (or God's) motivation in the matter. Is this deceiving spirit especially vindictive or cruel; is it merely mischievous? Perhaps more fundamentally, if the entire episode takes place under God's authorization (as indeed it seems), are the intentions of the spirit even significant? The theological implications are potentially alarming. As R. W. L. Moberly poignantly puts it: "Does God lie to his prophets?"[78]

Although some commentators have been morally or theologically scandalized by what seems like a collaborative act of sabotage between God and prophet, Moberly argues that these interpreters misunderstand Micaiah's intent. The vision of the heavenly court, in reality:

> might be revealing the true nature of the earthly court, i.e., that the manipulation, deception, and self-will might belong solely to Ahab and his prophets, and that they are being displayed to Ahab in an ironic and dramatic challenge.[79]

I find this part of Moberly's interpretation compelling for several reasons. For one, Moberly most adequately accounts for an aspect of the story that is repeatedly implied; namely, that Micaiah must make his message heard to a king who is unwilling to listen. In this reading, Micaiah's initial agreement with the other prophets (vv. 15–16) is no guileful sabotage but a gambit, designed to manipulate the king into demanding a truthful prophecy (and perhaps also force him to recognize the sycophancy of his advisors). The closest biblical analogue to Mi-

---

[77] Esther Hamori identifies the רוח שקר here as "the only specific spirit we see in the Hebrew Bible with individual identity and agency" (a notable exception being the [רוח ה']). Hamori, "The Spirit of Falsehood," 16.
[78] R. W. L. Moberly, "Does God Lie to His Prophets?: The Story of Micaiah Ben Imlah as a Test Case," *HTR* 96.1 (2003): 1–23.
[79] Moberly, "Does God Lie to His Prophets?," 22.

caiah's vision, then, is Nathan's parable to David (2 Sam 12:1–7).[80] With this striking description of divine deceit, Micaiah hopes to reveal to the king how the king's own prophetic servants have been manipulating him. Micaiah's goal, then, in employing a spirit myth is not to establish eternal truths about the metaphysical realities of the beings of the heavenly court, but to describe something that is happening interpersonally in the court of Israel.

Equally important is the effect of Micaiah's vision on how readers perceive the spirit possession practiced by Zedekiah and his fellow prophets. The myth, as related by Micaiah, not only explains but also serves to undermine the message of his rivals. However, unlike other stories of prophetic rivalry in the Hebrew Bible (e.g., Jer 27–28), Micaiah does not quite make an accusation of false prophecy—at least not in the conventional sense.[81] Rather than calling them frauds or madmen, Micaiah accepts the earnestness with which these other prophets practiced their craft; it is just that they have been deceived by the spirit that influenced them.

In 1 Kgs 22, discourse on myths about spirits is a way to contest spirit-experience performances. Zedekiah does not challenge the power or influence that Micaiah may have in the court; he acknowledges the legitimacy of the rival prophet's vision and surmises for himself a mythic explanation for the discrepancy of his own experience (i.e., that the spirit of the LORD has abandoned him in favor of Micaiah, 1 Kgs 22:24). Efforts by contemporary interpreters, then, to question the moral and theological fitness of the Micaiah story or to account for it systematically within a wider mythic worldview of ancient Israel/early Judaism miss the mark because it is a myth inseparable from the particular episode of spirit possession that it illuminates.

In 1 Kgs 22, the spirit-empowered prophecy delivered by Zedekiah and the other prophets can only be partially understood in light of a prophetic–symbolic act (i.e., the iron horns, the delivery of an oracle). As it is presented in this final form of the story, the vision (or myth) that Micaiah relates of the divine council is also necessary for understanding. Similarly, among the Sakalava, it is not enough merely to observe the activity of the human mediums; the identities and postures of the *tromba* must also be considered. In both instances, rather than reading the myths as causing human behavior, it is more informative to read the conflicts in the spirit and human realms as reflecting and mutually in-

---

80 We might say that "The LORD has decreed disaster for you" (1 Kgs 22:23) carries a similar rhetorical force to "You are the man!" (2 Sam 12:7).
81 See James L. Crenshaw, *Prophetic Conflict; Its Effect upon Israelite Religion*, BZAW 124 (Berlin: De Gruyter, 1971), 83–85.

forming one another.⁸² This understanding of the relationship between myth and ritual applies also when considering the myth of fallen angels.

3.5.3 The Myth of Fallen Angels and Prescriptive Etiologies

The tradition of the fallen angels, which survives most extensively in the collection of early Jewish writings that were assembled under the name 1 Enoch, is a mythic and exegetical narrative expansion of the curious episode of the "sons of God" or "divine beings" (בני־האלהים) in Gen 6:1–4.⁸³ According to the myth, these sons of God were, in fact, angels, who lusted after human women, descended to earth, and begat monstrous children. The angels then taught humanity forbidden knowledge, such as magic, warfare, astrology, and ornamentation. In this version, the spread of corruption from this divine invasion was disastrous enough to trigger the flood (cf. Gen 6:4; 5–7; 12) and a judgment on the angels (1 En. 12). The angels' giant offspring perish in the flood but live on non-corporeally as "evil spirits" who still hunger after humanity (1 En. 15–16; cf. Jub. 10:8–9). The myth survives also in several strands of late Second Temple literature, including the book of Jubilees and possibly the New Testament (e.g., 2 Pet 2:4; Jude 6), though the details and implied consequences of the myth are not consistent.⁸⁴

As discussed in the introduction, "evil" as a category oriented around the problem of "intelligibility" is an Enlightenment innovation and thus one that is framed quite differently in biblical and early Jewish literature. Instead,

---

82 Moberly, "Does God Lie to His Prophets?," 9.
83 Named after the patriarch Enoch who is mentioned in Genesis 5:18–24, the various writings that make up 1 Enoch were composed in Aramaic between the fifth or fourth century BCE and the turn of the millennium. The book is divided into five major sections, each with complex and interlinked compositional histories. For overviews see John J. Collins, *The Apocalyptic Imagination: An Introduction to Jewish Apocalyptic Literature*, 3rd ed. (Grand Rapids: Eerdmans, 2016), 52–94 and George W. E. Nickelsburg, "Enoch, Books of," *EDSS* 1:249–53. See also Loren T. Stuckenbruck, "Origins of Evil in Jewish Apocalyptic Tradition: The Interpretation of Genesis 6:1–4," in *The Myth of Rebellious Angels: Studies in Second Temple Judaism and New Testament Texts*, WUNT 335 (Tübingen: Mohr Siebeck, 2014), 1–33; Yoshiko Reed, *Fallen Angels and the History of Judaism and Christianity*; and John J. Collins, "The Origin of Evil in Apocalyptic Literature and the Dead Sea Scrolls," in *Congress Volume, Paris 1992*, ed. John A. Emerton, VTSup 61 (Leiden: Brill, 1995), 25–38.
84 See overview in Wright, *The Origin of Evil Spirits*, 169–93. See also a counterargument that 2 Pet 2:4 and Jude 6 do not reflect the Watcher myth in Kim Papaioannou, "The Sin of the Angels in 2 Peter 2:4 and Jude 6," *JBL* 140.2 (2021): 391–408.

these texts focus on oppositional figures who attempt to obstruct specific actions of God or God's people, rather than on a general system of categorical evil.[85] Strictly speaking, it is not necessary to grapple with the nature of ontological evil when evaluating spirit phenomena in the Hebrew Bible. Thus, when biblical scholars attempt to extrapolate an overarching theory of evil from across the varying and contradictory primary sources, it reveals an important modern assumption that ancient Second Temple era Jews may not have shared; namely, that a coherent mythic system is a necessary precursor to participating in possession and other spirit practices.[86]

In contemporary spirit-possession cults around the world, myths about spirits are rarely systematic or strictly enforced. Ethnographers have often noted that conceptions regarding the ontologies, origins, or identities of spirits are often quite varied and vague—even among participants in the same ritual. We find a comparable example again among the spirit-possession practices of the Sakalava in an annual festival called "the Great Service." Here, it is customary for humans and ancestral spirits (made present through human hosts) to celebrate together in the public, community-wide festival. In 2012, however, the usual activities were interrupted by a group of youthful spirits (hosted mostly by young men) dressed in red headbands and waistcloths and wearing white face paint. Although the festival is usually a raucous and noisy affair, these *jiriky* spirits were especially uproarious and numerous. More than one observer connected the presence of these spirits to reports of "brigands" in the nearby country, while others insisted that they were the spirits of animals. As Michael Lambek observed:

> People disagreed on who the *jiriky* were and where they came from, but they were not worried about this, and did not seem to need to know. Whether the *jiriky* were primarily human or nonhuman, brigands or guardians, or how one interpreted the difference, mattered less than what their sudden arrival indexed and what they did in front of people.[87]

This suggests, among other things, that beliefs about spirits among those who regularly consort with them are usually far less concrete and unanimous than some commentators would have it.

---

[85] See the discussion of the complex presentation of "evil" figures in the reception history of Genesis 22: Reed Carlson, "Provocateurs, Examiners, and Fools: Divine Opponents to the Aqedah in Early Judaism," *CBQ* 83.3 (2021): 373–89.
[86] The argument over the primacy of myth or ritual is an old one in the study of religion. For an overview, see Robert A. Segal, "Myth and Ritual," in *The Routledge Companion to the Study of Religion*, ed. John R. Hinnells, 2nd ed. (London: Routledge, 2010), 372–96.
[87] Lambek, "On Being Present to History," 333.

Returning to the myth of fallen angels, Lambek's observations suggest that a person's particular belief about the origins of spirit beings may not be the primary factor in determining how they participate in a possession ritual. Indeed, a myth about the continued threat of the invasive spirits of long-deceased giants is just as likely to arise as an *ex post facto* explanation for an already existing spirit-possession practice as it is to engender the innovation of such a practice by itself. It might also have developed as a rival or intended correction to other theories.

The analogy from Sakalava spirit possession demonstrates how the precise mapping of metaphysical realities is frequently a secondary concern for participants in spirit-possession practices. Thus, the purpose of myths connected to spirit-possession practices in early Judaism may be less that of *describing* why such phenomena occur—this despite the genre's inherent etymological tone—and more that of *prescribing* how such rituals ought to be practiced and/or what they should mean.

3.6 Conclusions

In this chapter I have outlined three heuristic and overlapping categories of spirit phenomena in the Hebrew Bible: (1) spirit language, (2) descriptions of spirit possession, and (3) myths about spirits. I have suggested that the term *rûaḥ* (רוח) is frequently portrayed as a material part of the body, an organ that is conceived as having considerable functional overlap with one's heart. The spirit, however, is more permeable than the heart and thus liable to outside influences, both good and bad. Additionally, I have shown that spirit phenomena in biblical literature are not limited to instances of the key term *rûaḥ* or to explicitly narrated possession events. Instead, taking cues from ethnographic research and, in particular, LeRhonda S. Manigault-Bryant's study on Gullah/Geechee women, I suggested that spirit possession can sometimes be a decidedly non-charismatic and even commonplace element of religious life and literature. Finally, I suggested that decoding myths about spirits has dominated much of the discussion regarding spirit phenomena in biblical literature, in part because it is in the nature of myth to claim an etymological and explanatory function. However, the link between myth and ritual is more tenuous and dynamic than many biblical scholars have recognized.

Having thus identified the range of spirit phenomena as they appear in biblical literature, I am now positioned to explore how these texts collaborate, correct, and contend with one another to construct notions of spirits and spirit experience.

4 When a Spirit Moves

4.1 The Exorcism of Robert Brigges

Robert Brigges's troubles started in Advent of 1573 after he attended a theological lecture at the Middle Temple in London.[1] A promising young law student, Brigges was on the verge of completing his studies when he attended the lecture, which concerned the topic of unforgivable sins. Distressed that he might already be damned, Brigges returned home that night in a melancholy mood. Over the next several months, Brigges became increasingly despondent toward his wife and baby and eventually attempted suicide on several occasions.

The nature of Brigges's ailment changed on Easter Sunday 1574 after he fainted and remained unconscious for twelve hours. Over the course of the following day, he lost his senses of sight, hearing, and feeling. Then, remarkably, he roused from his stupor and, seemingly unprovoked, quoted each of the Ten Commandments. Brigges then carried on for the next several hours in what was described by witnesses as a complicated theological debate. Brigges would offer arguments and then pause, as if listening to an unknown interlocutor. In his speeches, Brigges would quote long sections of scripture, though the law student had never been known to be an especially dedicated student of the Bible. This pattern continued for several days. Eventually, those around Brigges discerned that he was being antagonized by the forces of hell and debating with none other than Satan himself.

For the next twenty days, Brigges endured repeated torment from his possessors. In contrast to modern presentations of spirit possession as socially marginal and secretive, this ordeal was highly publicized and witnessed daily by a small crowd.[2] Immobilized, Brigges would debate with Satan as well as experience hallucinations and temptations. Notably, Brigges's fiercest debates with Satan concerned the heated controversies surrounding the ongoing English Reformation.[3]

---

1 The story of Robert Brigges is told by Kathleen R. Sands in *Demon Possession in Elizabethan England* (Westport: Praeger, 2004), 57–74; *An Elizabethan Lawyer's Possession by the Devil: The Story of Robert Brigges* (Westport: Praeger, 2002); and "John Foxe: Exorcist," *HT* 51.2 (2001): 37–43. The primary sources Sands consulted for this case are two unpublished manuscripts in the British Library: Harley MS 590, pp. 6–63 and Lansdowne MS 101, folios 165–75.
2 Sands, "John Foxe: Exorcist," 38.
3 At one point Satan threatened to rip Brigges to shreds if he himself did not rip up a copy of a printed sermon. It was likely a copy of a widely circulated sermon preached by John Foxe and already in its fourth printing by the time of Brigges's possession, *A Sermon of Christ Crucified*

Though most likely raised a Roman Catholic, Brigges took the Protestant position on such topics as prayers to saints and icons, the role of natural law in creation, and the possibility of good works as a means to salvation. In contrast, on each of these issues Satan was emphatically on the side of Rome. Yet this conflict was also intensely personal. Brigges was a law student. On the occasion that he was called to the bar, it would be expected of him to swear an oath of supremacy, effectively denouncing Rome and damaging his relationship with his prominent family.

The exorcism of Robert Brigges was accomplished suddenly. His ordeal eventually drew the attention of John Foxe, a popular martyrologist and outspoken critic of the Roman Catholic Church. For Brigges, Foxe conducted a public exorcism, strategically invoking the name of Jesus as a spiritual weapon (cf. Mark 9:38–41), which granted a temporary reprieve. Yet the possession would persist for another week, continuing in the same pattern. Then, one day, without an apparent climax, Satan inexplicably did not return. Brigges had seemingly exorcized himself. He eventually completed his studies, swore the oath of supremacy upon his call to the bar, and went on to enjoy a successful career as a barrister.

This sixteenth-century account of Robert Brigges's conflict with Satan may strike modern readers as almost comically sectarian, but those aspects of the story that feel like Reformation propaganda are by no means unique when we compare the Brigges story to other accounts of spirit possession in early modern Europe.[4] Europe was experiencing a period of rapid shift: new ecclesial structures, budding sciences, and the growing influence of printed media. It follows that spirit-possession practices would reflect those changing times.

Moreover, the story exhibits several aspects of spirit possession consistent with the observations of cultural anthropologists on analogous contemporary phenomena. For example, in contrast to what some may expect, Robert Brigges is a prominent member of the upper class. His possession event is neither marginal nor private, though his status as a likely Roman Catholic in a newly Protestant nation makes his position somewhat precarious. Moreover, though unusual and certainly a spectacle, Brigges's possession also exhibits a kind of structure (e.g., an awareness of the liturgical calendar and a genre of discourse consistent

---

(London: John Day, 1570). The contents of the sermon comment on many of the very issues that Brigges and Satan debated.

[4] See, for example, Andrew Cambers, "Demonic Possession, Literacy and 'Superstition' in Early Modern England," *PP* 202.1 (2009): 3–35; Marion Gibson, *Possession, Puritanism and Print: Darrell, Harsnett, Shakespeare and the Elizabethan Exorcism Controversy* (London: Pickering & Chatto, 2006); and Sarah Ferber, *Demonic Possession and Exorcism in Early Modern France* (New York: Routledge, 2004).

with Brigges's profession as a lawyer). We must admit that, whatever else it is, the episode also displays an aspect of performance, and in this way it functioned as an interpretation of current affairs—both those of society and, we might expect, those of Brigges's personal life. Indeed, Brigges, in his personal and professional affairs, embodies within himself the conflict among the powers that vie for control of Europe.[5]

Especially relevant, the possession of Robert Brigges also exhibits an extraordinary sensitivity to and engagement with scripture. This is true not only in its rehearsal of New Testament possession tropes (i.e., the demon/spirits seizing the host's body [e.g., Mark 5:3–4]; compulsion to self-destructive behavior [e.g., Mark 9:18]; and spirits speaking with the host's voice [Mark 1:24]), but also in Brigges's frequent quotation of scripture. Remarkably, by adopting the form of a theological debate, the entire possession episode is framed as a contest over the interpretation of scripture (compare Jesus's encounter with the devil in the wilderness [Matt 4:1–11/Luke 4:1–13]).

We can contrast Brigges's spirit possession with those of Cuban Espiritismo and practices of talking to the dead among Gullah/Geechee women. Unlike those, Brigges's possession is unwelcome and deeply disruptive. It is not cultivated but resisted. Further, it is temporary, and once he is exorcised, it seems that the ordeal does not reoccur. Here, then, are two differing conceptions of spirit possession. In one, represented by Espiritismo and Gullah/Geechee talking to the dead, the spirits abide, and their influences are more subtle. In the other, represented by Brigges (and to some degree the Sakalava), the influences of spirits are more dramatic, causing a public spectacle. The activities of the spirits in the latter conception spirits are more definite, with clear moments when they are present and absent. Although it would be a mistake to formalize such differences into complete systems, such models can be detected in various spirit-possession communities around the world. They are also present in biblical literature.

---

[5] The exorcism of Robert Brigges may be seen as emblematic of a final high point in mainstream spirit-possession practices in Europe. While it is difficult to catalogue when spirit-possession practices may or may not have "peaked" in the early modern period, there are indications that by the mid-seventeenth century, reports of possession had begun to give way to growing skepticism—especially among ecclesial authorities. See Thomas Freeman, "Demons, Deviance and Defiance: John Darrell and the Politics of Exorcism in Late Elizabethan England," in *Conformity and Orthodoxy in the English Church, c. 1560–1660*, ed. Peter Lake and Michael C. Questier, SMBRH (Woodbridge: Boydell, 2000), 34–63.

4.2 Chapter Overview

Taking cues from these contrasts in spirit possession, in this chapter I engage with an ongoing debate on the nature of spirits in biblical literature and propose a synthesis between two sides. Scholars have long made a distinction between two general descriptions of spirits in the Hebrew Bible: The first, an *animating* or *life-giving* spirit, is one that endows all living creatures; this is the "breath of life," so to speak. The second, *inspiring* or *charismatic* spirits, empower biblical figures at certain times for specific tasks or feats, but they can also be experienced as oppressive or chaotic. Notably, among the scholarly literature, the former is frequently discussed in the singular (i.e., "the animating spirit"), whereas the latter are often treated in the plural (i.e., "empowering spirits").[6]

More recently, however, some have questioned the utility of such a classification. John R. Levison, for example, has argued that this distinction has been grossly overstated, in part as a result of certain Christian theological interests.[7] Levison's warning against too strict a dichotomy is well-taken. However, in this chapter I suggest that there is still utility to this approach. The problem is not in the distinction itself but in the way the issue has been framed. Carol Newsom has already begun the discussion on reframing, recognizing that this contrast is not so much one of two differing types of spirits, but rather two—at-times rival —cognitive models for the individual agency of human beings.[8]

I thus propose a simpler way of distinguishing between two basic conceptions for spirits in biblical literature, which in turn reflect differing ideas about the functioning and agency of human bodies: spirits that *stay* and spirits that *move*. In the remainder of this chapter, I expound these two categories, referring to them as *abiding* spirits and *migrating* spirits, respectively. Through a philological analysis of the vocabulary and syntax used to describe spirit phenomena in the Hebrew Bible, I suggest that my model can more organically account for how spirits can alternate between both modes and how they can exist side-by-side, informing one another and, at-times, clashing.

---

[6] See a summary on some variations of these categories in the history of biblical scholarship in Levison, *Filled with the Spirit*, 8–13. See also Block, "The Prophet of the Spirit"; McCarter Jr., "Evil Spirit of God"; Lapsley, *Can These Bones Live?*, 164–67; Snaith, *Distinctive Ideas of the Old Testament*, 143–50; Robert Koch, *Der Geist Gottes im Alten Testament* (Bern: Lang, 1991), 19–31; and Hildebrandt, *An Old Testament Theology of the Spirit of God*, 28–66.
[7] Levison, *Filled with the Spirit*, 12.
[8] Newsom, *The Spirit Within Me*, 37–47.

4.3 Abiding Spirits

In general, we might say that an abiding spirit was seen as being imparted at birth to all living creatures and then departing at death. This spirit "abides" because it is always present, usually without a single or static moral charge, and is often connected to reflections on the inner life. Indeed, language concerning a person's abiding spirit is one of the primary ways that biblical literature articulates notions of the self and of personhood. Additionally, abiding spirits are often described as being material and a part of the body. They can be referred to as the "spirit/breath of life" (רוח/נשמת חיים) or simply as one's "spirit" with a suffixed personal pronoun (e.g., "his breath" רוחו). They can "depart" (יצ״א), "remain" (ית״ר), and, of course, be "breathed" (נפ״ח):

> Then the LORD God formed man from the dust of the ground, and breathed into his nostrils the breath of life; and the man became a living being. (Gen 2:7; cf. Isa 42:5)[9]

> For my part, I am going to bring a flood of waters on the earth, to destroy from under heaven all flesh in which is the breath of life; everything that is on the earth shall die. (Gen 6:17; cf. 7:15; 22)

> After this the son of the woman, the mistress of the house, became ill; his illness was so severe that there was no breath left in him. (1 Kgs 17:17)

> Just as you do not know how the breath comes to the bones in the mother's womb, so you do not know the work of God, who makes everything. (Qoh 11:5)

> "Remember that my life is a breath;
> my eye will never again see good." (Job 7:7)

In some of these texts, then, abiding spirits are so elemental to human animation that they are described as the very determiner for created life itself.

Even in these settings, however, the role of abiding spirits is not limited to their animating properties. Often, there is a dynamic and ongoing relationship between the creator and the creature, which is facilitated through one's abiding spirit.

> Into your hand I commit my spirit;
> you have redeemed me, O LORD, faithful God. (Ps 31:6 [NRSV v. 5])

---

9 "Breath of life" here is נשמת חיים. Newsom points out that while רוח and נשמה are not strictly synonymous, there is extensive overlap in their semantic ranges. This can be seen, for example, in their parallel usage by Elihu in Job 32:8; 33:4; 34:14–15. Newsom, *The Spirit Within Me*, 39.

> O Lord, by these things people live,
> and in all these is the life of my spirit.
> Oh, restore me to health and make me live! (Isa 38:16)
>
> You have granted me life and steadfast love,
> and your care has preserved my spirit. (Job 10:12)
>
> Teach me to do your will,
> for you are my God.
> Let your good spirit lead me
> on a level path. (Ps 143:10)
>
> ¹² Why does your heart carry you away,
> and why do your eyes flash,
> ¹³ so that you turn your spirit against God,
> and let such words go out of your mouth? (Job 15:12–13)

Clearly, then, although the abiding spirit is frequently connected to life itself, it is more than just a metaphor for animation. One's abiding spirit can be committed, led, and preserved. It can become intertwined with God's own abiding spirit; having become separated, one's abiding spirit can search for God or even turn away. Though abiding spirits are seen as originating with God and returning at death, they are not identical with Israel's God—at least not in a hypostatic sense.

Another significant attribute of abiding spirits beyond that of simply animating life is their function in descriptions of corporate spirit phenomena. This is especially prevalent in prophetic texts (e.g., Isa 44:3; 63:11; Ezek 11:19; 18:31; 36:26–27; Hos 4:12; 5:4; Joel 3:1–2; Hag 1:14; 2:5; Zech 12:10). In fact, it would seem that the default setting for spirit activity in biblical and early Jewish literature is within a community, and that individual spirit experiences are a special exception.

One instructive example can be found in the Community Rule scroll found near Qumran.[10] The following passage concludes the opening portion of the scroll, which concerns membership and initiation:

---

[10] There is a general consensus that the longest and possibly latest surviving version of the Community Rule, 1QS, was produced at the beginning of the first century BCE. However, the existence of several older and divergent copies suggests that the Community Rule has a complicated and multi-branched compositional history. For an overview, see Michael A. Knibb, "Rule of the Community," *EDSS* 1:793–97. More recently, see Alison Schofield, *From Qumran to the Yaḥad: A New Paradigm of Textual Development for The Community Rule*, STDJ 77 (Leiden: Brill, 2009); and Charlotte Hempel, *The Qumran Rule Texts in Context: Collected Studies*, TSAJ 154 (Tübingen: Mohr Siebeck, 2013), 109–19.

> ⁶... For it is through a spirit of true counsel (ברוח עצת אמת) with regard to the ways of man that all ⁷ his iniquities shall be wiped out so that he may look on the light of life. It is through a holy spirit (וברוח קדושה) uniting him to his truth that he shall be purified from all ⁸ his iniquities. It is through a spirit of uprightness and humility (וברוח יושר וענוה) that his sin shall be wiped out. And it is through the submission of his soul to all the statutes of God ⁹ that his flesh shall be purified, by being sprinkled with waters for purification and made holy by waters for cleansing. Let him, therefore, order his steps that he may walk perfectly ¹⁰ in all the ways of God in accordance with that which he commanded at the times (when he made known) his decrees, without turning to the right or left and without ¹¹ going against any one of all his commandments. Then he will be accepted through soothing atonement before God, and it will be for him a covenant ¹² of the eternal community. (1QS 3:6b–12)[11]

In this section of 1QS, initiation into the community is cast as a spirit phenomenon. "Spirit" (רוח) is mentioned three times, each with descriptors detailing the kind of spirit necessary for initiation.[12] As we might expect, the lines between God's spirit, the spirit of the community, and that of the initiate are blurred—perhaps, eventually, there was not meant to be a distinction.[13] Further, we cannot be sure how initiates might or might not have demonstrated their possession of the right spirit(s)—and what rituals might have accompanied these spirit diagnoses—but the passage is clear that the result of a right spirit was righteous action according to the interpretation of the community. The Yahad thus understood itself as a community permanently possessed by one or more abiding spirits (a holy spirit, a spirit of truth, and so on). The community initiated new members, in part, through the recognition of its own spirit(s) as they were active in others.

4.3.1 Paradigms of Self-Cultivation

Given the persistent association of abiding spirits with life itself, it is no wonder that they show up frequently in biblical texts that articulate notions of the self.

---

[11] Text and translations of 1QS are from Sarianna Metso, *The Community Rule: A Critical Edition with Translation*, EJL 51 (Atlanta: SBL Press, 2019).
[12] Anja Klein, "From the 'Right Spirit' to the 'Spirit of Truth': Observations on Psalm 51 and 1QS," in *The Dynamics of Language and Exegesis at Qumran*, ed. Devorah Dimant and Reinhard Gregor Kratz, FAT2 35 (Tübingen: Mohr Siebeck, 2009), 171–91.
[13] "The passage thus assembles three different notions of the spirit that carries out atonement and purification. Both the spirit of the true counsel of god and the holy spirit can safely be assumed to proceed from god, but it is clear that all three are considered to be a spirit that is present in the community and represents God's [sic] presence within the Yahad." Klein, "From the 'Right Spirit' to the 'Spirit of Truth,'" 177–78.

Although it is tempting in such occurrences to assume that modern conceptions of selfhood are operative also in biblical literature, it is worth pausing and examining our own cultural models for the self and asking whether they truly fit the primary texts.

One especially pervasive model in need of investigation is that of *self-cultivation*. In models of self-cultivation, one's personhood is perceived as being elastic and open to self-improvement or self-detriment. Especially within religious contexts, one can actively change or "work on" one's self through the use of certain strategies, thereby developing or progressing in ways deemed life-giving or spiritually edifying by tradition or personal experience. Michel Foucault calls such strategies for self-cultivation "technologies of the self":

> [Technologies of the self] permit individuals to effect by their own means or with the help of others a certain number of operations on their own bodies and souls, thoughts, conduct, and way of being, so as to transform themselves in order to attain a certain state of happiness, purity, wisdom, perfection, or immortality.[14]

Foucault's articulation can be helpful, for example, in revealing the functions that religious activity plays in determining identity. We might fruitfully analyze prayer practices using this model, especially since prayers are often explicitly oriented toward an anticipated outcome for the person or community. Scholars of religion have applied the self-cultivation model, for example, in the contemporary study of Islamic devotional practices.[15]

However, some scholars of religion have argued that "self-cultivation" should not be seen as an exhaustive category. In particular, Foucault's "technologies of the self"—like many other theories of the self in Western intellectual tradition—assumes a particular model of personhood oriented around *action* that can be limiting when assessing non-Western forms of religiosity. Anthropologist and Islamicist Amira Mittermaier has called this the "hegemonic paradigm of self-cultivation."[16] She points out that such conceptions are notably less effective in accounting for models of the person in which the self is *acted upon* at least as often as it *acts*:

---

14 Foucault, *Technologies of the Self*, 18.
15 See, for example, Saba Mahmood, *Politics of Piety: The Islamic Revival and the Feminist Subject* (Princeton: Princeton University Press, 2011); and Charles Hirschkind, *The Ethical Soundscape: Cassette Sermons and Islamic Counterpublics* (New York: Columbia University Press, 2006).
16 Amira Mittermaier, "Dreams from Elsewhere: Muslim Subjectivities beyond the Trope of Self-Cultivation," *JRAI* 18.2 (2012): 249.

> The paradigm of self-cultivation equips anthropologists with a vocabulary for describing and analytically engaging with practices such as veiling, attending mosque study groups, or listening to tape-recorded sermons. Yet it offers us little for engaging with a different axis of religiosity, one that valorizes being acted upon, one most vividly expressed in stories of dreams, visions, apparitions, spirit possession, prophecy, revelation, the miraculous, and, more broadly, stories that involve elements of surprise and awe.[17]

As Mittermaier illustrates, religious practices like visionary dreams or spirit possession (in Islam and beyond) are difficult to reconcile with the liberal idealization of the autonomous self and therefore also with the paradigm of self-cultivation. This is particularly true for religious practices whose principal means of participation is to be a witness, either as a spectator or as an observer of one's own experiences. Put simply, witnessing is neither especially "active" nor "passive."[18] Rather, it is another type of phenomenon wherein there is a convergence of seeing and being made to see.

Of course, this critique of the paradigm of self-cultivation requires one to take seriously the claim by a practitioner (or an ancient author) that in instances of religious experience, they are not *doing* anything, but, in fact, *something is being done* to them. For a reader locked into a self-cultivation model, the notion of passivity in religious experience might be seen as scandalous, or alternatively, impossible. After all, if spirit possession can only ever be self-instigated and then cloaked in self-deception to *seem* passive, what is there left to discuss? But that perspective fails not only to account adequately for human experiences that are characterized by passivity, but also to recognize how such postures can be constructed as enviable and virtuous. Further, this perspective may also lead to the mistaken assumption that such a value system can only exist within a strict, deterministic worldview.

However, many theorists have underestimated the complexity of notions of free will and determinism in communities that prioritize non-active religious experience. This is usually because, within the paradigm of the self-cultivation model, the question "who is doing this?" attains the utmost importance. But, when it is acknowledged and valued that a religious experience is originating from outside of a person, the question of agency not only becomes more difficult to determine, but also descends in priority. This is particularly true when a religious practice or experience is implicitly understood as having a consequence beyond itself.

---

17 Mittermaier, "Dreams from Elsewhere," 250.
18 "To serve as a witness is not to be passive." Michael Lambek, "Nuriaty, the Saint and the Sultan: Virtuous Subject and Subjective Virtuoso of the Post-Modern Colony," *AnthT* 16.2 (2000): 10.

The ambiguity of individual agency may be demonstrated through an example from Second Temple Jewish literature. 1QH^a, the Qumran scroll of Hodayot (Thanksgiving Psalms), has long fascinated scholars for its especially pronounced sense of the self.[19] Given the common function of spirit language as self-language in the Hebrew Bible, we should not be surprised to find it prevalent also in 1QH^a.[20] Additionally, many of these occurrences of spirit language contribute to what has often been called a deterministic theological framework that undergirds many of the Dead Sea Scrolls.[21]

> [Blessed are you, O God of compassi]on on account of the spirits that you have placed in me (מרוחות אשר נתתה בי). I will [f]ind a ready response, reciting your righteous acts and (your) patience. (1QH^a 4:29)[22]
>
> You yourself have formed the spirit and determined its activity [from of old] (אתה יצרתה רוח [ופעולתה הכינות]ה מעולם). And from you (comes) the way of every living being. (1QH^a 7:35a)
>
> ^{10}... You formed ^{11} every spirit, and [their] work [you determin]ed, and the judgment for all their deeds. (1QH^a 9:10c–11a)
>
> I wait hopefully, for you yourself have formed the spi[rit of your servant, and according to] your [wil]l you have determined me. (1QH^a 18:24a–b)[23]

As the name suggests, the *hodayot* are written not as petitions but as gratitude. Eileen Schuller has observed that "the very choice of the thanksgiving genre is an expression of a certain theological stance."[24]

---

[19] See Eileen M. Schuller, "Petitionary Prayer and Religion at Qumran," in *Religion in the Dead Sea Scrolls*, ed. John J. Collins and Robert A. Kugler, SDSSRL (Grand Rapids: Eerdmans, 2000), 29–45; Carol A. Newsom, "Apocalyptic Subjects: Social Construction of the Self in the Qumran Hodayot," *JSP* 12.1 (2001): 3–35; *The Self as Symbolic Space*; Angela Kim Harkins, "The Performative Reading of the Hodayot: The Arousal of Emotions and the Exegetical Generation of Texts," *JSP* 21.1 (2011): 55–71; *Reading with an "I" to the Heavens*; Jason Maston, "Anthropological Crisis and Solution in the Hodayot and 1 Corinthians 15," *NTS* 62.4 (2016): 533–48; and Shem Miller, "The Role of Performance and the Performance of Role: Cultural Memory in the Hodayot," *JBL* 137.2 (2018): 359–82.

[20] By my count there are more than eighty occurrences of רוח in the extant columns of 1QH^a.

[21] For a survey, see Mladen Popović, "Apocalyptic Determinism," in *The Oxford Handbook of Apocalyptic Literature*, ed. John J. Collins (Oxford: Oxford University Press, 2014), 225–70. See also Jonathan Klawans, "Josephus on Fate, Free Will, and Ancient Jewish Types of Compatibilism," *Numen* 56.1 (2009): 44–90.

[22] Text and translations of 1QH^a are from Carol A. Newsom and Eileen M. Schuller, *The Hodayot (Thanksgiving Psalms): A Study Edition of 1QH^a* (Atlanta: SBL Press, 2012).

[23] See also 1QH^a 7:26; 9:17; 9:30–31; 15:9; 18:24

[24] Schuller, "Petitionary Prayer and Religion at Qumran," 38.

Yet within a stance of gratitude over petition, there are opportunities for different types of determinism: a theology of supremacy does not require an anthropology of passivity. To recognize that God has ordered creation and will someday set it right is not the same as surrendering one's own participation in that culmination. Indeed, especially in the last twenty years, scholars have highlighted a relatively high degree of flexibility for human freedom in the Dead Sea Scrolls, despite what would seem to be their deterministic framework.[25] Jonathan Klawans has employed the philosophical term "compatibilism" to label the attempts in late Second Temple literature to maintain both determinism and free will.[26]

In 1QH^a, spirit language is often employed to communicate compatibilism. See, for example, this passage:

> [26] Blessed are you, O Lord, great in counsel and mighty in deed, because all things are your works. Behold you have determined to do me gr[eat]
> [27] kindness, and you have been gracious to me in your compassionate spirit and for the sake of your glory. Righteousness belongs to you alone, for you have done all these things.
> [28] Because I know that you have recorded the spirit of the righteous, I myself have chosen to cleanse my hands according to your wil[l.] The soul of your servant abhors every
> [29] malicious deed. I know that no one can be righteous apart from you, and so I entreat you with the spirit that you have placed in me (ואחלה פניך ברוח אשר נתתּה בּי) that you make
> [30] your kindness to your servant complete [for]ever, cleansing me by your holy spirit and drawing me nearer by your good favor, according to your great kindness [wh]ich you have shown. (1QH^a 8:26–30)[27]

Separating God's agency from the poet's in this prayer is quite impossible. On the one hand, God has determined to do the poet good because righteousness is God's alone. Indeed, the poet acknowledges that these petitions are in line with God's own will. Yet, at the same time, the poet speaks of choosing (בח״ר, ln. 28) and entreating (חל״ה, ln. 29) God. But all of this is done according to the spirit that God has already given to the poet (ln. 29).

As outlined earlier, throughout early Jewish literature and especially in the Dead Sea Scrolls, spirit language is often employed to describe the extreme emotion or passions—especially those which are perceived as originating outside of the self. Unlike the paradigm of self-cultivation, the goal of many of the *hodayot* prayers seems to be that of self-fallowing, or the abandonment of the self (to God). The abiding spirit here is both within one's control and outside of it, both intimately familiar and tragically foreign, both an aspect of one's own

---

25 See summary in Klawans, "Josephus on Fate," 57–58.
26 Klawans, "Josephus on Fate," 48.
27 See also 4:35–36

self and someone else's. "I entreat you with the spirit that you have placed in me," prays the poet. To see to one's own spirit, then, would be as misguided as simply to ignore it.

4.3.2 Filled with a Spirit

The prioritization of non-active religious experience is apparent also in a recurring idiom of spirit language in the Hebrew Bible and early Jewish literature. The idea of "filling with a/the spirit" or being "full of a/the spirit" appears across several genres and eras of biblical literature, frequently in reference to a spirit that abides. The extant examples in the Hebrew Bible are:

> And you shall speak to all who have ability, whom I have filled (*piel*, מִלֵּאתִיו)[28] with a spirit of wisdom[29], that they make Aaron's vestments to consecrate him for my priesthood. (Exod 28:3)
>
> And I have filled (*piel*, וָאֲמַלֵּא) him with a divine spirit, with ability, intelligence, and knowledge in every kind of craft. (Exod 31:3; cf. 35:31)
>
> Joshua son of Nun was full (*qal*, מָלֵא) of the spirit of wisdom, because Moses had laid his hands on him; and the Israelites obeyed him, doing as the LORD had commanded Moses. (Deut 34:9)
>
> But as for me, I am filled (*qal*, מָלֵאתִי) with power,
> with the spirit of the LORD,
> and with justice and might,
> to declare to Jacob his transgression
> and to Israel his sin. (Mic 3:8)

Additionally, the phrase appears in early Jewish literature written in Greek (e. g., πνεύματι συνέσεως ἐμπλησθήσεται, Sir 39:6) and is especially frequent in Luke-Acts.[30]

No scholar has written more extensively on spirit-filling language in biblical literature than John R. Levison. He understands "filled with the spirit," especially in the Hebrew Bible, to be a reference to "fullness" as a *state* rather than to any specific *event* or act of "filling."[31] Although he admits that the verb מל״א, when used with a direct object, can point to "an initial filling," he suggests that other

---

[28] Stem and diacritical marks are included to aid the discussion of verbal form below.
[29] NRSV: "whom I have endowed with skill"
[30] Luke 1:15, 41, 67; 4:14; Acts 2:4; 4:8, 31; 7:55; 9:17; 13:9; 13:52; cf. Eph 5:18.
[31] Levison, *Filled with the Spirit*, 56.

constructions more clearly communicate the endowment of a spirit (e.g., Judg 3:10 ותהי עליו רוח) and that these would have been chosen in Exodus and elsewhere had the *event* of filling been intended in these passages.³² Thus, Levison's final conclusions regarding Exod 31:3 and 35:31 may be taken as emblematic of his broader analysis:

> From the perspective of this simple verb *ml'*, then, the artisans responsible for the temple, and their leaders, Bezalel and Oholiab, are full to the brim with spirit of wisdom. When God says, "whom I have *filled* with spirit of wisdom," the emphasis lies upon the lavishness of this filling much more than upon the initial gift of this spirit. When, in fact, God filled these people is left entirely out of the picture.³³

In this way, Levison seeks to eliminate all charismatic or ecstatic understanding of "spirit-filling" in any of its occurrences in the Hebrew Bible.³⁴

However, Levison's emphasis on the static condition of fullness is only part of the significance of this phrase. In English, "filled with the/a spirit" is translated from varying stems of the Hebrew root מל״א (as Levison also notes). There are notable distinctions in meaning among these stems, especially when comparing the *qal* and the *piel*.³⁵ A broader survey of the root מל״א in the Hebrew Bible reveals that the *qal* is used most often to indicate the status of being full, whereas the *piel* denotes the event of filling.³⁶ There are exceptions, but these are best explained by recognizing that Hebrew, like English, will sometimes treat the same root as either fientive ("dynamic"; e.g., "was filled" Deut 34:9) or stative (e.g., "filled" Exod 40:34).³⁷ In short, מל״א functions precisely how we would expect it to in its various stems. In my view, then, Levison is correct in recognizing

---

32 Levison, *Filled with the Spirit*, 55.
33 Levison, *Filled with the Spirit*, 58.
34 Levison, *Filled with the Spirit*. See his discussions of other passages: Exod 28:1–3 (p. 57); Exod 31:1–6; 36:1–2; 35:30–35 (p. 62); and Num 27:18–23; Deut 34:9; Genesis 41:38; and Daniel 4:5, 6, 15 (pp. 68–80).
35 *Contra* Levison, *Filled with the Spirit*, 57 fn 22.
36 In the list of some twenty examples that Levison provides to show how מל״א means "the status of being full" only three examples are not in the *qal* but rather the *piel* (and one in the *niphal*, Hab 2:4). These three, however, indicate the keeping of a promise and are best translated as "fulfilled" (1 Kgs 8:15; 2 Chr 6:4; Jer 44:25). Levison, *Filled with the Spirit*, 56–57. There are several places where מל״א appears in the *qal* with a direct object even though we might expect the *piel* form. See, for example, texts regarding God's command to be fruitful, multiply and "fill": Gen 1:22; 1:28 cf. 9:1 and texts regarding God's glory or presence filling a space: Exod 30:34–35; 1 Kgs 8:10–11; Isa 6:1; Ezek 10:3–4; 2 Chr 5:14; 7:1–2. See also Jer 16:18; 19:4; Ezek 8:17; 30:11; Mic 3:8.
37 See *IBHS* 22.2.3.a.

the animating and permanent nature of spiritual "fullness" in these texts. However, it is not necessary to deny, as he does, the possibility of spirit-possession–type *events* in these texts in order to do so—especially in those instances in Exodus when מל"א appears in the *piel* stem.

To be animated by an abiding spirit of God in biblical literature is not a static state of fullness but an ongoing rhythmic existence of what can be experienced as alternating filling and emptying. This process is connected to the interplay between the activity of one's spirit and the ups and downs of life itself:

> But when they told him all the words of Joseph that he had said to them, and when he saw the wagons that Joseph had sent to carry him, the spirit of their father Jacob revived. (Gen 45:27)

> The LORD is near to the brokenhearted,
> and saves the crushed in spirit. (Ps 34:19 [NRSV v. 18])

> I think of God, and I moan;
> I meditate, and my spirit faints. *Selah.* (Ps 77:4 [NRSV v. 3])

> Therefore I will not restrain my mouth;
> I will speak in the anguish of my spirit;
> I will complain in the bitterness of my soul. (Job 7:11)

The fullness of one's abiding spirit can therefore vary, depending upon a variety of factors, including health, mood, and skill. Being full of an abiding spirit may indicate that there is no allowable space for any other kinds of spirits. In this, a loose analogue may be seen in how God's glory is said to fill (*qal*, מָלֵא) the cloud-covered tabernacle (Exod 40:34). The tent is so full that there is no room even for Moses when it is occupied (Exod 40:35).

Accordingly, it may come as no surprise that spirit-filling texts are frequently tied to ideas of wisdom. As already shown above, spirit language is a principal idiom for describing the skill of those who fashion the priestly garments and the shrine in the wilderness. Moreover, it is because Joshua is "filled with a spirit of wisdom" (מלא רוח חכמה) after Moses lays his hands on him that the Israelites recognize Joshua as Moses's successor (Deut 34:9). Similarly, Joseph's wisdom in Pharaoh's court is typified as spirit empowered (Gen 41:38–39). This is especially significant because Pharaoh's own "wise men" (חכמיה) are unable to equal him (Gen 41:8).

In these instances, "filling with a spirit" is not just an idiom for distinguishing between skilled and unskilled laborers or for appointing leaders. These persons are "filled" with an abiding spirit given to them by God. They are so full, in fact, that there is no room for any other kind of spirit that might compromise the tasks with which they have been entrusted. To use the language of classicist

Brooke Holmes, we might characterize these as infillings of the person that cannot be "seen," because they concern what is "felt" on the inside.[38] In sum: Biblical writers do not distinguish abiding spirits by their metaphysical qualities or their theological alignment but primarily through a cognitive model which explains their effects on human bodies; that is, the fact that they are persistently present—though of a dynamic character.

4.4 Migrating Spirits

Migrating spirits, in contrast to abiding spirits, are distinguished by their transience and temporary presence. Migrating spirits are not a necessary animating force for life; instead, they are frequently conceived as a force for uncommon power and charisma. God may choose to impart a migrating spirit for a specific purpose, but such spirits may also act independently of God for reasons that are their own.

In comparison with abiding spirits, migrating spirits are described using a much wider variety of language. Thus, I have organized a portion of my discussion by features of language so as to emphasize several broader strokes by which these phenomena can be described: (1) Locative Constructions, (2) Special Verbs, (3) "To Play the Prophet" (להתנבא), (4) God Causing Humans and Spirits to Interact, (5) Humans Acting Upon Spirits, (6) Polemics Against Spirit Possession, and (7) Spirits in Measure. My goal is not to uncover any kind of systematic or consistent pneumatology in the Hebrew Bible. Rather, I hope to uncover the frequently contradictory and usually unconscious cultural models that underlie conceptions of spirits in biblical literature.

4.4.1 Locative Constructions

One of the most frequent means of describing migrating spirits in biblical literature is through locative language, "a/the spirit was/is upon..." (רוח ותהי רוח על or רוח על). See, for example:

---

[38] Holmes uses "seen" versus "felt" instead of "mind/soul" versus "body" to describe the magico-religious divisions of the body in Homer's epics. The "seen" includes not only the externally visible elements of a person but also its human form, whereas the "felt" refers to "the conscious field that constitutes the unity of the self, as well as the daemonic energies that cut across it." Brooke Holmes, *The Symptom and the Subject: The Emergence of the Physical Body in Ancient Greece* (Princeton: Princeton University Press, 2010), 42.

> Balaam looked up and saw Israel camping tribe by tribe. Then the spirit of God came upon him, and he uttered his oracle, saying... (Num 24:2–3a; cf. 2 Chr 15:1; 20:14)

> A/The spirit[39] of the LORD came upon [Othniel], and he judged Israel; he went out to war, and the LORD gave King Cushan-rishathaim of Aram into his hand; and his hand prevailed over Cushan-rishathaim. (Judg 3:10; cf. 11:29)

> Then Saul sent messengers to take David. When they saw the company of the prophets prophesying,[40] with Samuel standing in charge of them, the spirit of God came upon the messengers of Saul, and they also played the prophet.[41] (1 Sam 19:20; cf. 19:23)

> The spirit of the Lord GOD is upon me,
> because the LORD has anointed me;
> he has sent me to bring good news to the oppressed,
> to bind up the brokenhearted,
> to proclaim liberty to the captives,
> and release to the prisoners. (Isa 61:1; cf. 59:21)

This locative construction seems to designate a variety of phenomena, including offering a prophetic oracle, providing charismatic leadership, and "playing the prophet" (להתנבא). It is also significant that this construction is applied equally to what are arguably positive or desirable spirits (e. g., Judg 3:10; 11:29; Isa 61:1), those that are detrimental and undesirable (e. g., 1 Sam 16:16), and those that are neutral or whose affects, positive or negative, are difficult to discern (e. g., 1 Sam 19:20).

Despite a wide variety of operative verbs, one of the more consistent features of migrating spirits is the preposition "on" or "upon" (על). As seen above, however, other prepositions can be used with "spirit" (רוח)—especially common is "in" (ב). In fact, one of the primary indicators for distinguishing between abiding spirits (which persist) and migrating spirits (which are transitory) in biblical literature is their coordinating use of ב or על respectively.[42] Although there are some potential exceptions, this distinction generally holds true.[43]

---

39 NRSV: "the spirit"
40 NRSV: "in a frenzy"
41 NRSV: "fell into a prophetic frenzy"
42 There are numerous examples of ב used with abiding spirits. See, for example, Gen 6:3a, 17; 7:15, 22 (cf. Ezek 37:5, 10, 14); Josh 2:11a; 5:1; Hag 2:5b; and Job 12:10; 32:8, 18; Isa 42:5; Zech 12:1. The idea to track the use of prepositions rather than the operative verbs was first suggested to me by Carol Newsom.
43 One exception that would seem to prove the rule is 2 Sam 23:2: "The spirit of the LORD speaks *through* (ב) me, / his word is upon my tongue." This verse appears to be more in line with a migrating spirit than an abiding one, even though it uses the ב preposition. In this case, however, the ב is instrumental (i.e., "by means of") rather than locative ("in"). Two other infrequent

Being able to distinguish types of spirits through the use of ב or על in locative constructions opens up new ways of interpreting previously ambiguous spirit texts. For example, the accounts of Joseph in Pharaoh's court (Gen 41:38) and Bezalel at the construction of the Tabernacle (Exod 31:2–3) have both been interpreted as examples of charismatic, possession-type spirit phenomena, yet both, in fact, use a ב construction, suggesting that the nature of their spirit was more abiding than migrating.

In other instances, however, charting the use of prepositions only complicates matters. See, for example, the curious episode of God luring Sennacherib, king of Assyria, away from Jerusalem:

> I myself will put a spirit in him (הנני נתן בו רוח), so that he shall hear a rumor and return to his own land; I will cause him to fall by the sword in his own land. (2 Kgs 19:7/Isa 37:7)

The spirit here would seem to be of the migrating kind in that it is imposed upon the king. Yet, it is articulated using the ב construction, which would suggest an abiding spirit. Sennacherib himself is unaware that the spirit is acting upon him and affecting his volition, which could be an attribute of either model (cf. Judg 9:23; Jer 51:11; Ezra 1:1). Further, the parallel with the deceiving spirit in 1 Kgs 22 is difficult to ignore, which may imply that the misleading spirit in 2 Kgs 19:7 is not actually active "in" Sennacherib, but rather through one of his advisors (cf. 1 Kgs 22:19–23). Alternatively, it may be the case that the passage is mixing the abiding and migrating conceptions together.

Accordingly, some texts evidently do combine aspects of both abiding and migrating spirits and mixing syntax could reflect this amalgam. Several texts fit into this category (e.g., Ezek 2:2; 3:24; 11:19a; cf. 18:31; 36:26–27; Ps 51:12; 1QH[a] 5:35b–36a; and some examples in 4QBarkhi Nafshi). The idea of biblical texts that mix these notions of spirits is developed further in the next chapter.

---

constructions should also be noted. The first is with אל: "The next day a harmful spirit of God seized Saul (ותצלח רוח אלהים רעה אל-שאול) and he played the prophet (ויתנבא) in the midst of his house" (1 Sam 18:10a, my translation; cf. 2 Kgs 2:9). In this instance, it is clear from context that this belongs with other similar examples of migrating spirits. The second construction to be noted is with עם: "But my servant Caleb, because there is a different spirit with him (היתה רוח אחרת עמו) and he has followed me fully, I will bring him into the land where he went, and his descendants will possess it" (Num 14:24, my translation). This instance to me is more unclear and could be read as either abiding or migrating.

4.4.2 Special Verbs

The prevalence and utility of the "a/the spirit was/is upon..." construction makes the occurrences of other, more specific verbs even more conspicuous. As many commentators have noticed, there is an especially high concentration of migrating spirit language in the book of Judges:

> But a/the spirit of the LORD *clothed*[44] Gideon (ורוח [ה'] לבשה את־גדעון); and he sounded the trumpet, and the Abiezrites were called out to follow him. (Judg 6:34; cf. 1 Chr 12:19; 2 Chr 24:20)[45]
>
> A/The spirit of the LORD began to *stir* [Samson] (ותחל רוח [ה'] לפעמו) in Mahaneh-dan, between Zorah and Eshtaol. (Judg 13:25)
>
> The spirit of the LORD *seized* upon [Samson][46] (ותצלח עליו רוח [ה']), and he tore the lion apart barehanded as one might tear apart a kid. But he did not tell his father or his mother what he had done. (Judg 14:6; cf. 14:19; 15:14; 1 Sam 10:6, 10; 11:6; 16:13; 18:10; 19:9)

The vagueness and infrequency of these constructions have not deterred interpreters from attempting to differentiate what specific ideas might be signaled by these verbs.[47] Without more information, however, offering technical definitions for distinguishing one from another is dubious. For example, it is hard to see a qualitative difference between a spirit *being upon* (ותהי עליו רוח־[ה']) Othniel but *clothing* Gideon (ורוח [ה'] לבשה את־גדעון), when both judges are similarly empowered to be victorious in battle against Israel's enemies.[48] Still, the color and vigor of this language should not be passed over, since it suggests that the richness of these experiences cannot be adequately described by any partic-

---

[44] NRSV: "took possession of"
[45] Typically, לבש in the *qal* stem means "to put on," which would suggest a meaning here of the spirit *wearing* Gideon. Most translations, however, render the verb as "clothe" (compare both meanings in Job 29:14). See the extended discussion of this issue in Lee Roy Martin, "Power to Save!?: The Role of the Spirit of the Lord in the Book of Judges," *JPT* 16.2 (2008): 34–37. For the counter argument, see Nahum M. Waldman, "The Imagery of Clothing, Covering, and Overpowering," *JANES* 19 (1989): 161–70.
[46] NRSV: "rushed on him"
[47] See, for example, Martin, "Power to Save!?" Jannes Reiling draws a distinction between "animistic" and "dynamistic" manifestations of spirits that is not dissimilar from my own "abiding" and "migrating" categories, "Holy Spirit," in *DDD*, ed. K. van der Toorn, Bob Becking, and Pieter Willem van der Horst, 2nd ed. (Leiden: Brill, 1999), 419–20.
[48] From a historical-critical perspective, it is best to think of these different verbal choices as the particular preferences of the various sources utilized by the editors of the book of Judges. See Blischke, *Der Geist Gottes*, 25–42, and Kratz, *The Composition of the Narrative Books of the Old Testament*, 202–08.

ular linguistic formula—an aspect of spirits in Judges that Lee Roy Martin calls "the untamable gift of the energizing presence of Yahweh."[49]

The use of specific verbs with a spirit as subject and humans as object is by no means limited to the book of Judges. A broader survey of texts in the Hebrew Bible reveals a wide range of verbs for which spirits are the subject:

> As soon as I have gone from you, the spirit of the LORD will *carry* you (ורוח [ה'] ישׂאך) I know not where. (1 Kgs 18:12a; cf. 2 Kgs 2:16)[50]

> When the company of prophets who were at Jericho saw him at a distance, they declared, "A/The spirit of Elijah *rests on* Elisha." (נחה רוח אליהו על־אלישׁע). (2 Kgs 2:15a; cf. Isa 11:2)

> For the mouth of the LORD has commanded,
> and his spirit has *gathered* them. (ורוחו הוא קבצן). (Isa 34:16b)[51]

> Like cattle going down into the valley,
> a/the spirit of the LORD *gave* them *rest* (רוח [ה'] תניחנו). (Isa 63:14a)

> And when he spoke to me, a spirit *entered into* me (ותבא בי רוח) and *set* me *on my feet* (ותעמדני על־רגלי); and I heard him speaking to me. (Ezek 2:2; cf. 3:24)

> The spirit *lifted* me *up* (ורוח נשׂאתני) and bore me away; I went in bitterness in the heat of my spirit, the hand of the LORD being strong upon me. (Ezek 3:14; cf. 12; 8:3; 11:1; 11:24; 43:5)

> Then the spirit of the LORD *fell upon* me (ותפל עלי רוח [ה']), and he said to me, "Say, Thus says the LORD: This is what you think, O house of Israel; I know the things that come into your spirit. (Ezek 11:5)[52]

> Teach me to do your will,
> for you are my God.
> Let your good spirit *lead* me (רוחך טובה תנחני)
> on a level path. (Ps 143:10)

---

[49] Martin, "Power to Save!?," 26. Martin shies away from using the term "possession," but he does not define the term as I have in this project.

[50] This example is exceptional for several reasons. First, it is described in the second-person voice, where one character (Obadiah) explains to another (Elijah) what he perceives to be the latter's interactions with a spirit of God. Second, it portrays not just altered behavior or internal experience as a result of spirit influence but a miraculous feat of translocation (cf. 1 Kgs 18:46; 2 Kgs 2:11). Nathan MacDonald suggests this may be what Ezekiel describes as well, but from a first-person perspective (Ezek 3:12, 14; 8:3; 11:1, 24; 37:1; 43:5), "The Spirit of YHWH: An Overlooked Conceptualization of Divine Presence in the Persian Period," in *Divine Presence and Absence in Exilic and Post-Exilic Judaism*, ed. Nathan MacDonald and Izaak J. de Hulster, 2 vols., FAT2 61 (Tübingen: Mohr Siebeck, 2013), 99–100.

[51] The textual transmission of this verse is complicated, and it is possible that the MT represents an effort at harmonization between different versions. Within the wider context of this passage, it is clear that the "them" that the spirit is gathering refers to the wilderness animals and demons described in vv. 11–15.

[52] For a fuller treatment of רוח in Ezekiel specifically, see Block, "The Prophet of the Spirit."

A spirit *glided past* my face (ורוח על־פני יחלף);
the hair of my flesh bristled. (Job 4:15)[53]

My intention is not to claim that each of these numerous examples represents identical notions of spirits.[54] Rather, they demonstrate the range with which spirits may be conceived as dynamic and transitory in biblical literature. Spirits *carry, rest upon, gather, lift, fall upon,* and *lead*. Moreover, these movements affect the people on whom they act in ways beyond those of abiding spirits.

4.4.3 "To Play the Prophet" (להתנבא)

A specific verb deserving of some extra attention is *ləhitnabbēʾ* (להתנבא), a construction that is frequently associated with spirit phenomena in the Hebrew Bible.[55] The root נב"א appears most often as a noun meaning "prophet" or as a verb in the *niphal* stem, usually meaning "to prophesy." It occurs in the *hithpael* stem comparatively less frequently: just under thirty times in the Bible, being especially prevalent in the books of 1 Samuel and Jeremiah.[56] Convention-

---

[53] On this translation, see Shalom M. Paul, "Job 4:15—a Hair Raising Encounter," *ZAW* 95.1 (1983): 119–21. David Clines argues that when רוח is masculine, it cannot mean "spirit" and must mean either "wind" or "breath" (but cf. 1 Kgs 22:21), *Job 1–20*, WBC 17 (Dallas: Word Books, 1989), 111. I am inclined to agree with James E. Harding, however, who argues that the phrase is intentionally ambiguous, evoking both "wind" and a figure in the divine council, "A Spirit of Deception in Job 4:15? Interpretive Indeterminacy and Eliphaz's Vision," *BibInt* 13.2 (2005): 137–66.

[54] Although some correspondences may be inevitable. For example, there may not be a large difference between the ותעמדני על- and ותשאני constructions in Ezekiel.

[55] See the review of scholarship in Klaus-Peter Adam, "'And He Behaved like a Prophet among Them.' (1 Sam 10:11b): The Depreciative Use of נבא Hitpael and the Comparative Evidence of Ecstatic Prophecy," *WO* 39.1 (2009): 3–57; and Christophe Nihan, "Saul Among the Prophets (1 Sam 10:10–12 and 19:18–24): The Reworking of Saul's Figure in the Contexts of the Debate on 'Charismatic Prophecy' in the Persian Era," in *Saul in Story and Tradition*, ed. Carl S. Ehrlich and Marsha C. White, FAT 47 (Tübingen: Mohr Siebeck, 2006), 88–118. See also: John Sturdy, "The Original Meaning of 'Is Saul Also Among the Prophets?' (1 Samuel X 11, 12; XIX 24)," *VT* 20.2 (1970): 206–13; Hildebrandt, *An Old Testament Theology of the Spirit of God*; Benjamin D. Sommer, "Reflecting on Moses: The Redaction of Numbers 11," *JBL* 118.4 (1999): 601–24; Levison, "Prophecy in Ancient Israel"; Martti Nissinen, "Prophetic Madness," in *Ancient Prophecy: Near Eastern, Biblical, and Greek Perspectives* (Oxford: University Press, 2017); and MacDonald, "The Spirit of YHWH."

[56] Num 11:25–27; 1 Sam 10:5–6, 10, 13; 18:10; 19:20–21, 23–24; 1 Kgs 18:29; 22:8, 10, 18/2 Chr 18:7, 9, 17; Jer 14:14; 23:13; 26:20; 29:27; Ezek 13:17; 37:10; 2 Chr 20:37. For an overview and extended bibliography, see Hans-Peter Mülller, "נביא," *TDOT* 9:129–50.

ally, the root in this stem should be understood as something like "to act like a prophet" or "to do the things commonly associated with prophets"—an idea I imperfectly render as "to play the prophet."[57] This basic understanding of the verb in the *hithpael* is not seriously disputed. What is less clear, however, is whether this word indicates any kind of spirit phenomenon, especially one of a charismatic type.

Scholars frequently understand the verb as denoting a kind of spirit-induced frenzy in connection to Saul (e.g., 1 Sam 10:5–6, 10, 13; 18:10; 19:20–21, 23–24). Compare, for example, my modifications with how the NRSV renders the verb when Saul is the subject:

> Then a/the spirit[58] of the LORD will seize you (וצלחה עליך)[59], and you will play the prophet (והתנבית)[60] along with them and be turned into a different person." (1 Sam 10:6)

> ¹⁰ The next day a harmful[61] spirit from God rushed upon Saul, and he raved (ויתנבא) within his house, while David was playing the lyre, as he did day by day. Saul had his spear in his hand; ¹¹ and Saul threw the spear, for he thought, "I will pin David to the wall." But David eluded him twice. (1 Sam 18:10–11)

Gunkel went so far as labeling these occurrences "glossolalia" and likening them to the events of Pentecost described in Acts 2.[62]

Yet, as others have noted, the conventional definition of "ecstasy" or "frenzy" is not fitting for every occurrence of the verb, and it may be a mistake to take the Saul examples in 1 Samuel as the normative conception for other instances.[63] Although it is true that several texts using this verb record no prophetic words or oracles (e.g., 1 Sam 18:10; 19:20–24), in other places, specific prophetic messages are explicitly associated with *ləhitnabbēʾ* (e.g., 1 Kgs 22:8a; cf. v. 18;/2 Chr 18:7; v. 17). This shows how one "playing the prophet" may utter recognizable prophetic oracles in a way not dissimilar from the *niphal* form of the verb.

The solution I propose is to understand the *niphal* form of נב"א as a specific formula for indicating the delivery of an oracle, and the *hithpael* stem as having a more diverse set of potential meanings depending on what one believes to be

---

57 See *IBHS* 26.2f; 26.4a. I use "playing" not necessarily in the sense of doing something disingenuously or poorly (i.e., "What are you playing at?") but more so in the sense of playing a part or a role at which a person can be skilled or unskilled, genuinely motivated or not.
58 NRSV: "the spirit"
59 NRSV: "possess you"
60 NRSV: "you will be in a prophetic frenzy"
61 NRSV: "evil"
62 Gunkel, *The Influence of the Holy Spirit*, 31.
63 See Levison, "Prophecy in Ancient Israel."

the typical behavior of prophets. This is consistent with other ways in which the *hithpael* form is utilized for other verbs in the Hebrew Bible.[64] This coordination of the two verbal forms may map especially well onto the use of the word in the book of Jeremiah:

> There was another man playing the prophet (*hithpael*, מִתְנַבֵּא)[65] in the name of the LORD, Uriah son of Shemaiah from Kiriath-jearim. He prophesied (*niphal*, וַיִּנָּבֵא) against this city and against this land in words exactly like those of Jeremiah. (Jer 26:20)

> And the LORD said to me: The prophets are prophesying (*niphal* נִבְּאִים) lies in my name; I did not send them, nor did I command them or speak to them. They are playing the prophet (*hithpael*, מִתְנַבְּאִים) for you[66] a lying vision, worthless divination, and the deceit of their own minds. (Jer 14:14; cf. 23:13; 29:26–27)

Yet, as helpful as this division in meaning may prove to be, it is only a partial solution.

In particular, a significant question remains unanswered: Does "playing the prophet" refer to an act of fraud in assuming a social status or office that is not one's own (i.e., the equivalent of impersonating a police officer at the scene of an accident)? Or rather, does it mean engaging in a particular behavior usually associated with prophets (i.e., temporarily electing oneself to direct traffic around the scene of an accident until professionals arrive)?

Klaus-Peter Adam argues that modern scholars are mistaken to associate *ləhitnabbēʾ* with ecstatic trance. Rather, in certain situations, it indicates assuming the role of prophet inappropriately. As he explains:

> From a pragmatic viewpoint, the meaning of the stem may serve to express an author's distance from a figure in a narrative. The author may deliberately make use of the Hitpael in order to declare a certain act as inappropriate or not suitable for the respective person.

---

64 For example: אב״ל in the *qal* means "to mourn." In 2 Samuel 14:2, Joab instructs the wise woman of Tekoa to play the mourner using the *hithpael* (התאבלי-נא); שכ״ר in the *qal* means to be(come) drunk. In 1 Sam 1:14, Eli chastises Hannah for playing the drunk (תשתכרין) at Shiloh. For more examples, see Adam, "'And He Behaved like a Prophet among Them.' (1 Sam 10:11b)," 8–12. Adam also suggests that the *hithpael* form usually implies fraud or inappropriate behavior. On this point we disagree, as I discuss below. See also Jonathan Deane Parker, "Moses and the Seventy Elders: Mosaic Authority in Numbers 11 and the 'Legend of the Septuagint'" (PhD diss., Durham University, 2015). Parker suggests that because the elders are recognized as having authority and import (especially in later interpretive tradition) it is likely not spirit possession that occurred in the tent but prophecy. However, I see no reason why it could not be both.
65 NRSV: "prophesying"
66 NRSV: "prophesying to you"

Falsely *pretending* to be in a certain social position of / to be in a certain status is the attached value judgment.[67]

Adam sees this meaning not only in Saul's behavior but also in the episode of the seventy-elders in Num 11 and with Micaiah son of Imlah in 1 Kgs 22.

John R. Levison also pushes back against the traditional ecstatic interpretation of *ləhitnabbēʾ* as well but chooses a different strategy. Referring to Num 11, he argues that *ləhitnabbēʾ* does indeed indicate a particular prophetic behavior— just not ecstasy. Rather, it is "a visionary experience within a controlled cultic setting to support Moses as he leads the Israelites."[68] He differentiates this story (and other instances of *ləhitnabbēʾ* in the Hebrew Bible) from those of Saul, who is a special exception since his brushes with prophecy result in violence, embarrassment, and madness.[69] Saul's is the negative example, according to Levison, proving that, despite his playing the prophet, Saul is not *among* (i.e., "one of") the prophets (1 Sam 10:12; 19:24).[70]

In my view, both scholars are right to recognize that a simple definition of "prophetic ecstasy" for *ləhitnabbēʾ* is inadequate. However, their respective analyses are distracted by attempting to load the verb with additional categories. Adam wishes to see *ləhitnabbēʾ* primarily as a pejorative term, despite the fact that at least three of its occurrences are indisputably positive.[71] Unlike Adam, I do not see why other texts (esp. 1 Sam 10 and Num 11) need be seen as depreciative uses of *ləhitnabbēʾ*.

Similarly, Levison's attempt to coordinate where there is and is not control, frenzy, and ecstasy in prophetic narratives goes beyond the evidence of the texts. As I demonstrated in chapter 1, there is no reason that a spirit-possession ritual— which, admittedly, may strike an uninitiated observer as chaotic—can nevertheless be orderly and ritualized from the perspective of participants. Levison argues that the conventional interpretation of *ləhitnabbēʾ* does not account for "the clear failure of uncontrolled prophetic behavior to provide Moses with

---

[67] Adam, "'And He Behaved like a Prophet among Them.' (1 Sam 10:11b)," 20. Emphasis original.
[68] Levison, "Prophecy in Ancient Israel," 504–05.
[69] Levison, "Prophecy in Ancient Israel," 511.
[70] Levison's analysis, taking cues from Wilson, *Prophecy and Society in Ancient Israel*, employs the theoretical models of anthropologist Ioan Lewis. I discuss the more recent critique of Lewis among cultural anthropologists in chapter 1.
[71] Adam does acknowledge these three instances (Jer 26:20; Ezek 37:10; and 2 Chr 20:37) and argues that the *hithpael* can be used to indicate the temporary nature of "playing the prophet"; see "'And He Behaved like a Prophet among Them.' (1 Sam 10:11b)," 19.

the administrative help he requested."[72] But his claim is valid only if one has a very limited view of what ecstatic possession experience might be able to accomplish within cults that practice it.[73]

Thus, I believe it is impossible to distinguish the social role of a prophet from its associated behaviors, especially when one is "playing the prophet." We may take as an example, 1 Samuel 10, an episode Adam interprets as a distanced, depreciative view of Saul and this group of prophets. Adam describes Saul as joining the other prophets in "pretending" to prophesy, but how might he do this without adopting certain recognizable prophetic behaviors?

It seems most likely then that *ləhitnabbēʾ* must refer to a range of activities commonly associated with prophets, which thereby elevate one to that status (e.g., spirit-induced ecstatic trance, perhaps, but maybe also criticizing a king). In contrast to Levison's and Adam's definitions, this meaning is broad enough to encompass the wide range of occurrences of *ləhitnabbēʾ* in the Hebrew Bible. For example, it can apply both to Saul's engaging in violence against David while "playing the prophet" (1 Sam 18:10), and Ezekiel's obeying God's command to prophesy to the spirit by "playing the prophet" in his vision (Ezek 37:10).

The verb *ləhitnabbēʾ*, and especially its occurrence in 1 Samuel 19, is noteworthy for another reason: this is one of the few clearly involuntary episodes of spirit possession to be found in the Hebrew Bible. As demonstrated throughout this book, most stories about spirits in biblical literature portray a spirit experience that is welcomed and often intentionally cultivated by the host. These accounts then proceed with the host's personality remaining present and more or less "in control." Saul and his messengers, however, are clearly at cross purposes with the spirit of God. From this, in comparison with the wealth of ethnographic literature surveyed thus far in the project, we may draw a tentative conclusion: In the majority of biblical episodes in which God's spirit influences a person, the host's experience is positive and empowering, provided that they are acting in accordance with God's will. Moreover, their personality remains present and in control throughout the experience. In contrast, spirit hosts who act at cross-purposes with God are more likely to experience possession as an invasion or deception (e.g., Judg 9:23; 1 Sam 16:14; 18:10; 1 Kgs 22:20–23; Isa

---

[72] Levison, "Prophecy in Ancient Israel," 504.
[73] For example, "playing at prophecy" may function as a God-ordained deputization of these seventy elders for duties previously reserved only for Moses; see Parker, "Moses and the Seventy Elders." As Levison notes, part of the difficulty in interpreting Numbers 11 is its composite nature and complicated literary history, including its relationships to other Pentateuchal texts like Exodus 18 and 24. See also Sommer, "Reflecting on Moses."

29:10). Additionally, their personalities may be suspended, and the episode may have embarrassing or even deadly consequences (e. g., 2 Kgs 19:7; but cf. Jer 51:11; Ezra 1:1).

4.4.4 God Causing Humans and Spirits to Interact

Another construction used for communicating migrating spirits has God as either the explicit or implied subject of a verb that brings humans and spirits into some kind of interaction. As noted above, these spirit phenomena are frequently corporate and not individual:

> But God sent a harmful[74] spirit between Abimelech and the lords of Shechem; and the lords of Shechem dealt treacherously with Abimelech. (Judg 9:23)

> Here is my servant, whom I uphold,
> my chosen, in whom my soul delights;
> I have put my spirit upon him;
> he will bring forth justice to the nations. (Isa 42:1)

> Draw near to me, hear this!
> From the beginning I have not spoken in secret,
> from the time it came to be I have been there.
> And now the Lord GOD has sent me and his spirit. (Isa 48:16)

> The LORD has stirred up the spirit of the kings of the Medes. (Jer 51:11b; Ezra 1:1)

> He said to me, "This is the word of the LORD to Zerubbabel: Not by might, nor by power, but by my spirit, says the LORD of hosts." (Zech 4:6)

> They made their hearts adamant in order not to hear the law and the words that the LORD of hosts had sent by his spirit through the former prophets. (Zech 7:12a; cf. Neh 9:20, 30; 1QS 8:19)

Like the examples listed above, these constructions attend a variety of phenomena, including both beneficial and detrimental occurrences of migrating spirits. Of special interest are those examples of uninvited and perhaps unconscious possession where God influences a foreign leader toward a particular action that is beneficial for God's people (e. g., Jer 51:11; Ezra 1:1; perhaps also Judg 9:23). Additionally, in several instances, God accomplishes tasks *by means of* a spirit (ברוחו; e. g., Zech 7:12; Neh 9:30).

Initially, it may seem an important distinction whether it is God or some kind of spirit that is the subject of a possessing verb. However, the same kinds of phe-

---

74 NRSV: "evil"

nomena are associated with both constructions. For example, prophets deliver oracles both when they are acted upon by a spirit (e.g., Num 24:2–3a; Ezek 11:5) and when God acts by means of a spirit (e.g., Zech 7:12). Especially in instances where the acting spirit is described as belonging to God (e.g., Isa 59:21; 61:1), it does not seem that the subject of a possessing verb (whether it is God or a spirit of God) is a principal distinction.

4.4.5 Humans Acting Upon Spirits

A smaller category describes humans acting upon spirits of various kinds. We have already seen this phenomenon to some degree in the discussion of abiding spirits above. Relatedly, there is considerable conceptual overlap between English and Hebrew in the rhetoric surrounding what might be called "self-control" or "self-possession":

> One who is slow to anger is better than the mighty,
> *One who rules his spirit* (ומשל ברוחו) is better than one who captures a city. (Prov 16:32)
> NRSV: "one whose temper is controlled"
> NJPS: "To have self-control"

> A fool *vents all his spirit* (כל־רוחו יוציא כסיל)
> but a wise one stills it back. (Prov 29:11)
> NRSV: "gives full vent to his anger"
> NJPS: "vents all his rage"

As exemplified here, English translations will often capture an aspect of the likely meaning of these phrases through the use of idioms. Such renderings do not misrepresent the general thrust of wisdom texts that patience is preferable to impetuousness. This being said, the poetic style of this spirit language is not merely aesthetic or conventional; it also recognizes that spirits can be overwhelming and wild—even when they are one's own. Such phrases reveal an underlying cognitive model that a spirit of any kind may require management and attention—even if it is not fully hypostasized as a separate being.

Humans can act upon spirits through other, less internalized means, particularly through the use of music:

> And whenever the [harmful] spirit from God came upon Saul, David took the lyre and played it with his hand, and Saul would be relieved and feel better, and the harmful[75] spirit would depart from him. (1 Sam 16:23)

---

75 NRSV: "the evil"

In this passage (already discussed in chapter 2), David soothes Saul in his spirit-induced ailment with music. In fact, the use of music is a broadly attested strategy in spirit-possession cults around the world, both ancient and contemporary.[76] A related passage appears in 2 Kgs:

> [15] [Elisha said,] "But get me a musician." And then, while the musician was playing, the hand of the LORD came on him. [16] And he said, "Thus says the LORD..." (2 Kgs 3:15–16a)

Although the word *rûaḥ* does not appear here, the surrounding context clearly suggests a spirit-possession–type ritual. In order to prophesy, Elisha requires the help of a harpist, perhaps because his skills are inhibited when used to aid the king of Israel (cf. v. 13).[77]

The last example I present of humans acting upon spirits appears in Isa 63:7–11. This text is somewhat more obscure than other examples in this category since it appears as a prophetic lament rather than as part of a narrative:

> [10] But they rebelled
> and grieved his holy spirit (ועצבו את־רוח קדשו);
> therefore he became their enemy;
> he himself fought against them.
> [11] Then they remembered the days of old,
> of Moses his servant.
> Where is the one who brought them up out of the sea
> with the shepherds of his flock?
> Where is the one who put within them
> his holy spirit (השם בקרבו את־רוח קדשו)? (Isa 63:10–11)

The holy spirit here is likely an aspect of God's own self—effectively *God's* abiding spirit. Thus, the gravity of Israel's rebellion is emphasized all the more by the intimacy with which God's wound is described. Likely alluding to this passage in Isaiah, the author of Ephesians explains that disunity in the early church is a cause of grief to the holy spirit (Eph 4:30), since the community is made up of "one body and one spirit" (v. 4).

---

[76] Judith Becker, "Listening Selves and Spirit Possession," *WM* 42.2 (2000): 25–50.

[77] The only other places where "the hand of the LORD was upon him" (ותהי עליו יד־[ה']) appears in the Hebrew Bible are in Ezekiel (Ezek 1:3; 3:22; 8:1; 37:1; 40:1), where it clearly signals spirit phenomena (e.g., "The hand of the LORD came upon me, and he brought me out by the spirit of the LORD... Ezek 37:1).

4.4.6 Polemics Against Spirit Possession

Several interpreters have suggested that ancient Israelite prophecy distinguished itself from surrounding cultures through intentionally avoiding charismatic or possession-type practices, or, alternatively, they have suggested that these phenomena were not native to Israelite religion.[78] These positions are contested, but it would seem that some polemics against ecstatic prophetic practices *can* be found in the Hebrew Bible:[79]

> The prophets are nothing but wind (והנביאים יהיו לרוח),
> for the word is not in them.
> Thus shall it be done to them! (Jer 5:13)

> The days of punishment have come,
> the days of recompense have come;
> Israel cries,
> "The prophet is a fool,
> the man of the spirit is mad!" (משגע איש הרוח) (Hos 9:7a–b)

> [27] At noon Elijah mocked them, saying, "Cry aloud! Surely he is a god; either he is meditating, or he has wandered away, or he is on a journey, or perhaps he is asleep and must be awakened." [28] Then they cried aloud and, as was their custom, they cut themselves with swords and lances until the blood gushed out over them. [29] As midday passed, they played the prophet (ויתנבאו)[80] until the time of the offering of the oblation, but there was no voice, no answer, and no response. (1 Kgs 18:27–29)

Nevertheless, an accusation of fraud or madness for a particular act of spirit possession should not be confused with condemnation of an entire practice. For ex-

---

[78] See, for example, Sigmund Mowinckel, "'The Spirit' and the 'Word' in the Pre-Exilic Reforming Prophets," *JBL* 53.3 (1934): 199–227; André Gunnel, "Ecstatic Prophecy in the Old Testament," in *Religious Ecstasy: Based on Papers Read at the Symposium on Religious Ecstasy Held at Åbo, Finland, on the 26th-28th of August 1981*, ed. Nils G. Holm, SIDA 11 (Stockholm: Almqvist & Wiksell, 1982), 187–200; Simon B. Parker, "Possession Trance and Prophecy in Pre-Exilic Israel," *VT* 28.3 (1978): 271–85; and Adam, "'And He Behaved like a Prophet among Them.' (1 Sam 10:11b)."

[79] On charismatic prophecy in ancient Israel compared to evidence from surrounding cultures, see especially, the work of Martti Nissinen, "Prophecy and Ecstasy," in *Ancient Prophecy: Near Eastern, Biblical, and Greek Perspectives* (Oxford: University Press, 2017); and "Prophetic Madness: Prophecy and Ecstasy in the Ancient Near East and in Greece."

[80] NRSV: "raved on"

ample, most possession cults contain some system for appraising good and bad practices, as well as evolving criteria for discerning fraud and legitimacy.[81]

Even the final example listed above from 1 Kgs 18 need not be seen as a condemnation of possession practices. It is true that the fruitless ecstasies of the prophets of Baal are an extreme foil to Elijah's own superbly efficacious and humble prayer (vv. 36–38). Elijah's ridicule of his opponents, however, may be understood not as a repudiation of their ritual approach; but rather, as Elijah sharing in it. As described by anthropologist Erika Bourguignon, mocking tones and theatrics are also a component of contemporary possession cults. Describing certain practices in Haiti, Bourguignon explains:

> It is interesting that the gods are approached with a very considerable mixture of banter and respect. There is respect, indeed, reverence and awe, in asking the gods for help, yet it is recognized that when they come during ceremonies, they wish to enjoy the drums and the dancing, the food and drink, and generally to have a good time, and a great deal of ribald talk and banter takes place. Not only do the spirits themselves approach their faithful in this manner, but they accept and expect such talk in return. Religious activity is not a solemn-faced affair, but one in which there is a good deal of humor and verbal fencing, aspects of behavior which are not foreign to everyday, human, social interactions.[82]

Against this background, the conflict at Carmel emerges not primarily as a contest of two separate rituals but as a joint ritual, which is designed to embattle two rival cults.

4.4.7 Spirits in Measure

Like abiding spirits, the migrating variety are also frequently conceived as material-like. Imagery of *pouring* and *filling* are especially prevalent:

> Then afterward
> I will pour out my spirit on all flesh;
> your sons and your daughters shall prophesy,
> your old men shall dream dreams,
> and your young men shall see visions. (Joel 3:1 [NRSV 2:28])

---

81 For example, see the discussions of strategies for legitimation in Brazilian Candomblé in Mattijs van de Port, "Circling around the Really Real: Spirit Possession Ceremonies and the Search for Authenticity in Bahian Candomblé," *Ethos* 33.2 (2005): 149–79.
82 Bourguignon, "The Self, the Behavioral Environment, and the Theory of Spirit Possession," 53.

> And I will pour out a spirit of compassion and supplication on the house of David and the inhabitants of Jerusalem, so that they might look to me whom they have pierced,[83] they shall mourn for him, as one mourns for an only child, and weep bitterly over him, as one weeps over a firstborn. (Zech 12:10)

> The LORD has poured into them
> a spirit of confusion;
> and they have made Egypt stagger in all its doings
> as a drunkard staggers around in vomit. (Isa 19:14; cf. 29:10)

> Until a spirit from on high is poured out on us (עד־יערה עלינו רוח ממרום),
> and the wilderness becomes a fruitful field,
> and the fruitful field is deemed a forest. (Isa 32:15; cf. יצ״ק in 44:3)

Additionally, spirits are often portrayed as measurable to some degree and limited. Frequently, they are distributed in portions:

> Then the LORD came down in the cloud and spoke to him, and took some of the spirit that was on him and put it on the seventy elders (ויאצל מן־הרוח אשר עליו ויתן על־שבעים איש הזקנים); and when the spirit rested upon them, they prophesied. But they did not do so again. (Num 11:25; cf. v. 29)

> When they had crossed, Elijah said to Elisha, "Tell me what I may do for you, before I am taken from you." Elisha said, "Please let me inherit a double share of your spirit." (ויהי־נא פי־שנים ברוחך אלי). (2 Kgs 2:9; cf. Sir 48:12)

A common link between these portioning texts is that of a prophetic mantle or office being passed from hand to hand (e.g., Num 27:18; Deut 21:17; 34:9; 1 Kgs 22:24; perhaps also 1 Sam 10:12a). It may be that a particular migrating spirit, one associated with prophetic leadership, must pass from person to person, ensuring God's persistent presence with the people.[84]

These examples indicate how, in some texts, spirits are conceived as being available only in a finite amount. We might loosely analogize this to a kind of economy of spirits, wherein there might be rationing, stimulus, hoarding, surplus, and deficit. As with any economy, individual actors and collectives have

---

[83] NRSV: "so that, when they look on the one whom they have pierced," The rendering of this phrase is disputed, not least because it is read as a messianic prophecy in John 19:37. I follow the MT here, *contra* the NRSV. For my purposes in this chapter, however, it is only necessary to recognize that the result of this pouring out is profound, corporate mourning. For an overview of text critical issues, see William Randolph Bynum, "Text-Critical Review of Zechariah 12:10," in *The Fourth Gospel and the Scriptures: Illuminating the Form and Meaning of Scriptural Citation in John 19:37*, NovTSup 144 (Leiden: Brill, 2012), 59–109.

[84] See MacDonald, "The Spirit of YHWH," 106.

varying degrees of agency and influence, but ultimately each remains subject to the "God of the spirits" (Num 27:16) who manages the whole.

Whereas the aforementioned texts notably differentiate spirits by means of quantity (e.g., doubling, portioning, and filling), others are more concerned with quality (e.g., good, bad, holy, unclean, and jealous). I have not been able to find an example in the Hebrew Bible where the two concepts indisputably function together.[85] Thus, it could be that both existed as alternative methods for recognizing and characterizing different spirit phenomena. Later, in Second Temple era literature, the two ideas did begin to function together. Some later texts take the unequal distribution of God's spirit in humanity as a given, and account for it as a consequence of God's will:

> [22] And you have caused your servant to have insight [... lo]ts of humankind. For according to (their) spirits you cast (the lot) for them between [23] good and evil, [and] you have determined [...]°°*tm* their recompense. And as for me, I know from the understanding that comes from you [24] that through your goodwill toward a p[er]son you mul[tiply his portion] in your holy spirit (ברצונכה בא[י]ש הרב[יתה נחלתו [ברוח קדושך]). Thus you draw him closer to your understanding. (1QH^a 6:22–24)
>
> while God added his testimony by signs and wonders and various miracles, and by gifts of the Holy Spirit, distributed according to his will. (Heb 2:4; cf. Titus 3:6)

Further, in these chronologically later examples, any distinctions between abiding and migrating spirits have also fallen away. As I discuss in the next chapter, this may be because by that time, the two conceptions were increasingly conflated.

4.5 Conclusions

In chapter 4, I have outlined two models for understanding spirits as presented in the Hebrew Bible, those that abide and those that migrate. These two models are not static or ideal types but rather loose associations of qualities that can cooperate, conflict, and overlap with one another. Abiding spirits are characterized as being the animating force for life and as departing at death. Though they abide, these spirits can have a dynamic character, pulsing with energy and alternatingly overflowing or emptying with ecstasy or sorrow. They occasionally get

---

85 A text like Joel 3:1, which references both "pouring" and God's spirit specifically, may have both systems functioning together, but the reference is so oblique it is difficult to know how developed either idea is.

out of control and must be tempered. In this, we find strategies that embolden the self to subdue or manage one's own abiding spirit. But we also see paradigms that valorize the abiding spirit influencing or conquering the self. Modern theorists may struggle to appreciate the significance of these latter conceptions if they operate within a paradigm wherein religious practice is primarily seen as an act of self-cultivation. In contrast to abiding spirits, migrating spirits are not strictly essential for life. They are temporary, of varying moral alignment, and often fickle. They are distinguished by verbs of motion and/or empowerment as well as use of the preposition עַל (whereas abiding spirits more frequently use the preposition בְּ). In texts discussing migrating spirits, we find evidence of their materiality and limitation. They are often portrayed as measurable, finite, and handed off from one person to another.

5 In Good Spirits

5.1 Umbanda Public Possession Ceremonies

Umbanda is an African-descended religion practiced most prominently in urban areas of Brazil, though it has spread throughout the Brazilian diaspora.[1] Similar in practice to other Yoruba-influenced traditions, Umbanda is notable for its elevation of Catholic and Spiritist symbols (and, likewise, its relative demotion of more conspicuous African imagery). A twentieth-century innovation that stems from older Afro-Brazilian religions like Candomblé, Umbanda is seen by some scholars of religion as operating "on the border between Afro-Indigenous ritual and Christian rationalism" due in part to its emphasis on psychological and medical therapy through spirit possession.[2]

The principal religious services of Umbanda take place at *centros*, gathering places founded by a *chefe* (chief) or *mãe/pai de santo* (mother/father of the saints) and administered by a team of mediums. The hierarchy of the administrative mediums is reflective of each medium's perceived skill in possession: those recognized as the most adept usually host the highest-ranking spirits (i.e., those spirits understood to be the most gifted in healing and counseling). The mediums dress for the ceremony in all-white outfits; the women even wear nurses' uniforms.[3] As congregants gather for the ceremony, many of them obtain a *ficha* (token) from an attendant, which will permit them to have a consultation with the spirit of their choice. As the ritual begins, the participants genuflect to an altar featuring Catholic saints and conduct the *defumacão* (smoking) of evil spirits with incense and cigar smoke. Participants begin to sing and move about the room. As they do so, the mediums intermittently stop dancing, jerk their bodies rapidly, and are eventually overcome by the presence of a spirit to whom they act as host. The mediums' bodies and voices become altered, and they are given certain ritual accoutrements, which, among other purposes, help to designate which spirit has possessed them.

The anthropologist Diana DeGroat Brown detailed her visit to one such centro in an affluent suburban community. In that instance, the chefe received the spirit of Pai João (Father John), a venerated *Preto Velho* (the spirit of an enslaved

---

[1] Rachel Harding, "Afro-Brazilian Religions," *ER* 1:124–25. See also Diana DeGroat Brown, *Umbanda: Religion and Politics in Urban Brazil*, 2nd ed. (New York: Columbia University Press, 1994); and Steven Engler, "Umbanda and Africa," *NovaRel* 15.4 (2012): 13–35.
[2] Harding, "Afro-Brazilian Religions," 124.
[3] Brown, *Umbanda*, 80, 96.

African ancestor) who was the highest ranking and most effective spirit healer present. His arrival was indicated by the chefe walking bent over with age, carrying a wooden staff, and smoking a pipe. Brown described what happened after each of the expected spirit visitors arrived:

> At this point, the singing and clapping stop. The ritual area appears to be the scene of restless disorganized activity, and to the inexperienced observer it may even appear that the service is ending. On the contrary, it is about to enter its most important phase, the period of *consultas* (consultations), when the members of the congregation are able to consult with the spirits about their problems. Spirit consultants, who possess high-ranking, fully initiated mediums, station themselves at intervals around the ritual area and prepare to give consultas... [Pai João's] first client is a woman who has not obtained a *ficha* (token) for a consulta but who is obviously very ill. She is led directly to Pai João, who greets her with a kindly air and listens attentively to her problem.[4]

Most of those seeking consultations were suffering in mind or spirit.[5] The therapies prescribed ranged from home remedies to more invasive interventions like exorcisms. These prescriptions were sometimes delivered in a ritual code that non-possessed attendants had to translate for the congregants.

In Brown's descriptions, the consultas were conducted with a "bureaucratic" precision.[6] Attendants directed congregants to the spirits indicated by their tokens in a decorous and sedate atmosphere. This environment was punctuated, however, by moments of intensely ecstatic possession. Nevertheless, these events were expected and controlled with a professionalism akin to a hospital triage room:

> Servants help to protect clients who may themselves become possessed during a consulta. Possession states often occur spontaneously among clients during consultas, or they may be induced by the spirit consultant as a part of the cure or evidence of spirit persecution. In contrast to the extremely controlled possession states achieved by experienced mediums, possession, when it occurs among those inexperienced in controlling it, is often violent, and clients must be protected from injury to themselves or to others.[7]

The parallels to medical professionals do not end there. As Brown observed, the white nurses' uniforms "give the ceremonies, particularly during the *consulta* pe-

---

4 Brown, *Umbanda*, 82.
5 In a survey of 465 visitors to an *Umbanda* centro, 64% of the problems brought for *consultas* were health related. Brown, *Umbanda*, 97.
6 Brown, *Umbanda*, 85.
7 Brown, *Umbanda*, 83.

riod, the appearance of large public medical clinics and reinforce their image as proper places for the treatments of illness."[8]

Umbanda ritual, as we can see, demonstrates many resonances of the medical idiom in communities that practice possession and related phenomena. It also exemplifies how spirit possession can be a cultivated practice with functions more complicated than simply expressing conceptions of personified evil. Umbanda is only one of the numerous contemporary possession cults to employ a medical idiom; however, its adoption of modern medical imagery is especially conspicuous. This is particularly true of the consultas, which are emblematic of the ways in which spirit possession mixes aspects of what western theorists might categorize as medicine, psychology, religious piety, or the performance of ethnic identity.

Since examples of possession in a medical idiom, like that of Umbanda, are notable, though not idiosyncratic, anthropologists have developed varying categories for comparing these phenomena cross culturally. Some of the more promising strategies can be found among theorists whose work is informed by neuroscience. Cognitive anthropologist Emma Cohen, for example, has developed two categories that she calls "executive" and "pathogenic" possession.[9] Cohen argues that her categories are "informed and constrained by recurrent features of evolved human cognition that guide perception, representation, thought and action."[10] In this, her categories may exhibit predilections that could be common across human religious expressions and experiences, both ancient and modern.

In Cohen's analysis, *executive possession* entails the perceived presence of an incorporeal agent within a person's body that temporarily affects the person's behavior and thoughts to the extent that the host's actions can be attributed to the agent rather than to the host. The executive type of possession engages cognitive functions that deal with the world of intentional agents. The executive type is what many readers may think of initially when imagining spirit possession, especially that aspect in which a host's personality is replaced by someone or something else. As I have argued, however, possession to the extent that the host is overwhelmed entirely is a relatively limited phenomenon in the Hebrew Bible, being most conspicuous in certain texts that utilize the verb ləhitnabbēʾ. In most instances of what might be called executive possession in the Hebrew

---

[8] Brown, *Umbanda*, 96.
[9] Emma Cohen, "What Is Spirit Possession? Defining, Comparing, and Explaining Two Possession Forms," *Ethnos* 73.1 (2008): 101–26.
[10] Cohen, "What Is Spirit Possession?," 103.

Bible, the host remains present and aware, while the co-present spirit or spirits have varying degrees of identity and will.

Most instances of spirit possession in the Hebrew Bible and in early Jewish literature have more in common with the *pathogenic* type. Cohen describes this type as the perceived presence of an agent (with or without a will or identity) that can cause physical effects like disease, as well as psychological effects such as hallucinations or depression. Such agents can also affect a person's luck, financial fortune, or the ways that they are perceived by others. Significantly, in the pathogenic model, spirits can have positive or relatively benign effects on a person. The pathogenic type, according to Cohen, engages human cognitive models having to do with representations of contamination.

Due to the dominance and spectacle of executive types of possession, pathogenic models for spirit possession have gone relatively unappreciated in biblical studies, especially in texts that connect spirit possession to notions of purity and impurity. That being said, both types, the executive and the pathogenic, are attested in early Jewish literature in a medical idiom.

5.2 Chapter Overview

In this final chapter of the book, I will argue two points. First, in contrast to many modern models for medicine, in biblical and early Jewish literature, medical treatment and spirit phenomena were not bifurcated conceptually. This created an inherent *therapeutic*—what might even be called *pastoral*—aspect to many spirit texts. Beyond merely mapping mythological realities or demonizing rival groups, such texts functioned to articulate the ties that bound a community together and to create frameworks for processing failure and loss. We recognize these dynamics when we survey Second Temple era literature, including 4Q242 The Prayer of Nabonidus and an Aramaic apotropaic text, 4Q560. I will also discuss how notions of "impure spirits" reflect ongoing debates in late Second Temple literature regarding the distinction or conflation between moral and ritual impurity.

Second, I will argue that a significant stream of medical language in the Hebrew Bible functioned to "unfamiliarize" aspects of the self that were seen as undesirable or morally compromised. These parts of the body—for example one's "heart" (לבב) or "spirit" (רוח)—are variously modified or exchanged in an effort to improve them (e.g., Deut 10:12–16, 30:6; Jer 31:33–34; Ezek 11:19–20, 18:31, 36:26–27). In some texts, the individual is charged with correcting their own body, while in others God is the principal surgeon. By the time these streams of interpretation reached the late Second Temple period, however, new vocabulary was developing for these unfamiliar selves; for example, one's "inclination" (יצר, 1QS 5:3b–6a). Moreover, these bodily vulnerabilities were no longer tolerated but exorcized completely as part of a process of total spirit-body reconstruction. I conclude that these texts and the traditions they represent provide a compelling origin for the more elaborate notions of spirit possession and exorcism seen in later texts and especially in early Christian tradition.

The final discussion of this chapter and this book concerns holy spirits. Continuing in the idiom of medical language, I suggest that in some late Second Temple texts, positive possession by a holy spirit from God was seen as a preventative solution to the problems caused by other kinds of spirits. However, this expectation had the potential to cause problems within a community when those who had received their holy spirit inoculation suffered nevertheless from the antagonism of spirits of another kind. The so-called Treatise on the Two-Spirits from 1QS is one such text that struggles with the problem of persistent less-than-holy activity in a community that is supposedly righteous. For an ethnographic analogue, I introduce a phenomenon in contemporary Ethiopian Pentecostal communities wherein someone who has been exorcised by the Holy Spirit nevertheless experiences recurring demonic antagonism. Through this comparison, I suggest that such situations, rather than causing moments of doubt or alienation, actually create opportunities in a community for the continued management and discernment of spirits.

5.3 Spirit Possession in a Medical Idiom

It is no great secret that ancient biblical texts and modern medical practices conceive of healing and bodily wholeness differently. To compare, in a conventional contemporary healthcare setting, the roles played by nurses and doctors, mental health care counselors, social workers, and hospital chaplains are distinct with separate programs for training and credentialing. In biblical literature, however, the various ailments treated by these professionals are less differentiated from one another and might all be seen as alternatively caused, managed, or cured by certain types of spirit phenomena. This much is relatively clear. What is less frequently acknowledged, however, is that the disparity between ancient and modern medicine is not simply one of a theistic worldview versus an agnostic one. More fundamentally, it is the operation of different and usually unexpressed cultural models for the human body that causes the disparity.

We can see the role that the conception of the body plays in determining therapeutic models by looking at a contemporary example. Anthropologist Thomas J. Csordas has written about the spirit healing practices of Charismatic

Roman Catholics in New England. As theists who practice spirit healing and read the Old Testament and other ancient writings as scripture, we might expect there to be considerable overlap between their views of the human body and those of biblical texts. Yet, when Csordas consulted with his subjects regarding the elemental anatomy that undergirded their conception of a person, he found a novel view altogether.

> Essential to the Charismatic healing system is a concept of the person as a tripartite composite of body, mind, and spirit. Conceptualization of a tripartite person creates a decisive cultural difference between Charismatic healing and conventional psychotherapy and medicine, insofar as the latter are predicated on a concept of the person as a dualistic composite of body and mind. For Charismatics the spiritual is, paradoxically, ineffable and empirical at the same time. Its ineffability was captured by an informant who said that the reason the spiritual could not easily be discussed was only because we have no language for it, and hence we are forced by default to describe it in the language of emotions. On the other hand, the spiritual is empirical in the sense that phenomena such as evil spirits, or the sense of divine presence, are experienced as real in their own domain, just as are viruses in the somatic and emotional traumas in the mental domains.[11]

Although this tripartite model of the person is informed by readings of scripture, its particular coordination of mind, body, and spirit are foreign to the cultural world of biblical spirit phenomena. Not only is this model still dependent on contemporary medical notions of the body; it also requires a uniquely modern partitioning of the different components of the person, defined by categories like ineffable and empirical. In contemporary communities such as the ones that Csordas describes, when God does impart miraculous healing, many see it as occurring in and through a separate "spiritual" component of a person, with the consequences of that intervention then spilling over into the physical and/or mental realms.[12] In short, these Charismatic Roman Catholics are still modern as far as it comes to their view of the body, even though they share the assumption along with biblical texts that spirits play a central role in healing.

To compare the conceptual differences between biblical and modern conceptions of the body, we can look at ancient Near Eastern parallels to the Hebrew Bible. Ingrid Lilly's comparisons of biblical *rûaḥ* language with ancient Near Eastern medicinal and cosmological texts are a good example.[13] Specifically,

---

[11] Csordas, *The Sacred Self*, 39–40.
[12] This dynamic is especially evident in the popular Pentecostal and Charismatic notion of "deliverance" in which a person is liberated from a demonic influence on their spirit, resulting in the easing or curing of certain psychosomatic symptoms. See Csordas, *The Sacred Self*, 41–42.
[13] Lilly, "Rûaḥ Embodied"; and "Conceptualizing Spirit."

Lilly has demonstrated how, in many ancient Mesopotamian texts, "personal wellbeing is contingent on the drama of divine winds."[14] The causes and matching treatments for various human ailments (including headaches, coughs, chills, intestinal problems, and fevers) are thus spirit related. We see this diagnosis also, for example, in the Babylonian *Ludlul Bēl Nēmeqi, The Poem of the Righteous Sufferer*, a text that tells of a Babylonian nobleman who suffers unjustly. Notably, this composition utilizes the imagery of Babylonian *chaoskampf* traditions but reimagines the drama as an internal struggle within the sufferer's body. To compare, in the Babylonian epic *Enuma Elish*, the storm god, Marduk, employs an *imḫullu* (wind) to defeat the watery chaos deity, Tiamat (Tablet IV). Yet, in the *Poem of the Righteous Sufferer*, the *imḫullu* is not a weapon in the heroic deity's arsenal but the very cause of the sufferer's internal distress.[15]

Similar connections between bodily maladies and the activities of spirits are also at work in certain biblical *rûaḥ* texts, especially those that seem inordinately concerned with spirit workings in and upon the human body. See, for example, Lilly's discussion of Job's conception of the body:

> Early in Job's second speech, he asks "is my flesh bronze?" (6:12). This question reveals the fundamental medical anxiety Job will confront in each of his subsequent speeches about his illness: his body does not have a hard boundary, leaving his internal *rûaḥ* vulnerable to dangerous penetrations. Indeed, Job's first statement about his own medical condition points to the dilemma of his *rûaḥ*, "the arrows of the Almighty are in me; my *rûaḥ* drinks their poison," (6:4) and in 7:20, Job asks, "why have you made me a target?" Job's skin is porous, his flesh is vulnerable, and as the target of a divine scourge, it is his *rûaḥ* that becomes sick.[16]

In Job, as in Babylonian literature, discerning a categorical distinction between winds and spirits is hardly possible when it comes to discerning them within one's body. Indeed, the symptoms of their presence are the same.[17] Thus, as porous bodies, human beings must attend to the dramas and whims of the spirit-winds that constantly move in and around us. As will be seen below, these ideas apply not only to the descriptions and diagnosis of pathological spirit possession ailments but also to their treatment.

---

[14] Lilly, "Conceptualizing Spirit," 838.
[15] Lilly, "Conceptualizing Spirit," 838.
[16] Lilly, "Rûaḥ Embodied," 330–31.
[17] Lilly, "Rûaḥ Embodied," 328.

5.3.1 Spirit Therapies in Second Temple Jewish Literature

As widespread as the connections between physical ailments and spirit pathologies were in the ancient Near East, the Hebrew Bible contains only a handful of extended reflections in this mode. The situation is different, however, in late Second Temple Jewish literature, which presents several examples of pathogenic spirit possession maladies. Since the pertinent texts originate in different historical and social contexts, they are not necessarily unified in their conceptions of spirits or in their proposed solutions. Nevertheless, a survey of some key examples can demonstrate the prevalence of these ideas and highlight their shared differences from modern conceptions of medicine and therapy. As I demonstrate below, one of the key differences is the integration of ritual purity and impurity into the medical treatment of spirit pathologies.

The first example is the fragmentary Aramaic document 4Q242 The Prayer of Nabonidus, a text likely composed by the sectarian community in the late second or early first century BCE.[18] In this first-person account, the Babylonian king Nabonidus describes the "evil boil" or "fever" (שחנא באישא, 4Q242 1 3:2) that afflicted him for seven years until he was cured by a Jewish "diviner" or "exorcist" (גזר, 4Q242 1 3:4).[19] Scholars have long recognized the likely connection between this fragmentary text and the account of Nebuchadnezzar in the book of Daniel, with most positing that 4Q242 is a witness to an earlier tradition on which Dan 4 is based.[20] Regardless of the precise literary relationship, the interweaving of various threads of theological tradition in 4Q242 is conspicuous, especially when compared to Daniel. Not only does the unnamed Jewish exorcist cure the Babylonian king's ailment through exorcism, but he also forgives his sins and restores him, correcting his false worship of idols.

We find fragments of other strategies for mitigating spirit ailments in a damaged Aramaic apotropaic text, 4Q560 (see also 11QApocryphal Psalmsᵃ [11Q11]).[21]

---

[18] Florentino García Martínez, "The Prayer of Nabonidus: A New Synthesis," in *Qumran and Apocalyptic: Studies on the Aramaic Texts from Qumran*, STDJ 9 (Leiden: Brill, 1992), 116–36; and Sidnie White Crawford, "Court Tales," *EDSS* 1:149–51. I am grateful to Matthew Rasure for suggesting I include a discussion of this text here.
[19] Text follows John J. Collins, "4QPrayer of Nabonidus ar," in *Qumran Cave 4.XVII: Parabiblical Texts, Part 3*, ed. James C. Vanderkam, DJD 22 (Oxford: Clarendon, 1996), 83–93. Translations of 4Q242 are my own.
[20] But see an argument that 4Q242 knows the book of Daniel, Andrew Steinmann, "The Chicken and the Egg: A New Proposal for the Relationship Between the Prayer of Nabonidus and the Book of Daniel," *RevQ* 20.4 (80) (2002): 557–70.
[21] Text and translations of 4Q560 are based on Douglas L. Penney and Michael O. Wise, "By the Power of Beelzebub: An Aramaic Incantation Formula from Qumran (4Q560)," *JBL* 113.4 (1994):

This document contains a number of typical features associated with ancient Near Eastern magic texts, which themselves go back perhaps as far as writing itself.[22] It also shares many features with a wealth of Jewish magic texts dating to the much later Byzantine period and after.[23] Despite this wide range of comparable texts, the fact that 4Q560 was found among the Dead Scrolls establishes that it was at least *in use* in the Second Temple period, however much older it may be.

The features of 4Q560 include direct address to both male and female demons, concern for safety in childbirth, and enumeration of specific spirit-caused diseases—especially "fever and chills" (אשא ועריא 4Q560 1 i 4).[24] Though the line is damaged, the phrase "iniquity and transgression" (עוֹאן ופשע, 4Q560 1 i 4) is noteworthy. Penney and Wise suggest that it is a quotation of Exod 34:7/Num 14:18, and thus a reference to the familiar formula for God's inclination to balance mercy and justice.[25] Speaking the full reference out loud may have been perceived as having a particular power.[26] This knitting together of what might be called moral or justice issues with a practical apotropaic text is illuminating: If we assume that the treatment matches the diagnosis, the depiction of physical spirit of 4Q560 is sensitive to the moral stakes in such a ritual operation.

We see in the Dead Sea Scrolls not only descriptions of spirit ailments and their treatments, but also what might be called strategies for diagnosis. For example, a section of the Damascus Document concerning anyone "ruled by the spirits of Belial" explains that such a person is to receive the same fate as the necromancer and the medium (i.e., death).[27] However, a period of observation is necessary, especially in instances of a serious but less egregious infraction:

627–50. See also Joseph Naveh, "Fragments of an Aramaic Magic Book from Qumran," *IEJ* 48.3/4 (1998): 252–61; and Philip S. Alexander, "The Demonology of the Dead Sea Scrolls," in *The Dead Sea Scrolls after Fifty Years: A Comprehensive Assessment*, ed. Peter W. Flint and James C. VanderKam, vol. 2 (Leiden: Brill, 1999).

22 Penney and Wise, "By the Power of Beelzebub," 630.

23 See Gideon Bohak, "Jewish Amulets, Magic Bowls, and Manuals in Aramaic and Hebrew," in *Guide to the Study of Ancient Magic*, ed. David Frankfurter, RGRW 189 (Leiden: Brill, 2019), 388–415.

24 David Lincicum, "Greek Deuteronomy's 'Fever and Chills' and Their Magical Afterlife," *VT* 58.4 (2008): 544–49.

25 Penney and Wise, "By the Power of Beelzebub," 639.

26 Alexander suggests that 4Q560 is a fragment of what have might been a much larger "recipe book" for apotropaic and exorcistic rituals. Alexander, "The Demonology of the Dead Sea Scrolls," 345.

27 I am grateful to Carol Newsom for recommending that I discuss this text.

> ³... However, anyone who strays ⁴ by profaning the Sabbath and the festivals shall not be put to death; rather let the people ⁵ keep him in custody. And if he desists from it (from going astray) they shall watch him for seven years, and afterwards ⁶ he is to be readmitted to the congregation. (CD 12:3b–6a)

Although this section is cryptic and short, it nevertheless reveals an underlying therapeutic goal in the law. If the person in question is "healed," restoration is possible and in fact preferable.

We find additional examples of spirit therapies designed for physical healing throughout the literature of the late Second Temple period. Josephus, for example, details how King Solomon was able both to cure diseases and to exorcise demons by means of composing "incantations" (ἐπῳδή, *Ant.* 8.45). In an episode evocative of the Prayer of Nabonidus, Josephus tells the story of a certain Eleazer of his own time, who was able to exorcise demons in the presence of Vespasian and his retinue by following Solomon's preserved methods and evoking the Israelite king's name.[28]

Gospel records of Jesus's ministry are replete with exorcistic healing accounts as well. For example, Jesus is described as rebuking the demon that afflicts a boy with seizures and muteness (Mark 9:25/Matt 17:18/Luke 9:42), and a woman who suffers from a bent back is said to be crippled by a spirit (Luke 13:11). Luke-Acts in particular frequently pairs the casting out of demons and the healing of diseases in summarizing statements about the ministries of Jesus and his early followers (e.g., Luke 6:18; 7:21; 8:2; Acts 5:16; 8:7; cf., Mark 6:). Against this backdrop, even healing stories that do not explicitly mention spirits or demons may imply spirit therapies, such as when Jesus heals a leper by uttering what might be an apotropaic command, "Be made clean!" (ἐκαθαρίσθη, Mark 1:40–45).[29] Clearly, a wide range of early Jewish writers, including those writing about the early Jesus movement, assumed a connection between physical healing and spirit therapy.

5.3.2 Unclean Spirits

In late Second Temple Jewish literature, notions of impurity are also widely associated with spirits and therapy. For example, in the synoptic Gospels, where

---

[28] Dennis C. Duling, "The Eleazar Miracle and Solomon's Magical Wisdom in Flavius Josephus's Antiquitates Judaicae 8:42–49," *HTR* 78.1–2 (1985): 1–25.
[29] Thomas Kazen, *Jesus and Purity Halakhah: Was Jesus Indifferent to Impurity?* Rev. Ed. (Winona Lake, IN: Eisenbrauns, 2010), 100–04.

spirit possession and exorcisms are especially prominent, the most frequent adjective used to describe detrimental possessing spirits is "impure" (τὰ πνεύματα τὰ ἀκάθαρτα).³⁰ Indeed, as Todd Klutz pointed out, the terms "demons" and "unclean spirits" are sometimes used interchangeably (e. g., Mark 3:22, 30; Luke 8:27, 29).³¹ The association in Jewish tradition of spirit activity with impurity, however, predates the New Testament. Further, these ideas are not uniform in their presentation, and it is debatable to what extent older purity ideas should be mapped onto later spirit texts.³²

In the Hebrew Bible, the roles of spirits and demons in purity laws and rituals is considerably more muted—though still present. Various obscure figures are mentioned by name or by an identifying characteristic, as, for example, "Azazel" (Lev 16:8, 10, 26), "goat-demons" (שעירם, Lev 17:7), and the "spirit of jealousy" (Num 5:14, 30). Even so, most scholars are in agreement that these characters are largely vestigial in the received forms of these rituals in the Priestly literature.³³ Whatever roles demonic or lesser-divine beings once played in such rituals, the monotheizing interests at work in biblical literature eventually relegated them to the realm of side characters with incomplete storylines. These demotions are so obvious, in fact, that Jacob Milgrom featured the "thoroughgoing evisceration of the demonic" as a principal descriptor of Priestly theology.³⁴

But does the Priestly literature protest too much? As several scholars have noted, from a historical perspective, it is unlikely that such beliefs disappeared altogether from ancient Israel and early Judaism.³⁵ Beliefs and rituals around

---

30 Some version of the phrase occurs at least twenty-one times in the New Testament. See Matthew Thiessen, *Jesus and the Forces of Death: The Gospels' Portrayal of Ritual Impurity within First-Century Judaism* (Grand Rapids: Baker Academic, 2020), 123–48.
31 Todd E. Klutz, "The Grammar of Exorcism in the Ancient Mediterranean World: Some Cosmological, Semantic, and Pragmatic Reflections on How Exorcistic Prowess Contributed to the Worship of Jesus," in *The Jewish Roots of Christological Monotheism: Papers from the St. Andrews Conference on the Historical Origins of the Worship of Jesus*, ed. Carey C. Newman, James R. Davila, and Gladys S. Lewis (Leiden: Brill, 1999), 161.
32 As Bazzana points out, on this point interpreters have too often employed a variety of anti-Jewish assumptions, including the inaccurate belief that Jews were the only people in antiquity who were concerned about purity laws. See *Having the Spirit of Christ*, 61–67.
33 Yehezkel Kaufmann was particularly adamant that "the Bible preserves no trace" of the pagan idea that such rituals are designed to protects gods and humans from "demonic or magical action of impurity." Kaufmann, *The Religion of Israel*, 103.
34 Jacob Milgrom, *Leviticus 1–16: A New Translation with Introduction and Commentary*, AB 3 (New York: Doubleday, 1991), 44.
35 See the argument in Kazen, *Jesus and Purity Halakhah*, 305–10. Baruch Levine maintained that magic, ritual, and legal matters coexisted in the cult and that this integration has been ar-

such figures undoubtedly persisted, though it remains murky to what extent and in what forms. The potent demonologies and spirit-filled worlds of Second Temple Jewish literature attest to this, even if their idioms were influenced by Persian or Hellenistic thought.[36] It is thus best to read the de-demonizing ideologies of Priestly literature as being at least as *prescriptive* as they are *descriptive*.

It should be no wonder, then, that when matters of purity are discussed in late Second Temple literature, the problems and solutions offered by spirit phenomena are featured prominently and often in connection to physical ailments. This is especially true in the Dead Sea Scrolls. One example is the Cave 4 fragments of the Damascus Document (i.e., 4Q266, 4Q268, and 4Q272), sometimes called 4QZadokite Fragments or Fragment on Skin Disease.[37] The fragments contain a prolonged exegetical expansion on the laws concerning "skin diseases" (נגיעים) in Lev 13–15. Of particular interest is what the text posits as the "etiological explanation for the genesis of skin disease."[38] Specifically, the document outlines in detail how healthy skin is maintained by a "spirit of life" and, conversely, skin disease is caused by other spirits.

> [17]... "And the priest shall order that they shave his head, but not the scall" (Lev 13:33). This is in order that [18] the priest may count the dead and live hair and see whether any has been added from [19] the live to the dead during the seven days, (in which case) he is unclean; while if none has been added from the live [20] to the dead, and the artery is filled with bl[ood] and the sp[ir]it of life (נמלא [ד]ם ור[ו]ח החיים) moves up and down in it, [21] the plague is [healed]. (4QZadokite Fragments on Skin Disease, lns. 17–21 [cf. 4Q266 f6 i 9–12; 4Q269 f7:6–8])[39]

The problem of the disease is described as a blockage of the flow of the spirit of life. This phrase is not merely an idiom for human blood but a description of the

---

tificially minimized, *In the Presence of the Lord: A Study of Cult and Some Cultic Terms in Ancient Israel* (Leiden: Brill, 1974), 55–56.

36 See discussion in chapter 1.

37 On provenance, see Joseph M. Baumgarten, "The 4Q Zadokite Fragments on Skin Disease," *JJS* 41.2 (1990): 153–65; and Elisha Qimron, "Qumran Corner: Notes on the 4Q Zadokite Fragment on Skin Disease," *JJS* 42.2 (1991): 256–59.

38 Baumgarten, "The 4Q Zadokite Fragments," 162.

39 Text and translations of 4Q266–273 are based on Baumgarten's composite reconstruction in "The 4Q Zadokite Fragments." While the Hebrew term רוח is posited as present in a damaged portion of this excerpt (and in several of the examples below), there is widespread agreement as to the general reconstructions presented here. See Baumgarten, "The 4Q Zadokite Fragments," 159–62; and Florentino García Martínez and Eibert J. C. Tigchelaar, *The Dead Sea Scrolls Study Edition* (Leiden: Brill, 1997), 588–89.

organ which allows for the free flow of blood. The presence of the spirit of life ensures that no other spirit can possess the system and obstruct it:

> ² … and the scab a blow of wood, stone, or any blow when the spi[rit comes and po]ssesses (הר[וח וא]חז[ה])⁴⁰ ³ of the artery, making the blood recede upwards and downwards, and the artery […]. (4QZadokite Fragments on Skin Disease, lns. 2–3 [cf. 4Q269 f7:2–3])

In contrast to the spirit of life, the spirit mentioned here physically tampers with the patient's internal bodily processes, which causes skin disease. Lilly's description of *rûḥôt* as *internal* winds is an especially apt model.

In the 4QZadokite Fragments, the management of spirits is essential to the maintenance of human physiology. Certainly, it would be difficult to tie directly the activity of these skin disease spirits to the cosmic conflicts involving Belial, the legions of darkness, or any of the other villains described in the Scrolls. Yet the descriptions in these fragments make the spirit language difficult to dismiss as merely idiomatic. In a very meaningful way, the purity rites of the priests are understood as a type of medically necessary exorcism.

A similar perspective on skin disease is articulated in the Genesis Apocryphon, this time in a narrative context.⁴¹ When the king of Egypt takes Sarai from Abram (cf. Gen 12:10–20), the Apocryphon elaborates on the "plagues" (נגעים, Gen 12:17) that afflicted the king and his household. After Abram prays, entreating God to protect Sarai from Pharaoh, God responds:

> ¹⁶… That night God Most High sent him a pestilential spirit (רוח מכדש) to afflict him and all the men of his house, an evil spirit (רוח באישא), ¹⁷ which kept afflicting him and all the men of his house. He was not able to approach her; nor did he have intercourse with her, though she was with him ¹⁸ for two years. (1QApGen 20:16–18)⁴²

---

40 Baumgarten has "takes hold" instead of "possess." See, "The 4Q Zadokite Fragments," 161–62. While "take hold" may be a more literal translation of אחז, I prefer "possess" here as it provokes the imagination to expand the types of phenomena that might fit under the banner of "spirit possession."
41 The Genesis Apocryphon was composed in Aramaic and has been dated between the second century BCE and the first century CE. Scholars have noted its interconnections with Enochic literature and the book of Jubilees. See Joseph A. Fitzmyer, *The Genesis Apocryphon of Qumran Cave 1 (1Q20): A Commentary*, 3rd ed., BibOr 18b (Rome: Pontificio Istituto Biblico, 2004), 16–25. But compare Michael Segal, "The Literary Relationship between the Genesis Apocryphon and Jubilees: The Chronology of Abram and Sarai's Descent to Egypt," *AS* 8.1–2 (2010): 71–88; and Klutz, "The Grammar of Exorcism," 156–65.
42 Text and translations of 1QApGen are from Fitzmyer, *The Genesis Apocryphon of Qumran Cave 1 (1Q20)*.

The affliction spreading from Pharaoh and across his household would likely have been understood as a kind of impure skin disease.⁴³

Similar to the fragments of the Damascus Document discussed above, the solution for this spirit-skin disease is a form of exorcism. Once he discovers the truth that Sarai is not Abram's sister but his wife, Pharaoh demands that Abram intervene to heal him:

> ²⁷... "Here is your wife. Take her away; go, depart from ²⁸ all the provinces of Egypt. Now pray for me and for my household that this evil spirit be expelled from us." (ותגער מנה רוחא דא באישתא) So I prayed for that [perse]cutor, ²⁹ and I laid my hands upon his [he]ad. The plague was removed from him, and the evil [spirit] was expelled [from him] (ואתפלי מנה מכתשא ואתגערת [מנה רוחא] באישתא), and he recovered. (1QApGen 20:27–29)

The identity of the "evil spirit" in this text remains impersonal and its actions seem somewhat instinctive rather than malicious. We might say that, in this, it is more like what we think of as a virus instead of a demonic force. Even with this medical analogue, however, we should not miss the fact that in the Genesis Apocryphon, the spirit-caused ailment is directly tied to a specific act of moral transgression. Indeed, such overlapping of different types of impurity and spirit phenomena are typical in the Dead Sea Scrolls.

Second Temple Jewish literature, in general, often conflates categories of purity that were separate (or separated) in older biblical literature.⁴⁴ For instance, many scholars recognize that the ritual laws of the Hebrew Bible detail two primary and intersecting types of purity, what Jonathan Klawans calls "ritual" and "moral" purity.⁴⁵ "Ritual" purity (commonly associated with the Priestly Penta-

---

43 See Klutz, "The Grammar of Exorcism," 157; but cf. Fitzmyer, *The Genesis Apocryphon of Qumran Cave 1 (1Q20)*, 210.
44 Susan Haber, "Ritual and Moral Purity and Impurity in Second Temple Judaism," in *They Shall Purify Themselves: Essays on Purity in Early Judaism*, ed. Adele Reinhartz (Atlanta: SBL Press, 2008), 31–46.
45 Jonathan Klawans, *Impurity and Sin in Ancient Judaism* (Oxford: Oxford University Press, 2000). The terms can be misleading since moral purity laws certainly contain important rituals and, likewise, the ritual purity system has a moral component. Klawans himself recognizes these problems but argues that the labels are still preferable to other options. For other versions of these divisions, which do not necessarily map exactly onto those of Klawans, see Adolph Büchler, *Studies in Sin and Atonement in the Rabbinic Literature of the First-Century* (Oxford: Oxford University, 1928); Tikva Frymer-Kensky, "Pollution, Purification, and Purgation in Biblical Israel," in *The Word of the Lord Shall Go Forth: Essays in Honor of David Noel Freedman in Celebration of His Sixtieth Birthday* (Winona Lake, IN: Eisenbrauns, 1983), 399–414; and David P. Wright, "The Spectrum of Priestly Impurity," in *Priesthood and Cult in Ancient Israel*, ed. Gary A. Anderson and Saul M. Olyan (Sheffield: Sheffield Academic, 1991), 150–81. Other important

teuchal source) concerns impurity resulting from tolerable and often unavoidable sources, such as through regular bodily functions, contact with a corpse, and skin disease. In general, such impurities are not presented as immoral in the Priestly literature of the Hebrew Bible, though they required responsible handling so as minimize contamination of others or the shrine.[46] In contrast, "moral" impurity (commonly associated with the Holiness or H source) was always the consequence of sin and could only be atoned for through sacrifice. It should be noted, however, that the field is not in agreement on the contours of these distinctions.[47]

Over the last thirty years, scholars have been especially productive in uncovering conceptions of purity and impurity in the Dead Sea Scrolls.[48] In general, there is widespread agreement that notions of purity played a central role in the sectarian community and that these ideas were integrated into other emphases commonly associated with the literature of the sectarian community, including their eschatological and dualistic concerns. In general, the purity system(s) of the Dead Sea Scrolls are especially strict when compared to earlier biblical or later rabbinic traditions. Nevertheless, as with other Second Temple era literature, a variety of perspectives on the particulars of the purity system are found among the Qumran scrolls. Certain of these texts, such as the Community Rule, the Hodayot, and the War Scroll, merge the categories of "ritual" and "moral" purity. At the same time, other texts seem to maintain these older distinctions, or to show an interest only in one type of impurity or the other.[49]

---

studies that do not follow this mold include Jacob Neusner, *The Idea of Purity in Ancient Judaism* (Leiden: Brill, 1973); Milgrom, *Leviticus*; and Mary Douglas, *Leviticus as Literature* (Oxford: Oxford University Press, 1999). See overviews in Susan Haber, "Ritual and Moral Purity and Impurity in the Hebrew Bible," in *They Shall Purify Themselves: Essays on Purity in Early Judaism*, ed. Adele Reinhartz (Atlanta: SBL Press, 2008), 9–29; and Wil Rogan, "Purity in Early Judaism: Current Issues and Questions," *CBR* 16.3 (2018): 309–39.

46 See discussion in Joel S. Baden and Candida R. Moss, "The Origin and Interpretation of Ṣāraʿat in Leviticus 13–14," *JBL* 130.4 (2011): 643–62.

47 See the critique of Klawans using a cognitive science informed approach in Thomas Kazen, *Emotions in Biblical Law: A Cognitive Science Approach* (Sheffield: Sheffield Phoenix, 2011). See also Jacob Milgrom, "Systemic Differences in the Priestly Corpus: A Response to Jonathan Klawans," *RB* 112.3 (2005): 321–29.

48 See summaries in Susan Haber, "Ritual and Moral Purity and Impurity in the Dead Sea Scrolls," in *They Shall Purify Themselves: Essays on Purity in Early Judaism*, ed. Adele Reinhartz (Atlanta: SBL Press, 2008), 47–74; Jonathan Klawans, "Purity in the Dead Sea Scrolls," in *The Oxford Handbook of the Dead Sea Scrolls*, ed. Timothy H. Lim and John J. Collins (Oxford: Oxford University Press, 2010), 377–402; and Hannah K. Harrington, *The Purity Texts*, CQS 5 (New York: T & T Clark, 2004).

49 See Klawans, "Purity in the Dead Sea Scrolls," 384–88.

These inconsistencies have driven some scholars to question how severe any erasure of the distinction could really have been. These questions, however, are wrapped up in theories regarding the historical development of the scrolls, an issue which does not concern us here.[50]

What is of interest is how frequently the Dead Sea Scrolls articulate the maintenance of purity using spirit language. This is exemplified well in 1QH^a where purification of sin is portrayed as an internal spirit phenomenon that concerns a person's moral organ:

> [22] ... And a perverted spirit you have purified from great sin (ורוח נעוה טהרתה מפשע רב) that it might take its place with [23] the host of the holy ones and enter into community with the congregation of the children of heaven. And you cast for a person an eternal lot with the spirits [24] of knowledge, that he might praise your name in a common rejoicing and recount your wonderful acts before all your works. (1QH^a 11:22–24; cf. 4:38; 9:34)

In achieving its heightened state of purity, the community must depend on divine intervention for fighting sources of impurity. Additionally, lest we make the mistake of assuming such language concerns merely the abstract, the *hodayot* are adamant that the effects of malignant spirit tampering are not just damning but also excruciating:

> [6]... For Belial (is present) when their destructive intention manifests itself. [7] All the foundations of my frame groan, and my bones are dislocated. My bowels are to me like a ship in a raging [8] storm, and my heart beats wildly to the point of destruction. A spirit engulfs me because of the devastation caused by their sin. (1QH^a 15:6b–8)

The effects of spirit-induced sin on the community thus require a spirit-infused treatment, one that is implemented directly by the deity with only minimal contributions from the individual affected self or their community.

Such expressions of excessive helplessness are consistent with an overarching tendency toward outlandish self-rebuff in 1QH^a. Indeed, this seems to be an intentional strategy within the composition. As Carol Newsom explains:

> [I]n the Hodayot the self enacts its own nothingness in radical contrast to the being of God. To its pollution corresponds the holiness of God; to its guilt, God's righteousness; to its inability to will and to do, God's uniquely autonomous will and creative power; to its lowliness among the works of God, God's own absolute incomparability.[51]

---

50 See Hannah K. Harrington, "Purity and the Dead Sea Scrolls: Current Issues," *CBR* 4.3 (2006): 397–428.
51 Newsom, *The Self as Symbolic Space*, 220.

Newsom labels these expressions "masochistic sublime."⁵² Within such a system, even the means of diagnosing truth is out of human hands since each person is dependent on the insight granted by God's own spirit:

³⁵... I, your servant, know ³⁶ by means of the spirit which you have placed within me (ברוח
אשר נתתה בי). (1QHª 5:35b–36a; cf. 6:36)

Thus, in contrast to many of the other texts we have surveyed in this book, in the Hodayot there is only minimal collaboration or co-management of spirits (but cf. 1QHª 8:29–31). In general, the spirits at work in the world are perceived as simply too strong. Ultimately, either the spirits of Belial or God's spirit will overwhelm the person. The appropriate posture in such circumstances, according to the Hodayot, is the desperate and gracious subjugation of the self to God.

5.3.3 From Spirit Disability to Spirit Gain

Given the persistent inseparability of spirit language from medical and moral matters (whether in biblical literature or in contemporary spirit possession practicing communities), it might be asked, what is gained socially and culturally by diagnosing diseases and transgressions alike principally as spirit problems? Yet to some degree, this is to get the question backwards. Since for many societies it is simply assumed that spirits are a factor in illness (as they are in so many aspects of human life), we are much more accurate in considering modern interpreters as the innovators when we separate medicine and spirits into different spheres. A more appropriate question, then, would be to ask what has been lost.

Cultural models that understand illnesses and disabilities as embodied spirit phenomena provide more than just tools for diagnosis and treatment. They also reflect a broader pneumatological anthropology in which health, ability, and power are seen as spirit phenomena. Disability studies scholars have uncovered how such systems for understanding human bodies underlie biblical social complexes as far reaching as kingship, sacrifice, purity, and charisma.⁵³ A person's bodily status, then, is integrally tied to their social status, and in biblical literature the presentation of one can often become a kind of map of the other, as in, for example, the respective depictions of Saul, David, and Mephibosheth in the

---

52 Newsom, *The Self as Symbolic Space*, 220.
53 For overviews, see Hector Avalos, "Disability Studies and Biblical Studies: Retrospectives and Prospects," *Int* 73.4 (2019): 343–54; and Candida R. Moss and Jeremy Schipper, "Introduction," in *Disability Studies and Biblical Literature* (New York: Palgrave Macmillan, 2011), 1–11.

books of Samuel.[54] Within such a cultural model, spirit hygiene does not just maintain health; it can also elevate the body to new heights of spirit ability.

These assumptions about spirits, bodies, and spirits in bodies may help to explain how, in contemporary spirit possession as well as in biblical literature, an ordeal that begins as a spirit ailment can be transformed into one of spirit empowerment.[55] An analogue borrowed from Disability studies is that of "deaf gain," the idea that in *losing* one's hearing one also *gains* deafness and with it new perception and insight.[56] Likewise, a person whose body is especially susceptible to spirit influence may come to discover that with the right treatments and rituals, a different spirit (or a different relationship with the invading spirit) can lead to new abilities.

One example of *spirit gain* in biblical literature may be the belief that the body of a spirit-afflicted person provides insights into the activity of divine powers. Ingrid Lilly demonstrates how this might be possible in her comparison of Ezekiel's spirit-induced prophecy with ancient Near Eastern combat literature:

> Mesopotamian and West Asian combat myths portray a protagonist deity at war, often with destructive consequences for rebellious lands or mountain tribes who have grown too strong and no longer need the gods. Ezekiel's combat rhetoric assumes this mytho-setting, his voice enacting a strident moral and ethical assault on his native mountain home – accusing it of rebellion and godless self-sufficiency. Even as his voice draws on the martial power of triumphant ANE combat gods though, his body is distressed, weak, and mutilated. The spirit does not strengthen, but rather weakens his body.[57]

In this way, the spirit affliction caused by Ezekiel's prophecy *is* its power and not a side effect. The drama of spirits that the prophet experiences within his body is a chart of the unseen activities in the heavens. Further, through cultivated attention to his own impairment, the prophet gains the ability to speak with the moral authority of the possessing power.

---

54 Jeremy Schipper, *Disability Studies and the Hebrew Bible: Figuring Mephibosheth in the David Story*, LHBOTS 441 (New York: T & T Clark, 2006), 61–99.
55 See Masquelier, "From Hostage to Host," and my discussion in chapter two.
56 H-Dirksen L. Bauman and Joseph J. Murray, eds., *Deaf Gain: Raising the Stakes for Human Diversity* (Minneapolis: University of Minnesota, 2014).
57 Ingrid Lilly, "A Moral Voice from a Spirit-Possessed Body?: Babylonian Medical Cosmology in the Hebrew Prophet Ezekiel" (paper presented at the Biennial Meeting of the Society for the Anthropology of Religion, San Diego, CA, 17 Apr, 2015), 1–2.

5.4 Unfamiliar Selves

In the previous chapter, I described two basic cultural models for understanding spirits in the Hebrew Bible, those of abiding and migrating spirits. I suggested that these models were differentiated not by their theological and anthropological ontology (e.g., a "soul" versus a "spirit," a "divine" spirit versus a "human" one, etc.) or by a particular moral charge (i.e., the good part of a person and the bad part) but simply by their effects on people. In some biblical literature these effects were conceived in terms of quiescence or movement. Abiding spirits provided the animating power of life and energized aspects of the inner life, such as desire and will. Migrating spirits meanwhile were more temporary and empowering—but also fickle. They were more likely to take some measure of control of a person, though rarely to the extent that the individual's personality would abscond completely. Even though these two models can be differentiated, it does not necessarily mean that they are mutually exclusive or rivaled. In fact, especially in late Second Temple literature, the crisis caused by a harmful spirit that lingers instead of moves on (or, conversely, the marvel of a newly arrived holy spirit that will never leave) becomes cause for focused attention.

In the section that follows, I will extend my analysis of this dichotomy by outlining a related body of texts where the two conceptions are intertwined. Beginning in texts of the Hebrew Bible that describe "circumcision of the heart" as a kind of moral renewal, I show how the addition of spirit language to such conceptions recasts this transformation as a type of spirit possession. In many of these inner transformation texts, the faulty components of the body (and of the self) have been unfamiliarized to such an extreme degree that the only solution to their lingering presence is exorcism.

5.4.1 Surgery on the Self

The image of circumcising the heart occurs frequently in biblical literature as a motif to describe inner moral transformation.[58] Given the ways in which this

---

[58] See an overview, Werner E. Lemke, "Circumcision of the Heart: The Journey of a Biblical Metaphor," in *A God So Near: Essays on Old Testament Theology in Honor of Patrick D. Miller*, ed. Brent A. Strawn and Nancy R. Bowen (Winona Lake, IN: Eisenbrauns, 2003), 299–319. See also, Thomas Krüger, "Das menschliche Herz und die Weisung Gottes: Elemente einer Diskussion über Möglichkeiten und Grenzen der Tora-Rezeption im Alten Testament," in *Rezeption und Auslegung im Altem Testament und in seinem Umfeld: ein Symposion aus Anlass des 60. Ge-

book has explored the materiality of self-language in biblical literature, the notion of a physical and moral surgery of this kind should not surprise us. Indeed, such an idea need not be wholly figurative but likely reflects a cognitive model for the anatomical location of volition, one not dissimilar from those that inform the Mesopotamian medical texts discussed above.

Although the motif of the circumcised heart is recurring, it is not always employed to the same affect—not even within the same book. We see this, for example, in Deuteronomy:

> [12] So now, O Israel, what does the Lord your God require of you? Only to fear the Lord your God, to walk in all his ways, to love him, to serve the Lord your God with all your heart and with all your soul, [13] and to keep the commandments of the Lord your God and his decrees that I am commanding you today, for your own well-being... [16] Circumcise, then, the foreskin of your heart, and do not be stubborn any longer. (Deut 10:12–13, 16; cf. Lev 26:41)

In this occurrence of the motif, the Israelites are adjured to circumcise their own hearts; that is, to see that they maintain their relationship with God through obedience, devotion, and fear of the Lord. These emphases are consistent with other parts of the hortatory prologue (Deut 5–11) and with much of Deuteronomy more broadly.

In a subsequent occurrence of the motif in Deuteronomy, however, this "self-surgery" aspect is upended. It is God, and not Israel, that accomplishes this moral surgery on the self:

> Moreover, the Lord your God will circumcise your heart and the heart of your descendants, so that you will love the Lord your God with all your heart and with all your soul, in order that you may live. (Deut 30:6)

The subtle but significant shift is easy to miss since the language in Deut 10:12–16 and 30:6 is so similar. Yet as Marc Brettler pointed out over twenty years ago, in Deut 30 we are not in the genre of sermon but of something more like prophecy.[59] Verses 1a–2, which concern acts of returning/repenting (שו״ב) on the part of Israel, are typically understood as the protasis of a condi-

---

burtstags von Odil Hannes Steck, ed. Reinhard G. Kratz and Thomas Krüger, OBO 153 (Göttingen: Universitätsverlag, 1997), 65–92.

[59] *Contra* popular interpretations which cast the passage as a conditional. Marc Zvi Brettler, "Predestination in Deuteronomy 30.1–10," in *Those Elusive Deuteronomists: The Phenomenon of Pan-Deuteronomism*, ed. Linda S. Schearing and Steven L. McKenzie, JSOT 268 (Sheffield: Sheffield Academic Press, 1999), 171–88. See a more recent discussion critiquing what he calls the assumption of a modern idea of agency in Lambert, *How Repentance Became Biblical*, 123–24.

tional statement (i.e., *if* you repent; cf., NRSV). Brettler argued, however, these verses are better understood as part of the apodosis (i.e., *then* you *will* repent).⁶⁰ Returning/repenting to God, then, is not a necessary condition for restoration but a foreshadowing of it. Moreover, instead of obedience guaranteeing the circumcised state of the heart (Deut 10), it is the circumcised heart that makes obedience possible (Deut 30).

We see a similar interpretive movement with regard to circumcised hearts in the book of Jeremiah, and it is likely that these passages from both books influenced one another in their respective histories of composition.⁶¹

> Circumcise yourselves to the LORD,
> remove the foreskin of your hearts,
> O people of Judah and inhabitants of Jerusalem,
> or else my wrath will go forth like fire,
> and burn with no one to quench it,
> because of the evil of your doings. (Jer 4:4)

Here the prophet has adapted the language of circumcision into a metaphor for willful orientation either toward or away from God's will. The image appears elsewhere in Jeremiah as well. In chapter 6, the reference is not to one's heart but to ears that are not able to listen (Jer 6:10; cf., Exod 6:12). In chapter 9, Judah is included in a list of nations that are circumcised "only in the foreskin" (Jer 9:24). Indeed "all the house of Israel" is specified as "uncircumcised in heart" (Jer 9:25).

The tone of these passages in Jeremiah is similar to that of Deut 10:16 in that God's people are either charged to complete their own inner organ circumcision or promised punishment for failing to do so. But, just as in Deuteronomy, there is another place in the book where the prophet identifies God as the agent for triggering internal moral transformation:

> ³³ But this is the covenant that I will make with the house of Israel after those days, says the LORD: I will put my *tōrâ*⁶² within them, and I will write it on their hearts; and I will be their God, and they shall be my people. ³⁴ No longer shall they teach one another, or say to each other, "Know the LORD," for they shall all know me, from the least of them to the greatest,

---

60 In Hebrew, it is ambiguous. However, comparative evidence from related biblical passages as well as early interpretive tradition suggest this reading (e.g., Neh 1:6–11 and 4QMMT [4Q398 11 13:1–7]). Brettler, "Predestination in Deuteronomy 30.1–10," 175–78.
61 See Lemke, "Circumcision of the Heart," 300–07. Lev 26:41 may be a connected text, though Krüger makes the case that it is later, Krüger, "Das menschliche Herz…," 80.
62 NRSV: "law".

says the LORD; for I will forgive their iniquity, and remember their sin no more. (Jer 31:33–34)

Here, the language of circumcision is absent, but the metaphorical connection between moral transformation and organ modification remains. God, the divine surgeon-scribe, writes the *tōrâ* upon the peoples' hearts, thereby cementing their covenantal relationship. As if to emphasize the complete elimination of Israel's agency in the endeavor, God's act even abolishes the need for teachers of God's *tōrâ*. With this new and modified heart, Israel will no longer be physically capable of regarding the word of the LORD as a reproach and of failing to take pleasure in it (Jer 6:10; cf. Jer 32:37–41). All will simply know God by heart.[63]

The motif of metaphorically or metaphysically circumcising parts of the inner body and sense organs continued well into the late Second Temple period. See, for example, not only the circumcised "heart" (1QpHab 11:12–13; 1QS 5:25–26), but also "lips" (1QH^a 10:9, 20) and "ear" (1QH^a 21:6).[64] Early Christian groups also took up the imagery:

> Rather, a person is a Jew who is one inwardly, and real circumcision is a matter of the heart— it is spiritual and not literal. Such a person receives praise not from others but from God. (Rom 2:29 NRSV; cf. Ep. Barn. 9:1–8; 10:12)

Of special note is 1QS, which describes the circumcision of the inner "inclination" (יצר):

> ⁴… Let no man walk in the stubbornness of his heart so as to go astray after his heart ⁵ and his eyes and the thought of his inclination (מחשבת יצרו)! Rather, they shall circumcise in the community the foreskin of their inclination and of their stiff neck that they may lay a foundation of truth for Israel, for the community of the eternal covenant. (1QS 5:4b–5)[65]

---

63 "In its more pessimistic moments, biblical literature seems to doubt that human beings can bring about the necessary internalization or refortification on their own.... To get Israel back into the mode of covenantal service therefore requires nothing less than God's own gracious intervention, an act of divine *ḥesed* that replaces their hardened disposition or, as some biblical texts put it, their 'uncircumcised heart,' with an orientation that facilitates the love of him." Jon D. Levenson, *The Love of God: Divine Gift, Human Gratitude, and Mutual Faithfulness in Judaism* (Princeton: Princeton University Press, 2016), 27.
64 See also more fragmentary examples: 4Q177 9 8 and 4Q504 4 11.
65 Cf. the version in 4QS^d, which does not have the idea of circumcising "the foreskin of their inclination." Metso, *The Community Rule*, 27.

The "inclination" (יצר) is discussed in more detail below. For now, it is enough to recognize the wide-ranging deployment of this more idiomatic understanding of "circumcision" and to begin to examine its implications with regard to spirit possession.

Envisioning God, and not the self, as mohel for the inner moral organ was not the only adaptation of this motif in biblical literature. In particular, biblical writers came to describe the spirit as also needing modification. Such an interpretive move should not be surprising. As already discussed in chapter three, the heart and spirit frequently function together in the Hebrew Bible to indicate a variety of aspects of self-reflection, including motivation, enthusiasm, and thought life (e.g., Pss 77:7; 78:8; 143:4; Isa 57:15; Zech 7:12). It would follow that any alterations to the heart might eventually be applied also to the spirit. Yet in this transfer, cultural models for describing spirit phenomena also become available and with them new ways of conceiving of inner transformation beyond circumcision. These include spirit renewal, spirit exchange, and eventually exorcism.

5.4.2 Transplanting the Spirit Organ

The motif of divine body modification becomes a type of spirit possession, not only through the addition of spirit language but also through its function as a platform for conceiving of God's presence and absence. In many texts, especially those originating in the postexilic and Second Temple periods, God's immanence comes to be seen not just as *contingent upon* but actually *determinative of* the status of Israel's spirit. Nathan MacDonald has characterized texts in this tradition as reflecting "a hope of a new inner disposition."[66] He suggests that

> Many of those who wrote in the Persian period had the sense that God's presence had eluded them and that Israel's experience fell short of what she had known prior to the fall of Jerusalem. Consequently, in this period the hope was expressed that God's spirit would be active more widely, amongst all Israelites and perhaps even the whole world. This hope was typically expressed as something that would occur at, or as a precursor to, the breaking in of God's final salvation.[67]

---

[66] MacDonald, "The Spirit of YHWH."
[67] MacDonald, "The Spirit of YHWH," 107–08.

Emblematic of this movement are texts that turn towards recognizing the spirit *in addition to* (and eventually *instead of*) the heart as the foundation of moral orientation. MacDonald sees the book of Ezekiel as a turning point in this regard.[68]

Although the aforementioned texts from Deuteronomy and Jeremiah utilize the motif primarily with reference to the heart, the book of Ezekiel introduces spirit language as a new element.[69] The association appears prominently in three occurrences:

> [19] I will give them one heart, and put a new spirit within them; I will remove the heart of stone from their flesh and give them a heart of flesh, [20] so that they may follow my statutes and keep my ordinances and obey them. Then they shall be my people, and I will be their God. (Ezek 11:19–20)
>
> Cast away from you all the transgressions that you have committed against me, and get yourselves a new heart and a new spirit! Why will you die, O house of Israel? (Ezek 18:31)
>
> [26] A new heart I will give you, and a new spirit I will put within you; and I will remove from your body the heart of stone and give you a heart of flesh. [27] I will put my spirit within you, and make you follow my statutes and be careful to observe my ordinances. (Ezek 36:26–27)[70]

As in Jeremiah and Deuteronomy, Ezekiel has examples both of Israel enacting (or being urged to enact) their own inner transformation (Ezek 18:31) and God enacting it (Ezek 11:19–20 and 36:26–27).

Two innovations are notable in the Ezekiel texts. First, Ezekiel has couched these moral transformations in spirit language: it is not enough for Israel to modify their heart—they must also obtain a new spirit. Second, in contrast to Deuteronomy and Jeremiah, the moral organ has not simply been circumcised or written upon, but completely replaced. As Jacqueline Lapsley observes,

> The language of the new heart and the new spirit most clearly reveals what is at stake for Ezekiel: the *internal* recreation of the people. The language of the heart transplant reveals the deep concern for a total transformation of the inner life... The distinctly human quality of the heart ... and the distinctly divine origin of the heart make for a curious image. A heart truly human in substance must be wholly divine in origin.[71]

---

[68] MacDonald, "The Spirit of YHWH," 103.
[69] It is likely that Ezekiel was the first to introduce the idea of spirit to this motif. On the literary relationships, see Anja Klein, *Schriftauslegung im Ezechielbuch: redaktionsgeschichtliche Untersuchungen zu Ez 34–39*, BZAW 391 (Berlin: De Gruyter, 2008) esp. 81–110.
[70] Klein points out that Ezek 36:23b–32 is missing from an early textual witness in the Greek (Pap. 967), suggesting that this portion may be a later addition. Klein, "From the 'Right Spirit' to the 'Spirit of Truth,'" 174.
[71] Lapsley, *Can These Bones Live?*, 165–66. Emphasis in the original.

The transformation is reminiscent of Saul's coronation narrative, where the change is specifically associated with spirit possession: "God gave him another heart" (ויהפך־לו אלהים לב אחר, 1 Sam 10:9) and "a spirit of God seized him" (ותצלח עליו רוח אלהים, 1 Sam 10:10, *my translation*). In 1 Sam 10, the transformation empowers Saul to lead Israel as military commander and king. By contrast, as Lapsley points out, the emphasis in Ezekiel is not on the resulting power or might, but on the divine origin of the new heart itself.

In prescribing a complete transplant for both the heart and the spirit, the prophet has gone beyond language merely in the mode of "spirit as other." Coping with or even healing the damage is no longer an option. The heart and spirit have become so morally problematic that they must be removed completely. This transformation prescribed by Ezekiel, especially in chapter 36, is nothing short of a prophecy of spirit possession. It is described, however, not as a narrative of ritual but as a pneumatic, quasi-medical procedure.

In Ps 51, the casting of inner moral transformation as a spirit possession phenomenon is even more pronounced.

> [12] Create in me a clean heart (לב טהור ברא), O God,
> and put a new and right spirit within me (רוח נכון חדש בקרבי).
> [13] Do not cast me away from your presence,
> and do not take your holy spirit from me (ורוח קדשך אל־תקח ממני).
> [14] Restore to me the joy of your salvation,
> and sustain in me a willing spirit (ורוח נדיבה תסמכני). (Ps 51:12–14 [NRSV. vv. 10–12])

Anja Klein has argued that Ps 51 is literarily dependent on Ezek 36:26–27 and that it represents a further evolution on the continuum of inner moral transformation texts:

> Considering the exegetical trail that leads from Jeremiah 31 via Ezekiel 36 to Psalm 51, an increasing interest in the spirit can be discerned: While the new covenant in Jeremiah solely intends an inner restoration of the heart, the new heart is supplemented with the new spirit in Ezekiel 36, and Psalm 51 eventually speaks of the new creation, in which the clean heart steps back in favour of the spiritual disposition.[72]

In particular, the psalmist's use of the verb "create" (בר״א) in verse 12 is conspicuous since the term is almost exclusively associated with God's creative power. Thus, in Ps 51, the psalmist casts the renewal of the spirit as a fundamental act of creation.

---

72 Klein, "From the 'Right Spirit' to the 'Spirit of Truth,'" 176.

The word "spirit" occurs four times in Ps 51: (1) an "upright spirit" (רוח נכון, v. 12); (2) "[God's] holy spirit" (רוח קדשך, v. 13); (3) a "willing spirit" (רוח נדיבה, v. 14); and (4) a "broken spirit" (רוח נשברה, v. 19). Especially because the passage is poetry, any attempt to track pneumatological distinctions between each term would be difficult to control methodologically. Even so, in light of the spirit traditions upon which the Psalm is dependent, a certain coordination of old models can be discerned. In verse 12, the plea for God to renew an upright spirit is paired with a prayer for a clean heart. It is likely that the two organs function here as synonymous parallels. Further, this pairing in Ps 51 is reminiscent of what I have called the abiding model for spirits; that is, following the promise of Ezek 36:26, the psalmist in verse 12 requests a renewal of the very organ(s), heart and spirit, that animate his life. We can interpret the reference to God's holy spirit in Ps 51:13 as the analogous animating organ of God's own being, its intervention having also been promised (i.e., "my spirit" in Ezek 36:27). The "willing spirit" of verse 14, then, is what results when God's holy spirit migrates to and abides within the psalmist. But what does the prescribed spirit transformation now enable the psalmist to do? We can see one answer through the lens of the expansive interpretive history of this passage.

For over two millennia, Jews and Christians have understood Ps 51 as a paradigmatic text for understanding repentance.[73] We see this trend already in the supplementary superscription, which situates the text as David's response to Nathan's moral chastisement following the Bathsheba debacle. Yet despite the roles that Ps 51 has played ritually and theologically for modeling and enacting penitential acts throughout the centuries, ultimately the psalmist is profoundly pessimistic about humanity's ability to restore itself to right moral status. In its plain sense, the Psalm acknowledges that the only actual hope is that God might miraculously intervene. David Lambert has thus argued that Ps 51 should be characterized not as a "penitential" psalm but as a "plea for help just like other prayers."[74] Indeed, Ps 51 describes a kind of repentance that is accomplished without human agency—a complete abdication of personal will. Lacking even the correct

---

[73] David Lambert has questioned whether this is an accurate reading of Ps 51, and indeed, whether the traditional theological idea of repentance is appropriate to ascribe to any biblical text. Lambert, *How Repentance Became Biblical*, 39, 62, 65. This argument is rooted in Lambert's belief that the biblical texts do not portray the idea of a "self" in any way that could be meaningfully discussed by modern interpreters. In chapter three I dispute this idea and suggest that spirit language often functions as self-language in the Hebrew Bible. See Reed Carlson, "Review of Lambert, David A. *How Repentance Became Biblical: Judaism, Christianity, and the Interpretation of Scripture*," *SynTh* 3.6 (2016): 43–46.

[74] Lambert, *How Repentance Became Biblical*, 39.

moral organs to begin the process, the psalmist prays that these parts will be replaced by those of God's own creation.

In light of this renunciation of personal agency, it becomes apparent that, more than any other text discussed in this section, Ps 51 is the one most in line with that traditional idea of spirit possession in which a host's own volition is suspended. Put into Emma Cohen's terminology, it is indeed very close to "executive" possession.[75] Yet it is a spirit possession not feared or resisted but actively sought out and earnestly prayed for.

Spirit language appears again in verses 18–19 as part of a critique of rituals of sacrifice.

> [18] For you have no delight in sacrifice;
> if I were to give a burnt offering, you would not be pleased.
> [19] The sacrifice acceptable to God is a broken spirit;
> a broken and contrite heart, O God, you will not despise. (Ps 51:18–19 [NRSV vv. 16–17])

It is unlikely that Ps 51 rejects the entirety of the cult in these verses. Rather, this is a more limited critique, asserting that conventional sacrifice should not be practiced without accompanying spiritual transformation. In this, these stanzas evoke a well-established strain of prophetic tradition in the Hebrew Bible, which excoriates the cult for carrying out sacrifices without also maintaining societal justice (e.g., Isa 1:10–17; Hos 6:6; Amos 5:21–24; Mic 6:6–8).[76] Psalm 51, however, does not mention prophetic highpoints like rescuing the oppressed or having justice roll down like waters. Rather, the contingency for effective sacrifice is not social justice, but rather the sacrifice of one's "broken spirit" (רוח נשברה).[77] Recalling verses 12–14, the psalmist can only attain such a state through divine intervention and spirit possession.

In problematizing his own spirit, the psalmist has "othered" an aspect of the self to such an excessive degree that it has become unfamiliar. The internal spirit is compromised, and only an outside force can remedy it. In this case, the out-

---

[75] Cohen, "What is Spirit Possession?," 110–14.
[76] See Ronald S. Hendel, "Away from Ritual: The Prophetic Critique," in *Social Theory and the Study of Israelite Religion: Essays in Retrospect and Prospect*, ed. Saul M. Olyan (Atlanta: SBL Press, 2012), 59–79; Bryan D. Bibb, "The Prophetic Critique of Ritual in Old Testament Theology," in *The Priests in the Prophets: The Portrayal of Priests, Prophets and Other Religious Specialists in the Latter Prophets*, ed. Lester L. Grabbe and Alice Ogden Bellis, JSOTSup 408 (London: T&T Clark, 2004), 31–43. I am grateful to Ethan Schwartz for alerting me to the substantial connection between Ps 51 and this tradition.
[77] The foil for the "broken spirit" (רוח נשברה) may be that of the "stubborn" or "stiff-necked" spirit (קש″ה; e.g., Deut 2:30).

side force is another spirit, a holy one, which originates with God. Although Ps 51 is not describing an exorcism explicitly, we can see that, phenomenologically, all of the necessary pieces are there. Indeed, subsequent Second Temple period interpreters made use of the psalm in just this way.

We see this interpretive tradition continuing, for example, in 4QBarkhi Nafshi, a nonsectarian fragmentary prayer text found at Qumran that was composed no later than the second–first centuries BCE.[78] Like the biblical texts discussed above, Barkhi Nafshi utilizes the motif of inner body modification to indicate God's mediation, but in this text the interventions have become even more severe.

> [5]... You have commanded my heart, and my inmost parts you have taught well, lest your statutes be forgotten [6] [On my heart] you [have enjoined] your law, on my inmost parts you have engraved it; and you have prevailed upon me, so that I pursue after you[r] ways. (4Q436 1 i 5b–6)[79]

---

[78] This date was obtained paleographically since the text contains minimal internal chronological indicators. David Rolph Seely, "Barkhi Nafshi," *EDSS* 1:76–77; "The Barki Nafshi Texts (4Q434–439)," in *Current Research and Technological Developments on the Dead Sea Scrolls: Conference on the Texts from the Judean Desert, Jerusalem, 30 April, 1995*, ed. D. W. Parry and S. D. Rick (Leiden: Brill, 1996), 194–214, 206–08; "The 'Circumcised Heart' in '4Q434 Barki Nafshi,'" *RevQ* 17.1–4 (1996): 527–35; Lawrence H. Schiffman et al., eds., "Implanting Pious Qualities as a Theme in the Barkhi Nafshi Hymns," in *The Dead Sea Scrolls Fifty Years after Their Discovery: Proceedings of the Jerusalem Congress, July 20–25, 1997* (Jerusalem: Israel Exploration Society, 2000), 322–31; George J. Brooke, "Body Parts in Barkhi Nafshi and the Qualifications for Membership of the Worshipping Community," in *Sapiential, Liturgical and Poetical Texts from Qumran: Proceedings of the Third Meeting of the International Organization for Qumran Studies, Oslo, 1998*, ed. Daniel K. Falk, Florentino García Martínez, and Eileen M. Schuller, STDJ 35 (Leiden: Brill, 2000), 79–94; Rosen-Zvi, *Demonic Desires*; Brand, *Evil Within and Without*, 44–48; Menahem Kister, "Body and Purification from Evil: Prayer Formulas and Concepts in Second Temple Literature and Their Relationship to Later Rabbinic Literature," *Megillot* (2010): 243–84; Eibert Tigchelaar, "The Evil Inclination in The Dead Sea Scrolls, with a Re-Edition of 4Q468I (4QSectarian Text?)," in *Empsychoi Logoi: Religious Innovations in Antiquity; Studies in Honour of Pieter Willem van Der Horst*, ed. Alberdina Houtman, Albert de Jong, and Magda Misset-van de Weg, AJEC 73 (Brill: Leiden, 2008), 347–55; and Daniel K. Falk, "Willing Heart and Broken Spirit: Psalm 51 in the Dead Sea Scrolls," in *Reading the Bible in Ancient Traditions and Modern Editions: Studies in Memory of Peter W. Flint*, ed. Andrew B. Perrin et al. (Atlanta: SBL Press, 2017), 521–48.

[79] Text and translations of Barkhi Nafshi are based on Moshe Weinfeld and David Rolph Seely, "4QBarkhi Nafshi," in *Qumran Cave 4.XX Poetical and Liturgical Texts, Part 2*, ed. E. G. Chazon et al.; DJD 29 (Oxford: Clarendon, 1999), 255–334.

Working along the same trajectory as other texts I have discussed in this section, Barkhi Nafshi quotes, alludes to, or otherwise integrates Deut 30, Jer 31, Ezek 36, and Ps 51.[80] It does so in order to describe God's act of repairing the petitioner's faulty moral organs.

However, the poet in Barkhi Nafshi also extends this interpretive trajectory, going beyond the individual moral organ transplant described in previous texts by systematically disassembling the human body. The poet lists each problematic part and notes how it has been modified. What was only a spirit and heart transplant in Ps 51, becomes a complete moral overhaul in Barkhi Nafshi:

> ^{i 10} [the heart of stone] you have [e]xorcized from me (לב האבן ג[ערתה ממני])[81], and have set a pure heart in its place. The evil inclination [you] have exorcized[82] [from my inner parts] (יצר רע גער[תה מן כליותי) ^{ii 1} [and a ho]ly [spirit] (ורוח קוד[ש])[83] you have set in my heart. Adulterousness of the eyes you have removed from me, and it gazed upon [all] ² [your ways. The s]tiffness of neck you have sent away from me, and you had made it into humility. Wrathful anger you have removed [from me, and have set] ³ [in me a spirit of lo]ng-suffering. Haughtiness of heart and arrogance of eyes you have for[got]ten to reckon to me. [A spirit of deceit] ⁴ [you have destroyed] and a [bro]ken heart you have given to me. The inclina[tion... (4Q436 1 i 10–ii 4; cf., 4Q435 2 i 1–5)

The word "exorcize" or "rebuke" (גע״ר), which appears twice here, is especially conspicuous. In Aramaic as well as Hebrew, the verb can have a moral-medical connotation, as in, for example, the Genesis Apocryphon, where Abraham "exorcizes" (גע״ר) Pharaoh's skin disease (1Q20:27–29). Elsewhere it has a distinctly militant overtone, as in, for example, God's eschatological act of banishing Belial and his armies in the War Scroll (1QM 14:10).[84] Evoking nuances from both contexts, the poet in Barkhi Nafshi uses the verb to describe how God has exorcized a part of the body.[85]

The first exorcism described in this passage expels what text critics have suggested is a "heart of stone" (cf. Ezek 36:26). If this reconstruction is correct, it is notable that the subsequent replacement heart is described not as "flesh" (as we might expect from reading Ezekiel) but rather as one that is "pure." Informed by Ps 51, it would seem that 4QBarkhi Nafshi has conflated notions of purity with

---

80 See Seely, "The 'Circumcised Heart' in '4Q434 Barki Nafshi,'" and Brooke, "Body Parts."
81 Weinfeld and Seely render this, "you have removed from me," "4QBarkhi Nafshi," 299.
82 Weinfeld and Seely render this, "[you] have driven with rebukes," "4QBarkhi Nafshi," 299.
83 Weinfeld and Seely render this, "the spirit of ho]liness."
84 Tigchelaar connects this to God's "rebuke" גע״ר of the satan in Zech 3:2. Tigchelaar, "The Evil Inclination in The Dead Sea Scrolls," 73:351–52.
85 As an additional benefit, the exchanges described in Barkhi Nafshi also provide a practical defense against נגע, "plague" (4Q434 1 i 10–11).

those of righteousness and prescribed exorcism as the most effective way to obtain both within the self.

The second exorcism mentioned in this section expels an "evil inclination" (יצר רע), and it reveals the end result of such exhaustive self-othering in the poem. As Miryam Brand argues,

> [...] in 4Q436 1 i–ii the evil inclination is paralleled on the one hand with the heart and on the other with sinful inclination such as the "lechery of eyes" removed by God in 4Q436 1 ii.1. This indicates that despite the use of the verb *g'r*, the *yēṣer raʿ* here is an *internal* evil inclination and not an external spirit.[86]

This internal spirit, then, is a possessing, detrimental spirit, with symptoms consistent with what many might call a demon. It causes pain both mental and physical and manipulates its host into engaging in unwanted thoughts and actions (in this case sin and disobedience). The twist on the conventional formula, however, is that this demon originated within the person rather than invading it from outside.

Ishay Rosen-Zvi in his book *Demonic Desires* has treated the "evil inclination" extensively, tracing it through its relatively infrequent occurrences in biblical and Second Temple Jewish literature into its maturing as a complex theological concept in rabbinic sources.[87] Rosen-Zvi argues that the Qumran texts occupy a middle ground between biblical notions of the *yeṣer* as "thoughts" or "plans" and those of rabbinic literature as a reified, quasi-independent being.[88]

Against this backdrop, Rosen-Zvi notes that the *yeṣer* in 4QBarkhi Nafshi is treated differently from other internal components in this passage. The "evil inclination" is not repaired, replaced, or fortified, but removed completely. This usage dovetails with the only other place in the extant Dead Sea Scrolls where the phrase occurs:

> 15 אל תשלט בי שטן ורוח טמאה מכאוב ויצר 16 רע אל ירשו בעצמי
> [15] Let not Satan rule over me, nor an unclean spirit;
> Neither let pain nor the [16] evil inclination take possession of my bones. (11QPsalms Scroll[a] [11Q5] 19:15–16)[89]

---

[86] Brand, *Evil Within and Without*, 47.
[87] Rosen-Zvi, *Demonic Desires*.
[88] Rosen-Zvi, *Demonic Desires*, 44.
[89] Text and translation follows J. A. Sanders, *The Psalms Scroll of Qumrân Cave 11*, DJD 4 (Oxford: Clarendon, 1965), 76–79.

From the perspective of these two Dead Sea Scroll *yeṣer* texts, it would seem that although every human is born with a *yeṣer*, we could live just fine (or better) without it. This is in contrast to the "heart" and "spirit," which cannot be removed completely but only replaced.[90] In this, we might tentatively liken the *yeṣer* to an inflamed appendix, which now causes more trouble than it is worth and must be removed. The fact that this troublesome component finds its mythic origin within the person rather than from the heavens does not diminish its damage or alter the prescribed treatment it shares with that of demonic possession: exorcism.

5.5 Holy Spirits as Preventative Care

A recurring phenomenon across communities both ancient and modern that practice dualism-informed spirit possession and exorcism is the problem of persistent antagonistic spirit influence. Put simply, if an exorcist claims that a person has been made free of adverse spiritual conditions, how do they make sense of the fact that sometimes the old circumstances return? Contrary to what some readers may expect, crises of this nature are not usually destabilizing forces in such communities. Rather, these episodes are often the very occasions when leaders establish their spiritual expertise and reinforce community identity. In this final discussion of the book, I demonstrate the evidence for these negotiations in early Jewish texts where God's holy spirit functions primarily as a possessing and exorcizing agent. In describing the activities of such a spirit, these texts achieve the essential tasks of mapping out community boundaries and establishing religious authority.

Before displaying these dynamics at work in biblical texts, we will consider a loose contemporary parallel: the long-standing theological debate among Pentecostal Christians over whether "born-again" and "[Holy] Spirit-filled" Christians are susceptible to demonic possession. As Jörg Haustein has argued, this debate reveals both a fundamental disagreement over the nature of the self (particularly in its relation to one's body) and a strategic tolerance for spiritual ambiguity—this, despite the firm dualism of traditional Pentecostal pneumatology.[91] In the context of his ethnographic analysis of Pentecostals in Ethiopia, Haustein outlined how church members frequently adduce the finality of casting out demons

---

90 Kister, "Body and Purification from Evil," 243–84.
91 Jörg Haustein, "Embodying the Spirit(s): Pentecostal Demonology and Deliverance Discourse in Ethiopia," *Ethnos* 76.4 (2011): 534–52.

in Jesus's name as one of the defining characteristics of Pentecostal exorcism.[92] Their purpose, in part, is to make a special point of contrast to traditional *zār* rituals and other rival treatments, which must sometimes be repeated (and might even then provide only measured relief). Claiming improvement upon the limited effectiveness of traditional practices, the majority of Ethiopian Pentecostals assert that their method of exorcism is needed only once. They account for the difference not only due to the immense power ascribed to the name of Jesus, but also to the presence of the Holy Spirit within the born-again Christian's body, which precludes the cohabitation of any other kind of spirit.

Despite this official line, a significant minority, which Haustein (following Thomas Csordas) labeled "deliverance Pentecostals," claim that regular entanglement with demonic forces in the forms of illness, mental distress, and excessive emotion are part of each Christian's lifelong spiritual battle. Through case studies, Haustein demonstrated that beneath the outer layer of doctrinal uniformity, a substantial amount of spiritual ambiguity persists, which he argued is the result of practical necessity and tenacious counter-doctrinal experience. Pentecostal Christians who have experienced the infilling of the Holy Spirit (as evidenced by the miraculous gift of speaking-in-tongues) are still at times tormented by their old spirits, suffering physically, mentally, or emotionally. Such relapses (which evoke Jesus's parable of the return of the unclean spirit, Luke 11:24–26/Matt 12:43–45) call into question the efficacy of the original deliverance and provoke cognitively dissonant interrogation: *Is this a repossession, or was the old exorcism just incomplete? Was it really the Holy Spirit that caused me to enter an ecstatic state, or was it instead a deceitful spirit mimicking God's work?* According to some voices, doctrinally speaking at least, such gray areas of spirit possession should be impossible. Nevertheless, the lived experiences of some Ethiopian Pentecostals can cause them to look elsewhere for spiritual help.

As Haustein argued, this communal negotiation and interpretation of spiritual anomalies has as much to do with establishing religious authority as it does with providing spiritual therapy. Far from undermining such structures, spiritual uncertainty creates a need for the careful "discernment" of spirits. This is the realm in which leaders can arise as spirit experts, dictating which phenomena are the result of holy or demonic spirits, what communal or individual behaviors have led to the activity of such presences, and what steps the community might take in order to ameliorate them. When the coordination of unseen spirit activity is a necessary precursor for authority, exposition on theological anthro-

---

92 Haustein, "Embodying the Spirit(s)," 538.

pology becomes more than just speculation on the metaphysical nature of being a human in relation to the divine. It is also a negotiation of power, a way of claiming one's own mastery in perceiving spiritual realities that others miss.

This case study taken from Pentecostal communities in Ethiopia demonstrates how persistent antagonistic spirit influence can cause both problems and opportunities for religious communities that practice spirit possession and exorcism. It can also prove instructive for our analysis of early Jewish spirit texts, where we see analogous issues. To be clear, in drawing this parallel, I do not assume an equivalence between what an Ethiopian Pentecostal might mean when they say, "Holy Spirit" and what such a phrase could mean when translated from a Second Temple era text. The parallel is drawn not along the lines of theological or dogmatic belief but of performed religious experience.

This latter point is important to clarify, given the legacy of misleading Christian interpretation of Old Testament spirit passages (see my comments in chapter 1). Yet, although caution against anachronistic Nicene interpretation is more than warranted, it should not prevent us from recognizing that some early Jewish literature did indeed attribute a distinct moral and cultic function to God's holy spirit. The flourishing of such speculation in some Jewish circles of the Second Temple period undoubtedly contributed to the fascination that early Christian interpreters had with holy spirits.[93]

With this disclaimer in place, we might wonder what the term "holy spirit" signifies in early Jewish literature. The Hebrew phrase most frequently rendered into English as "holy spirit" is the construct chain רוח קדש. It appears only three times in the Hebrew Bible: twice in Isa 63:10–11 and once in Ps 51:13. In all three occurrences it is referred to as *God's* holy spirit using a pronominal suffix, "your" (רוח קדשך) or "his" (רוח קדשו).[94] In Isaiah 63, it would seem that the phrase "holy spirit" describes God's persistent presence with Israel in the wilderness, a reference to God's own abiding spirit.[95] In Ps 51, God's holy spirit has a primarily exorcistic or apotropaic purpose: by replacing the existing faulty moral organs, God's holy spirit makes the psalmist's body uninhabitable for impure spirits (and perhaps any other spirit at all).

A holy spirit is not the only spirit associated with God's person in the Hebrew Bible, nor the only one that God is capable of deploying. The "divine spirit" or "spirit of God"/"spirit of the LORD" are prominent examples, but there are oth-

---

[93] See, for example, the recent work by Levison, *The Holy Spirit before Christianity*.
[94] The phrase is best understood as an attributive genitive (i.e., "your holy spirit" and not "[the] spirit of [your] holiness"). See *IBHS* 9.5.3. An adjectival form is attested as well but only in later literature (e.g., רוח קדושה, 1QS 3:7; 4Q418 8:6). The OG is adjectival: τὸ πνεῦμα τὸ ἅγιον.
[95] It may also be a reference to the story of the seventy elders in Num 11:25–29.

ers.⁹⁶ Since this holy spirit is associated with God, it would be an understatement to call it ordinary. Even so, when compared to other types of spirits that we encounter in the Hebrew Bible, God's holy spirit is one of many.

This changes in later Second Temple Jewish literature, however—especially in the Dead Sea Scrolls. Not only do the Dead Sea Scrolls contain more references to God's holy spirit, but they also distinguish it more sharply. The Damascus Document, for example, attributes the activity of Israel's prophet to the work of God's holy spirit (CD 2:12, cf. 1QS 8:16). In 1QHᵃ, the poet prays that God's holy spirit might be a cleansing agent ridding the body of unrighteousness (1QHᵃ 8:30). This sanitizing function is even more pronounced in Barkhi Nafshi, where God's holy spirit effectively inoculates the poet against sin (4Q436 1 i 10–ii 4, see above).

The role that spirits play in the Treatise of the Two Spirits section of the Community Rule (1QS 3:13–4:26) is especially significant for this discussion since it seems to struggle directly with the problem of persistent spirit antagonism. God's holy spirit is mentioned only once (1QS 4:21), and it is two dualistically opposed spirits—the spirit of truth and that of perversity or falsehood—which play the major roles. Even so, the Treatise is preceded by a section concerning membership, where 1QS explicitly mandates possession by a holy spirit (1QS 3:6–9). As with other texts that mention multiple types of spirits in quick succession, the lines between such are often blurred, especially in subsequent interpretive tradition.

Scholarly opinion on the compositional history of the Treatise has evolved considerably since its discovery. Initially thought to depict one of the central theological doctrines of the sectarian community, subsequent scholarship has concluded that the Treatise is an independent composition that was inserted

---

96 The "divine spirit" or "spirit of God" (רוח אלהים, Num 24:2; 1 Sam 10:10; 11:6; 16:15–16, 23; 19:20, 23; Ezek 11:24; 2 Chr 15:1; 24:20; cf. רוח אלוה, Job 27:3; רוח־אל, Job 33:4); a/the "spirit of the LORD" (רוח [ה'], Jdg 3:10; 6:34; 11:29; 14:6, 19; 15:14; 1 Sam 10:6; 16:14; 2 Sam 23:2; 1 Kgs 18:12; 1 Kgs 22:24/2 Chr 18:23; Isa 11:2; 40:13; 63:14; Ezek 11:5; 37:1; Mic 3:8; 2 Chr 20:14; cf. Num 11:29; Isa 59:21); a "harmful spirit" (רוח רעה, Jdg 9:23; cf. 1 Sam 16:14–23; 18:10; 19:9); "lying spirit" (רוח שקר, 1 Kgs 22:23/2 Chr 18:22); "spirit of justice" (רוח משפט, Isa 4:4; 28:6); "spirit of wisdom and understanding" (רוח חכמה ובינה, Isa 11:2); "spirit of counsel and might" (רוח עצה וגבורה, Isa 11:2); "spirit of knowledge and the fear of the LORD" (רוח דעת ויראת [ה'], Isa 11:2); "spirit of confusion" (רוח עועים, Isa 19:14); "spirit of deep sleep" (רוח תרדמה, Isa 29:10); "spirit of compassion and mercy" (רוח חן ותחנונים, Zech 12:10); and "new spirit" (רוח חדשה, Ezek 11:19; 36:26). My translations.

5.5 Holy Spirits as Preventative Care — 157

into the document relatively late in the compositional history of 1QS.[97] Such a reconstruction suggests that scholars should consider the likelihood that the Treatise is more a response to the practices of the community than it is their theological foundation.

The subject matter of the Treatise is provocative: two diametrically opposed spirits are said to influence human beings, dictating their behaviors and determining their fates:

> [17]... He created man to rule [18] all the world, and he assigned two spirits to him that he might walk by them until the appointed time of his visitation; they are the spirits [19] of truth and of injustice. From a spring of light come the generations of truth, and from a well of darkness the generations of injustice. [20] Control over all the sons of righteousness lies in the hand of the prince of lights, and they walk in the ways of light; complete control over the sons of injustice lies in the hand of the angel [21] of darkness, and they walk in the ways of darkness. It is through the angels of darkness that all the sons of righteousness go astray, [22] and all their sins, their iniquities, their guilt, and their deeds of transgression are under his control [23] in the mysteries of God until his time. (1QS 3:17b–23a)

Scholars have appropriately recognized this moral-cosmological outlook as "dualistic."[98] Even so, the Treatise takes important steps to avoid complete separation. First, and most definitively, God is portrayed as the ultimate source of both spirits. Second, and more subtly, the Treatise explains that God has allowed the spirit of perversity and his lot to antagonize the children of righteousness "in the mysteries of God until his time" (לפי רזי אל עד קצו, 1QS 3:23). As Miryam Brand has observed, the Treatise takes the unusual step of attributing *all* the iniquities of the children of light to these spirits.[99] Moreover, in contrast to Barkhi Nafshi, although the Treatise does discuss an eventual purification from all sin, it is not set to be accomplished until God's appointed era begins in the future. In the meantime, the children of righteousness must struggle against the hostile spiritual forces within that cause them to sin.

---

97 See summary in Charlotte Hempel, "The Treatise on the Two Spirits and the Literary History of the Rule of the Community," in *Dualism in Qumran*, ed. Géza G. Xeravits, LSTS 76 (London: T & T Clark, 2010), 102–20.
98 E.g., Mladen Popović, "Light and Darkness in the Treatise on the Two Spirits (1QS III 13–IV 26) and in 4Q186," in *Dualism in Qumran*, ed. Géza G. Xeravits, LSTS 76 (London: T & T Clark, 2010), 148–65; and Loren T. Stuckenbruck, "The Interiorization of Dualism within the Human Being in Second Temple Judaism: The Treatise of the Two Spirits (1QS III:13–IV:26) in its Tradition-Historical Context," in *Light against Darkness: Dualism in Ancient Mediterranean Religion and the Contemporary World*, ed. Armin Lange (Göttingen: Vandenhoeck & Ruprecht, 2011), 145–68.
99 Brand, *Evil Within and Without*, 260.

This coexistence and dueling influence of spirits that are supposedly counteractive, parallels aspects of the Ethiopian Pentecostal situation that I have described above. Like the debates in this church today, the role of spirit discernment is utilized in the Treatise both to establish authority and to diagnose the enduring problems of spiritual ambiguity. Like the so-called deliverance Pentecostals, the Treatise describes the present time as one of metaphysical conflict for the faithful, when some spiritual battles may be won or lost, even as the ultimate outcome of the war is never in doubt. The spirits of darkness exist with the sole purpose of causing the sons of light to stumble (1QS 3:24). Tragically and seemingly incomprehensibly to all but God, they sometimes succeed. God's supernatural agents, meanwhile, grant excessive virtues and promise eternal rewards (1QS 4:2–8). Even so, for the present age at least, the best they can do is "help" (עזר, 1QS 3:24) the sons of light in their struggle.

Stepping back to consider the context of the Treatise in 1QS, I find it significant that the composition would make such an allowance for the sinful liability of the righteous, since 1QS and other related compositions contain strict expectations for members' behavior and ritual practice. Acknowledging the problem of persistent spirit antagonism, Loren Stuckenbruck has argued that the recurrent failure of members to live up to the expectations of the community may have been precisely what prompted the eventual inclusion/creation of the Treatise in 1QS in the first place:

> [The Treatise]'s theological anthropology, which envisions the human being as the battleground between cosmic forces, is an interiorization of a socio-religious conflict that, given the strict ideals of the community, could no longer be circumscribed by physical boundaries. The internalized socio-religious conflict does not at this stage, however, threaten the community with internal "de-combustion." The Treatise provided its original community, and subsequently the Qumran community, with a theological framework that enabled these groups to come to terms with discrepancies between the ideology and identity they claimed for themselves on the one hand and realities of what they experienced on the other.[100]

Some may criticize Stuckenbruck for oversimplifying the Treatise as little more than a practical compromise on the community's unreachable ideals. In light of Haustein's analysis, however, I choose to read it differently.

The factors behind why the Treatise may have been included in 1QS are undoubtedly complex. One of these could very well have been that the Treatise offered a compelling theological anthropology that made sense of religious expe-

---

[100] Stuckenbruck, "The Interiorization of Dualism within the Human Being in Second Temple Judaism."

rience in the community. Because both righteousness and sin were believed to result from pathological spirit possession of one kind or another, their constant coexistence among the supposedly holy-spirit-initiated required apologetic explanation. In acknowledging that the spirit of perversity still caused the sons of light to stumble, the sectarian community effectively demonized itself. The purpose behind such disparagement was therapeutic, however, since it contextualized spiritual failures within a broader eschatological narrative in which the ultimate victory of God's transformative power was never in doubt.

5.6 Conclusions

In this last chapter of the book, I have identified several trends in the spirit texts of the Hebrew Bible and traced how they developed in select examples of Second Temple Jewish literature. Specifically, I identified how medical language and spirit language exist side-by-side in this literature (as they do in contemporary spirit possession cults around the world), thereby creating discourses around therapy and group identity. I argued that the literary tradition of unfamiliarizing aspects of the self, which began in the Hebrew Bible, flourished in Second Temple Jewish literature, and offers a compelling phenomenological origin for notions of demonic possession and exorcism found in later Jewish and Christian literature. This theorized provenance is an alternative (or at least a complement) to the conventional assumption that notions of exorcism stem from increased speculation on the mythic origins of evil beings. I also suggested that before Christian theology went on to deify it, early Jewish groups conceived of God's holy spirit as a possessing power that would purify both the self and one's community morally and ritually by exorcising the influence of other kinds of (impure) spirits. In cultivating holy spirit possession, a person embodied carnally God's eschatological victory over the opposing powers threatening both the cosmos and the self.

As this is not only the conclusion to this chapter but also to the book, a few final comments on what I hope are the lasting contributions of the project are warranted.

First, in this monograph I have defined and illuminated "spirit phenomena" as a rich and underappreciated theological category in the Hebrew Bible. I have done so by mapping the functions of spirit language, rituals, and myths in biblical and in Second Temple literature. Whereas most studies of these phenomena aim to decode them using modern categories, I have applied models from cultural anthropology and ethnography on possession, trance, and other similar practices from around the world in order to reveal functions not usually associated with spirit texts in the Bible (e.g., a system of communication, social commentary, therapeutic self-othering, systems of healing). More broadly, my research into ancient texts in which the self is conceived as unbuffered from outside forces has raised a new question: How did modern interpreters come to deny such permeability?

Second, beyond enriching our understanding of ancient Israel and early Judaism, this project also has implications for public discourse and for contemporary faith communities in the Western world—especially those whose beliefs about spirits differ radically from those found in the Global South. By positively comparing biblical texts with contemporary spirit possession, I have challenged colonial stereotypes characterizing many non-Western religious practices as primitive or harmful. Western biblical scholars in particular have often failed to recognize how the literary presentation of religious experience in the Bible very frequently resonates with people of faith around the world in ways we do not always validate or value.

Third, I have endeavored to explore spirit texts in the Hebrew Bible and in Second Temple literature without utilizing Christian theological tradition as a norming lens. This was a necessary task for the field because so many of the most prominent treatments of spirit material in the Hebrew Bible are what amount to the "background" sections for studies focused on early Christian pneumatology. Additionally, this approach was required because so much of the biblical and Second Temple material diverges considerably from how it was received both in later Jewish and Christian traditions.

Fourth, I have introduced a framework for understanding the developing concepts of evil in Second Temple Jewish literature that is informed by mythological texts but not based in them. Rather, I have rooted my discussion of evil in the vibrant conversations currently ongoing in biblical scholarship surrounding notions of the self. As originally conceived, this was, in fact, one of the more significant contributions I sought to make in this project. Although I believe that I have largely accomplished this task, having now reached the conclusion, I wonder if it has turned out to be one of the least interesting aspects of the book.

The more time I have spent in this literature, the more I have become convinced that dealing with "evil" in the modern sense of the word is a secondary concern in many of the spirit phenomena texts in biblical literature—even those that explicitly discuss demons, exorcism, and eschatological conflict. It is not that the problem of evil is not a concern of these texts—of course it is. Rather, it is that notions of evil and its activity in the world are so thoroughly integrated into other religious and communal concerns that to focus only on evil (primarily as an intellectual problem and not also as one of religious experience) is to miss the forest for the trees. As Richard J. Bernstein has observed,

> When theologians and philosophers of religion speak about 'the problem of evil,' they typically mean something quite specific—the problem of how to reconcile the appearance of evil with a belief in a God who is omniscient, omnipotent, and beneficent. Even this discourse has become specialized and professionalized, and remote from the lived experiences of ordinary people. ... The main issue of the so-called problem of evil is not really the characterization of evil and its varieties. It is rather the problem of how to reconcile evil (however it is described) with religious beliefs and convictions."[101]

Bernstein's pragmatic approach to framing the problem of evil recalls for us the anthropological dimension of this very theological issue.

Many of the biblical and Second Temple Jewish texts surveyed in this book are not struggling to identify where evil exists or how it might be defined. They are wrestling rather with the undeniable truth that they are surrounded by evil, even within themselves, and that its influence is obvious. Thus, they ask: *Do our existing practices and beliefs adequately address this reality? Can these resources be strengthened or transformed in order to ameliorate the problem more effectively? Are those who do not follow our community's prescriptions for dealing with evil our enemies?* Such were the kinds of therapeutic concerns that motivated many early Jewish and Christian literary engagements with the problem and origin of evil.

As I have striven to demonstrate in this book, the bountiful heritage of spirit phenomena in biblical literature was a significant conceptual and textual resource that outfitted these theoretical excursions—as were the associated spirit practices that accompanied them. Contemporary Jewish and Christian communities that struggle with the problem of evil today make use of many of the same texts and practices—though not always in the same ways or forms. They use these resources to *manage* evil, since by now it should be clear that evil is a problem we cannot *solve*. Further, these spirit phenomena are intertwined with the cycles of birth and death, communal identity formation, and the engendering of hope in the midst of adversity, which animate so much of human religious experience. In these efforts, Jews and Christians for millennia have found allies in God's spirit, the human spirit, holy spirits, the communal spirit, the Holy Spirit, and many other pneumatological entities and powers. Some write books about these phenomena in order to better understand them. Others experience them daily without any concern for explaining or proving their existence. A number of people do both. Likely no one will know who has the clearer view on the nature of spirit phenomena until God sets all spirits to right in the end.

---

101 Richard J. Bernstein, *Radical Evil: A Philosophical Interrogation* (Cambridge: Polity Press, 2002), 2.

Bibliography

Primary Sources

Baumgarten, Joseph M. "The 4Q Zadokite Fragments on Skin Disease." *JJS* 41.2 (1990): 153–65.
Collins, John J. "4QPrayer of Nabonidus ar." Pages 83–93 in *Qumran Cave 4.XVII: Parabiblical Texts, Part 3*. Edited by James C. Vanderkam. DJD 22. Oxford: Clarendon, 1996).
Fitzmyer, Joseph A. *The Genesis Apocryphon of Qumrân Cave 1 (1Q20): A Commentary*. 3rd ed. BibOr 18b. Rome: Pontificio Istituto Biblico, 2004.
Metso, Sarianna. *The Community Rule: A Critical Edition with Translation*. EJL 51. Atlanta: SBL Press, 2019.
Newsom, Carol A., and Eileen M. Schuller. *The Hodayot (Thanksgiving Psalms): A Study Edition of 1QHa*. Atlanta: SBL Press, 2012.
Sanders, J. A. *The Psalms Scroll of Qumrân Cave 11*, DJD 4. Oxford: Clarendon, 1965.
VanderKam, James C. *The Book of Jubilees*. CSCO 511. Louwain: Peeters, 1989.
Weinfeld, Moshe and David Rolph Seely. "4QBarkhi Nafshi." Pages 255–334 in *Qumran Cave 4.XX Poetical and Liturgical Texts, Part 2*. Edited by Esther Chazon, Torleif Elgvin, Esther Eshel, Daniel Falk, Bilhah Nitzan, Elisha Qimron, Eileen Schuller, David Seely, Eibert Tigchelaar, and Moshe Weinfeld. DJD 29. Oxford: Clarendon, 1999.

Secondary Sources

Abernethy, Andrew T. "The Spirit of God in Haggai 2:5: Prophecy as a Sign of God's Spirit." *VT* 70.4–5 (2020): 511–20.
Abusch, Tzvi. "Ghost as God: Some Observations on a Babylonian Understanding of Human Nature." Pages 363–83 in *Self, Soul, and Body in Religious Experience*. Edited by Albert I. Baumgarten, Jan Assmann, and Guy G. Stroumsa. SHR 78. Leiden: Brill, 1998.
Adam, Klaus-Peter. "1 Sam 28: A Comment on Saul's Destiny from a Late Prophetic Point of View." *RB* 116.1 (2009): 27–43.
Adam, Klaus-Peter. "'And He Behaved like a Prophet among Them.' (1 Sam 10:11b): The Depreciative Use of נבא Hitpael and the Comparative Evidence of Ecstatic Prophecy." *WO* 39.1 (2009): 3–57.
Adams, Karin. "Metaphor and Dissonance: A Reinterpretation of Hosea 4:13–14." *JBL* 127 (2008): 291–305.
Ahlström, G. W. "1 Samuel 1,15." *Biblica* 60.2 (1979): 254.
Ahmed, Durre S., ed. *Gendering the Spirit: Women, Religion & the Post-Colonial Response*. New York: Palgrave, 2002.
Alexander, Philip S. "The Demonology of the Dead Sea Scrolls." *The Dead Sea Scrolls after Fifty Years: A Comprehensive Assessment*. Edited by Peter W. Flint and James C. VanderKam. Vol. 2. Leiden: Brill, 1999.
Alter, Robert. "How Convention Helps Us Read: The Case of the Bible's Annunciation Type-Scene." *Prooftexts* 3.2 (1983): 115–30.

American Psychiatric Association. *Diagnostic and Statistical Manual of Mental Disorders*. 4th ed. Washington, DC: American Psychiatric Publishing, 1994.
American Psychiatric Association. *Diagnostic and Statistical Manual of Mental Disorders*. 5th ed. Arlington: American Psychiatric Publishing, 2013.
Amit, Yairah. "The Delicate Balance in the Image of Saul and its Place in the Deuteronomistic History." Pages 71–79 in *Saul in Story and Tradition*. Edited by Carl S. Ehrlich. FAT 47. Tübingen: Mohr Siebeck, 2006.
Anderson, Arnold A. "The Use of 'Ruah' in 1QS, 1QH and 1QM." *JSS* 7.2 (1962): 293–303.
Anderson, Bernhard W. *Creation Versus Chaos: The Reinterpretation of Mythical Symbolism in the Bible*. New York: Association Press, 1967.
Anderson, Gary A. *Sin: A History*. New Haven: Yale University Press, 2009.
Ankarloo, Bengt, and Stuart Clark, eds. *Witchcraft and Magic in Europe: The Twentieth Century*. 6 vols. Philadelphia: University of Pennsylvania Press, 1999.
Arichea, Daniel C. "Translating Breath and Spirit." *BT* 34.2 (1983): 209–13.
Arnold, Bill T. "Soul-Searching Questions About 1 Samuel 28: Samuel's Appearance at Endor and Anthropology." Pages 75–83 in *What about the Soul?: Neuroscience and Christian Anthropology*. Edited by Joel B. Green. Nashville: Abingdon, 2004.
Asad, Talal. *Genealogies of Religion: Discipline and Reasons of Power in Christianity and Islam*. Baltimore: Johns Hopkins University Press, 1993.
Asamoah-Gyadu, J. Kwabena. "Spirit and Spirits in African Religious Traditions." Pages 41–53 in *Interdisciplinary and Religio-Cultural Discourses on a Spirit-Filled World: Loosing the Spirits*. Edited by Veli-Matti Kärkkäinen, Kirsteen Kim, and Amos Yong. New York: Palgrave Macmillan, 2013.
Asher-Greve, Julia M. "The Essential Body: Mesopotamian Conceptions of the Gendered Body." *Gender & History* 9.3 (1997): 432–61.
Assmann, Jan. *Death and Salvation in Ancient Egypt*. Ithaca: Cornell University Press, 2005.
Auffarth, Christoph, and Loren T. Stuckenbruck, eds. *The Fall of the Angels*. TBN 6. Leiden: Brill, 2004.
Auld, A. Graeme. *I & II Samuel: A Commentary*. OTL. Louisville: Westminster John Knox Press, 2011.
Aune, David E., and John McCarthy. *The Whole and Divided Self: The Bible and Theological Anthropology*. New York: Crossroad, 1997.
Avalos, Hector. "Disability Studies and Biblical Studies: Retrospectives and Prospects." *Int* 73.4 (2019): 343–54.
Baden, Joel S., and Candida R. Moss. "The Origin and Interpretation of Ṣāraʻat in Leviticus 13–14." *JBL* 130.4 (2011): 643–62.
Bailliot, Magali. "Rome and the Roman Empire." Pages 175–97 in *Guide to the Study of Ancient Magic*. Edited by David Frankfurter. RGRW 189. Leiden: Brill, 2019.
Ballard, Jaimie. "About Half of Americans Believe Ghosts and Demons Exist." *YouGov*, 30 October 2020. https://today.yougov.com/topics/philosophy/articles-reports/2020/10/30/ghosts-demons-exist-poll-data.
Baranski, Lynne. "In a Connecticut Murder Trial, Will (Demonic) Possession Prove Nine-Tenths of the Law?" *People*, 26 October 1981. https://people.com/archive/in-a-connecticut-murder-trial-will-demonic-possession-prove-nine-tenths-of-the-law-vol-16-no-17/.
Barnard, George William. *Exploring Unseen Worlds: William James and the Philosophy of Mysticism*. Albany: State University of New York Press, 1997.

Barr, James. "Jewish Apocalyptic in Recent Scholarly Study." *BJRL* 58.1 (1975): 9–35.
Barr, James. *The Garden of Eden and the Hope of Immortality: The Read-Tuckwell Lectures for 1990*. London: SCM, 1992.
Barr, James. "The Question of Religious Influence: The Case of Zoroastrianism, Judaism, and Christianity." *JAAR* 53.2 (1985): 201–35.
Barr, James. *The Semantics of Biblical Language*. London: SCM, 1991.
Barton, John. *Oracles of God: Perceptions of Ancient Prophecy in Israel after the Exile*. 2nd ed. London: Darton, Longman, & Todd, 2007.
Bauman, H-Dirksen L., and Joseph J. Murray, eds. *Deaf Gain: Raising the Stakes for Human Diversity*. Minneapolis: University of Minnesota, 2014.
Baumgarten, Albert I., Jan Assmann, and Guy G. Stroumsa, eds. *Self, Soul, and Body in Religious Experience*. SHR 78. Leiden: Brill, 1998.
Bazzana, Giovanni B. *Having the Spirit of Christ: Spirit Possession and Exorcism in the Early Christ Groups*. Synkrisis. New Haven: Yale University Press, 2020.
Becker, Eve-Marie, Jan Dochhorn, and Else Kragelund Holt, eds. *Trauma and Traumatization in Individual and Collective Dimensions: Insights from Biblical Studies and Beyond*. SAN 2. Göttingen: Vandenhoeck & Ruprecht, 2014.
Becker, Judith. "Listening Selves and Spirit Possession." *WM* 42.2 (2000): 25–50.
Beliso-De Jesús, Aisha M. *Electric Santería: Racial and Sexual Assemblages of Transnational Religion*. Gender, Theory, and Religion. New York: Columbia University Press, 2015.
Ben Zvi, Ehud. "A Contribution to the Intellectual History of Yehud: The Story of Micaiah and its Function within the Discourse of Persian-Period Literati." Pages 89–102 in *The Historian and the Bible: Essays in Honour of Lester L. Grabbe*. Edited by Philip R. Davies and Diana Vikander Edelman. LHBOTS 530. New York: T & T Clark, 2010.
Benjamin, Don C. "An Anthropology of Prophecy." *BTB* 21.4 (1991): 135–44.
Ben-Noun, Liubov. "What Was the Mental Disease that Afflicted King Saul?" *CCS* 2.4 (2003): 270–82.
Berman, Joshua A. *Inconsistency in the Torah: Ancient Literary Convention and the Limits of Source Criticism*. Oxford: Oxford University Press, 2017.
Berman, Joshua A. "The Legal Blend in Biblical Narrative (Joshua 20:1–9), Judges 6:25–31, 1 Samuel 15:2, 28:3–25, 2 Kings 4:1–7, Jeremiah 34:12–17, Nehemiah 5:1–12)." *JBL* 134.1 (2015): 105–25.
Bernstein, Richard J. *Radical Evil: A Philosophical Interrogation*. Cambridge, UK: Polity Press, 2002.
Berquist, Jon L. "Psalms, Postcolonialism, and the Construction of the Self." Pages 195–202 in *Approaching Yehud: New Approaches to the Study of the Persian Period*. Edited by Jon L. Berquist. SemeiaSt 50. Atlanta: SBL Press, 2007.
Bhayro, Siam, and Catherine Rider, eds. *Demons and Illness from Antiquity to the Early-Modern Period*. MRLLA 5. Leiden: Brill, 2017.
Bhogal, Harman. "The Post-Reformation Challenge to Demonic Possession." Pages 359–75 in *Demons and Illness from Antiquity to the Early-Modern Period*. Edited by Siam Bhayro and Catherine Rider. MRLLA 5. Leiden: Brill, 2017.
Bibb, Bryan D. "The Prophetic Critique of Ritual in Old Testament Theology." Pages 31–43 in *The Priests in the Prophets: The Portrayal of Priests, Prophets and Other Religious Specialists in the Latter Prophets*. Edited by Lester L. Grabbe and Alice Ogden Bellis. JSOTSup 408. London: T&T Clark, 2004.

Blenkinsopp, Joseph. "Saul and the Mistress of the Spirits." Pages 49–62 in *Sense and Sensitivity: Essays on Reading the Bible in Memory of Robert Carroll*. Edited by Alastair G. Hunter and Philip R. Davies. JSOTSup 348. London: Sheffield, 2002.

Blenkinsopp, Joseph. "The Social Roles of Prophets in Early Achaemenid Judah." *JSOT* 25.93 (2001): 39–58.

Blischke, Mareike Verena. *Der Geist Gottes im Alten Testament*. FAT2 112. Tübingen: Mohr Siebeck, 2019.

Bloch, Maurice. *Placing the Dead: Tombs, Ancestral Villages and Kinship Organization in Madagascar*. SSA 1. London: Seminar Press, 1971.

Block, Daniel I., ed. *By the River Chebar: Historical, Literary, and Theological Studies in the Book of Ezekiel*. Cambridge, UK: James Clarke Company, 2014.

Block, Daniel I. "The Prophet of the Spirit: The Use of רוּחַ in the Book of Ezekiel." *By the River Chebar: Historical, Literary, and Theological Studies in the Book of Ezekiel*. Edited by Daniel I. Block. Cambridge, UK: James Clarke Company, 2014.

Blount, Benjamin. "Situating Cultural Models in History and Cognition." Pages 271–98 in *Approaches to Language, Culture, and Cognition: The Intersection of Cognitive Linguistics and Linguistic Anthropology*. Edited by Masataka Yamaguchi, Dennis Tay, and Benjamin Blount. London: Palgrave Macmillan, 2014.

Boase, Elizabeth, and Christopher G. Frechette, eds. *Bible through the Lens of Trauma*. SemeiaSt 86. Atlanta: SBL Press, 2016.

Boddy, Janice. "Spirit Possession Revisited: Beyond Instrumentality." *ARAnth* 23 (1994): 407–34.

Boddy, Janice. *Wombs and Alien Spirits: Women, Men, and the Zār Cult in Northern Sudan*. NDAW. Madison: University of Wisconsin Press, 1989.

Bohak, Gideon. "Jewish Amulets, Magic Bowls, and Manuals in Aramaic and Hebrew." Pages 388–415 in *Guide to the Study of Ancient Magic*. Edited by David Frankfurter. RGRW 189. Leiden: Brill, 2019.

Bolívar Aróstegui, Natalia, Carmen González, and Natalia del Río Bolívar. *Corrientes Espirituales en Cuba*. Havana: Editorial José Martí, 2007.

Bottéro, Jean. *Religion in Ancient Mesopotamia*. Translated by T. L. Fagan. Chicago: The University of Chicago Press, 2001.

Bourguignon, Erika. *Possession*. San Francisco: Chandler & Sharp, 1976.

Bourguignon, Erika. *Religion: Altered States of Consciousness, and Social Change*. Columbus: Ohio State University Press, 1973.

Bourguignon, Erika. "The Self, the Behavioral Environment, and the Theory of Spirit Possession." Pages 39–60 in *Context and Meaning in Cultural Anthropology*. Edited by Melford E. Spiro. New York: Free Press, 1965.

Bourke, Joseph. "The Spirit of God in the Old Testament." *LotS* 13.156 (1959): 538–50.

Bouyer, Louis. "'Mysticism': An Essay on the History of the Word." Pages 42–55 in *Understanding Mysticism*. Edited by Richard Woods. 1st. ed. Garden City, NY: Image Books, 1980.

Brakke, David, Michael L. Satlow, and Steven Weitzman, eds. *Religion and the Self in Antiquity*. Bloomington: Indiana University Press, 2005.

Brand, Miryam T. *Evil Within and Without: The Source of Sin and Its Nature as Portrayed in Second Temple Literature*. JAJSup 9. Göttingen: Vandenhoeck & Ruprecht, 2013.

Breed, Brennan W. *Nomadic Text: A Theory of Biblical Reception History.* Bloomington: Indiana University Press, 2014.

Brettler, Marc Zvi. "Predestination in Deuteronomy 30.1–10." Pages 171–88 in *Those Elusive Deuteronomists: The Phenomenon of Pan-Deuteronomism.* Edited by Linda S. Schearing and Steven L. McKenzie. JSOT 268. Sheffield: Sheffield Academic Press, 1999.

Briggs, Charles A. "The Use of רוח in the Old Testament." *JBL* 19.2 (1900): 132–45.

Briggs, Richard S. "Reading the Sotah Text (Numbers 5:11–31): Holiness and a Hermeneutic Fit for Suspicion." *BI* 17.3 (2009): 288–319.

Briggs, Robin. *Witches & Neighbors: The Social and Cultural Context of European Witchcraft.* New York: Viking, 1996.

Brittle, Gerald. *The Devil in Connecticut.* New York: Bantam, 1983.

Brock, Rita Nakashima. *Soul Repair: Recovering from Moral Injury after War.* Boston: Beacon Press, 2012.

Broida, Marian W. "Apotropaic Intercession in the Hebrew Bible and the Ancient Near East." Pages 19–38 in *Studies on Magic and Divination in the Biblical World.* Edited by Helen R. Jacobs, Anne Katrine de Hemmer Gudme, and Philippe Guillaume. BibInters 11. Piscataway: Gorgias, 2013.

Broida, Marian W. *Forestalling Doom: "Apotropaic Intercession" in the Hebrew Bible and the Ancient Near East.* AOAT 417. Münster: Ugarit-Verlag, 2014.

Brooke, George J. "Body Parts in Barkhi Nafshi and the Qualifications for Membership of the Worshipping Community." Pages 79–94 in *Sapiential, Liturgical and Poetical Texts from Qumran: Proceedings of the Third Meeting of the International Organization for Qumran Studies, Oslo, 1998.* Edited by Daniel K. Falk, Florentino García Martínez, and Eileen M. Schuller. STDJ 35. Leiden: Brill, 2000.

Brooke, George J. *Reading the Dead Sea Scrolls: Essays in Method.* EJL 39. Atlanta: SBL Press, 2013.

Broome, Edwin Cornelius. "Ezekiel's Abnormal Personality." *JBL* 65.3 (1946): 277–92.

Brown, Derek R. "Images of Satan in Biblical and Second Temple Jewish Traditions." Pages 21–60 in *The God of This Age: Satan in the Churches and Letters of the Apostle Paul.* WUNT2 409. Tübingen: Mohr Siebeck, 2015.

Brown, Derek R. *The God of This Age: Satan in the Churches and Letters of the Apostle Paul.* WUNT2 409. Tübingen: Mohr Siebeck, 2015.

Brown, Diana DeGroat. *Umbanda: Religion and Politics in Urban Brazil.* 2nd ed. New York: Columbia University Press, 1994.

Brown, John Pairman. "The Mediterranean Seer and Shamanism." *ZAW* 93.3 (1981): 374–400.

Brown, Karen McCarthy. *Mama Lola: A Vodou Priestess in Brooklyn.* Rev. ed. CSRS 4. Berkeley: University of California Press, 2001.

Brueggemann, Walter. *Theology of the Old Testament: Testimony, Dispute, Advocacy.* Minneapolis: Fortress, 1997.

Büchler, Adolph. *Studies in Sin and Atonement in the Rabbinic Literature of the First-Century.* Oxford: Oxford University Press, 1928.

Büchsel, Friedrich. *Der Geist Gottes im Neuen Testament.* Gütersloh: Bertelsmann, 1926.

Budde, Karl. *Die Bücher Samuel,.* Tübingen: Mohr Siebeck, 1902.

Burkes, Shannon. *God, Self, and Death: The Shape of Religious Transformation in the Second Temple Period.* JSJSup 79. Leiden: Brill, 2003.

Burton, Ernest DeWitt. *Spirit, Soul, and Flesh.* Chicago: University of Chicago Press, 1918.

Bush, Stephen S. "Are Religious Experiences Too Private to Study?" *JR* 92.2 (2012): 199 – 223.
Bynum, William Randolph. "Text-Critical Review of Zechariah 12:10." Pages 59 – 109 in *The Fourth Gospel and the Scriptures: Illuminating the Form and Meaning of Scriptural Citation in John 19:37*. NovTSup 144. Leiden: Brill, 2012.
Caciola, Nancy Mandeville. *Discerning Spirits: Divine and Demonic Possession in the Middle Ages*. Cornell University Press, 2015.
Cambers, Andrew. "Demonic Possession, Literacy and 'Superstition' in Early Modern England." *PP* 202.1 (2009): 3 – 35.
Cardeña, Etzel. "Trance and Possession as Dissociative Disorders." *TPRR* 29.4 (1992): 287 – 300.
Cardeña, Etzel, and Michael Winkelman. *Altering Consciousness: Multidisciplinary Perspectives*. 2 vols. Santa Barbara: Praeger, 2011.
Carlson, Reed. "Hannah at Pentecost: On Recognizing Spirit Phenomena in Early Jewish Literature." *JPT* 27.2 (2018): 245 – 58.
Carlson, Reed. "Provocateurs, Examiners, and Fools: Divine Opponents to the Aqedah in Early Judaism." *CBQ* 83.3 (2021).
Carlson, Reed. "Review of Bazzana, Giovanni B. Having the Spirit of Christ: Spirit Possession and Exorcism in the Early Christ Groups." *Pneuma* 42.2 (2020): 269 – 71.
Carlson, Reed. "Review of Levison, John R. The Holy Spirit Before Christianity." *WW* 40.1 (2020): 98 – 99.
Carr, David M. *The Formation of the Hebrew Bible: A New Reconstruction*. New York: Oxford University Press, 2011.
Carter, Warren. "Cross-Gendered Romans and Mark's Jesus: Legion Enters the Pigs (Mark 5:1 – 20)." *JBL* 134.1 (2015): 139 – 55.
Cazelles, Henri. "Prolégomènes à une étude de l'Esprit dans le Bible." Pages 75 – 90 in *Von Kanaan bis Kerala: Festschrift für Prof. Mag. Dr. Dr. J.P.M. van der Ploeg O.P. zur Vollendung des siebzigsten Lebensjahres am 4. Juli 1979: überreicht von Kollegen, Freunden und Schülern*. Edited by W. C. Delsman and J. P. M. van der Ploeg. AOAT 211. Neukirchen-Vluyn: Neukirchener, 1982.
Charlesworth, James H. *The Old Testament Pseudepigrapha*. 2 vols. New Haven: Yale University, 1983.
Charlesworth, James H. *The Old Testament Pseudepigrapha and the New Testament: Prolegomena for the Study of Christian Origins*. Cambridge: Cambridge University Press, 1985.
Chaves, Michael. *The Conjuring: The Devil Made Me Do It*. Warner Bros. Pictures, 2021.
Chesnut, R. Andrew. *Born Again in Brazil: The Pentecostal Boom and the Pathogens of Poverty*. New Brunswick: Rutgers University Press, 1997.
Chidester, David. "Material Terms for the Study of Religion." *JAAR* 68.2 (2000): 367 – 79.
Childs, Brevard S. *Introduction to the Old Testament as Scripture*. Philadelphia: Fortress, 1979.
Childs, Brevard S. *Myth and Reality in the Old Testament*. SBT 27. Eugene: Wipf & Stock, 1960.
Childs, Brevard S. "Speech-Act Theory and Biblical Interpretation." *SJT* 58.4 (2005): 375 – 92.
Chireau, Yvonne P. *Black Magic: Religion and the African American Conjuring Tradition*. Berkeley: University of California Press, 2003.

Clark, Stuart. *Thinking with Demons: The Idea of Witchcraft in Early Modern Europe*. Oxford: Oxford University Press, 1999.

Clarke, Clifton, ed. *Pentecostal Theology in Africa*. ACSS 6. Eugene: Pickwick, 2014.

Clendinen, Dudley. "Defendant in a Murder Puts the Devil on Trial." *New York Times*, 23 March 1981. http://www.nytimes.com/1981/03/23/nyregion/defendant-in-a-murder-puts-the-devil-on-trial.html?pagewanted=all.

Clines, David J. A. *Job 1–20*. WBC 17. Dallas: Word Books, 1989.

Cogan, Mordechai. "The Road to En-Dor." Pages 319–26 in *Pomegranates and Golden Bells: Studies in Biblical, Jewish, and Near Eastern Ritual, Law, and Literature in Honor of Jacob Milgrom*. Edited by David P. Wright, David Noel Freedman, and Avi Hurvitz. Winona Lake, IN: Eisenbrauns, 1995.

Cohen, Emma. "What Is Spirit Possession? Defining, Comparing, and Explaining Two Possession Forms." *Ethnos* 73.1 (2008): 101–26.

Cohen, Naomi G. "'דברי בי'...': An ›Enthusiastic‹ Prophetic Formula." *ZAW* 99.2 (1987): 219–32.

Collins, Adela Yarbro. "Paul's Disability: The Thorn in His Flesh." Pages 165–83 in *Disability Studies and Biblical Literature*. Edited by Candida R. Moss and Jeremy Schipper. New York: Palgrave Macmillan, 2011.

Collins, John J. *The Apocalyptic Imagination: An Introduction to Jewish Apocalyptic Literature*. 3rd ed. Grand Rapids: Eerdmans, 2016.

Collins, John J. "The Origin of Evil in Apocalyptic Literature and the Dead Sea Scrolls." Pages 25–38 in *Congress Volume, Paris 1992*. Edited by John A. Emerton. Supplements to VTSup 61. Leiden: Brill, 1995.

Cook, L. Stephen. *On the Question of the "Cessation of Prophecy" in Ancient Judaism*. TSAJ 145. Tübingen: Mohr Siebeck, 2011.

Cortés, Juan B., and Florence M. Gatti. *The Case Against Possessions and Exorcisms: A Historical, Biblical, and Psychological Analysis of Demons, Devils, and Demoniacs*. New York: Vantage, 1975.

Craffert, Pieter F. *The Life of a Galilean Shaman: Jesus of Nazareth in Anthropological-Historical Perspective*. Matrix 3. Eugene: Cascade Books, 2008.

Crapanzano, Vincent. "Spirit Possession: An Overview." *ER* 13:8687–94.

Crawford, Sidnie White. "Court Tales." *EDSS* 1:149–51.

Crenshaw, James L. *Prophetic Conflict; Its Effect upon Israelite Religion*. BZAW 124. Berlin: De Gruyter, 1971.

Cryer, Frederick H. *Divination in Ancient Israel and Its Near Eastern Environment: A Socio-Historical Investigation*. JSOTSup 142. Sheffield: Sheffield Academic, 1994.

Csordas, Thomas J. *The Sacred Self: A Cultural Phenomenology of Charismatic Healing*. Berkeley: University of California Press, 1997.

Dan, Joseph. "Samael, Lilith, and the Concept of Evil in Early Kabbalah." *AJSR* 5.5 (1980): 17–40.

Darling, Lynn. "By Demons Possessed." *Washington Post*, 13 September 1981. https://www.washingtonpost.com/archive/lifestyle/1981/09/13/by-demons-possessed/3479fa6b-eee3-4233-a2fc-b9defa403504/.

Davies, Philip R., and Diana Vikander Edelman, eds. *The Historian and the Bible: Essays in Honour of Lester L. Grabbe*. LHBOTS 530. New York: T & T Clark International, 2010.

Davis, Andrew R. "Rereading 1 Kings 17:21 in Light of Ancient Medical Texts." *JBL* 135.3 (2016): 465–81.

Day, John. *God's Conflict with the Dragon and the Sea: Echoes of a Canaanite Myth in the Old Testament*. UCOP 35. Cambridge: Cambridge University Press, 1985.
De Vries, Simon J. *Prophet against Prophet: The Role of the Micaiah Narrative (I Kings 22) in the Development of Early Prophetic Tradition*. Grand Rapids: Eerdmans, 1978.
Derrett, J. Duncan M. "Contributions to the Study of the Gerasene Demoniac." *JSNT* 2.3 (1979): 2–17.
Di Vito, Robert A. "Old Testament Anthropology and the Construction of Personal Identity." *CBQ* 61.2 (1999): 217–38.
Dickens, Charles. *A Christmas Carol*. Edited by Richard Kelly. Peterborough: Broadview, 2003.
Dieleman, Jacco. "The Greco-Egyptian Magical Papyri." Pages 283–321 in *Guide to the Study of Ancient Magic*. Edited by David Frankfurter. RGRW 189. Leiden: Brill, 2019.
Dimant, Devorah. "Between Qumran Sectarian and Non-Sectarian Texts: The Case of Belial and Mastema." Pages 235–56 in *The Dead Sea Scrolls and Contemporary Culture: Proceedings of the International Conference Held at the Israel Museum, Jerusalem (July 6–8, 2008)*. Edited by Adolfo D. Roitman, Lawrence H. Schiffman, and Shani Tzoref. STDJ 93. Leiden: Brill, 2011.
Dimant, Devorah. "'The Fallen Angels' in the Dead Sea Scrolls and in the Apocryphal and Pseudepigraphic Books Related to Them (Hebrew)." PhD. diss., Hebrew University, 1974.
Dobroruka, Vicente. *Second Temple Pseudepigraphy: A Cross-Cultural Comparison of Apocalyptic Texts and Related Jewish Literature*. Ekstasis 4. Berlin: De Gruyter, 2014.
Douglas, Mary. *Leviticus as Literature*. Oxford: Oxford University Press, 1999.
Douglas, Mary. *Purity and Danger: An Analysis of Concept of Pollution and Taboo*. London: Routledge, 1966.
Dreytza, Manfred. *Der theologische Gebrauch von RUAH im Alten Testament: eine wort- und satzsemantische Studie*. 2nd ed. Basel: Brunnen, 1992
Duhaime, Jean. "Dualism." *EDSS* 1:215–20.
Duling, Dennis C. "The Eleazar Miracle and Solomon's Magical Wisdom in Flavius Josephus's Antiquitates Judaicae 8:42–49." *HTR* 78.1–2 (1985): 1–25.
Eagleton, Terry. *On Evil*. New Haven: Yale University Press, 2010.
Eliade, Mircea. *The Sacred and the Profane: the Nature of Religion*. New York: Harper & Row, 1961.
Ellens, Deborah L. "Numbers 5.11–31: Valuing Male Suspicion." Pages 55–82 in *God's Word for Our World Volume I: Theological and Cultural Studies in Honor of Simon John De Vries*. Edited by J. Harold Ellens, Deborah L. Ellens, Rolf P. Knierim, and Isaac Kalimi. JSOTSup 388. London: T & T Clark, 2004.
Engberg-Pedersen, Troels. *Cosmology and Self in the Apostle Paul: The Material Spirit*. Oxford: Oxford University Press, 2010.
Eshel, Esther. "Apotropaic Prayers in the Second Temple Period." Pages 69–88 in *Liturgical Perspectives: Prayer and Poetry in Light of the Dead Sea Scrolls: Proceedings of the Fifth International Symposium of the Orion Center for the Study of the Dead Sea Scrolls and Associated Literature, 19–23 January, 2000*. Edited by Esther G. Chazon. STDJ 48. Leiden: Brill, 2003.
Eshel, Esther. "Demonology in Palestine during the Second Temple Period (Hebrew)." PhD. diss., Hebrew University, 1999.
Espírito Santo, Diana. *Developing the Dead: Mediumship and Selfhood in Cuban Espiritismo*. Gainesville: University Press of Florida, 2015.

Espírito Santo, Diana. "Imagination, Sensation and the Education of Attention Among Cuban Spirit Mediums." *Ethnos* 77.2 (2012): 252–71.
Espírito Santo, Diana. "Spiritist Boundary-Work and the Morality of Materiality in Afro-Cuban Religion." *JMC* 15.1 (2010): 64–82.
Falk, Daniel K. "Willing Heart and Broken Spirit: Psalm 51 in the Dead Sea Scrolls." Pages 521–48 in *Reading the Bible in Ancient Traditions and Modern Editions: Studies in Memory of Peter W. Flint*. Edited by Andrew B. Perrin, Kyung S. Baek, Daniel K. Falk, and Peter W. Flint. Atlanta: SBL Press, 2017.
Fee, Gordon D. *God's Empowering Presence: The Holy Spirit in the Letters of Paul*. Peabody: Hendrickson, 2009.
Feinstein, Eve Levavi. *Sexual Pollution in the Hebrew Bible*. Oxford: Oxford University Press, 2014.
Feldman, Louis H. "Josephus' Portrait of Solomon." *HUCA* 66 (1995): 103–67.
Ferber, Sarah. *Demonic Possession and Exorcism in Early Modern France*. New York: Routledge, 2004.
Firth, David G., and Paul D. Wegner. *Presence, Power, and Promise: The Role of the Spirit of God in the Old Testament*. Downers Grove: IVP Academic, 2011.
Fischer, Irmtraud. *Gotteskünderinnen: zu einer geschlechterfairen Deutung des Phänomens der Prophetie und der Prophetinnen in der Hebräischen Bibel*. Stuttgart: Kohlhammer, 2002.
Fischer, Stefan. "1 Samuel 28: The Woman of Endor – Who Is She and What Does Saul See?" *OTE* 14.1 (2001): 26–46.
Fisher, Philip. *The Vehement Passions*. Princeton: Princeton University Press, 2002.
Fitzmyer, Joseph A. *The Genesis Apocryphon of Qumran Cave 1 (1Q20): A Commentary*. 3rd ed. BibOr 18b. Rome: Pontificio Istituto Biblico, 2004.
Fjelstad, Karen, and Nguyễn Thị Hiền. *Spirits without Borders: Vietnamese Spirit Mediums in a Transnational Age*. New York: Palgrave Macmillan, 2011.
Flannery, Frances, Colleen Shantz, and Rodney A. Werline. *Experientia, Volume 1: Inquiry into Religious Experience in Early Judaism and Christianity*. SBLSS 40. Atlanta: SBL Press, 2008.
Flannery, Frances, Colleen Shantz, and Rodney A. Werline. "Introduction: Religious Experience, Past and Present." Pages 1–10 in *Experientia, Volume 1: Inquiry into Religious Experience in Early Judaism and Christianity*. Edited by Frances Flannery, Colleen Shantz, and Rodney A Werline. SBLSS 40. Atlanta: SBL Press, 2008.
Flusser, David. "Qumrân and Jewish 'Apotropaic' Prayers." *IEJ* 16.3 (1966): 194–205.
Foster, Benjamin R. "The Person in Mesopotamian Thought." Pages 117–39 in *The Oxford Handbook of Cuneiform Culture*. Edited by Karen Radner and Eleanor Robson. Oxford Handbooks. Oxford: Oxford University Press, 2011.
Foucault, Michel. *History of Madness*. Edited by Jean Khalfa. Translated by Jonathan Murphy and Jean Khalfa. London: Routledge, 2006.
Foucault, Michel. *Technologies of the Self: A Seminar with Michel Foucault*. Edited by Luther H. Martin, Huck Gutman, and Patrick H. Hutton. Amherst: University of Massachusetts Press, 1988.
Foxe, John. *A Sermon of Christ Crucified*. London: John Day, 1570.

Frankfurter, David. "Ancient Magic in a New Key: Refining an Exotic Discipline in the History of Religions." Pages 3–20 in *Guide to the Study of Ancient Magic*. Edited by David Frankfurter. RGRW 189. Leiden: Brill, 2019.

Frankfurter, David., ed. *Guide to the Study of Ancient Magic*. RGRW 189. Leiden: Brill, 2019.

Freedman, David Noel. *The Anchor Bible Dictionary*. 6 vols. New York: Doubleday, 1992.

Freeman, Thomas. "Demons, Deviance and Defiance: John Darrell and the Politics of Exorcism in Late Elizabethan England." Pages 34–63 in *Conformity and Orthodoxy in the English Church, c. 1560–1660*. Edited by Peter Lake and Michael C. Questier. SMBRH 2. Woodbridge: Boydell, 2000.

Freud, Sigmund. "A Seventeenth-Century Demonological Neurosis (1923 [1922])." Pages 72–105 in *The Ego and the Id and Other Works*. Translated by James Strachey. Vol. 19 of *The Standard Edition of the Complete Psychological Works of Sigmund Freud*. London: Hogarth, 1961.

Frey, Jörg. "Paul's View of the Spirit in the Light of Qumran." Pages 239–62 in *The Dead Sea Scrolls and Pauline Literature*. Edited by Jean-Sébastien Rey. STDJ 102. Leiden: Brill, 2013.

Friebel, Kelvin G. *Jeremiah's and Ezekiel's Sign-Acts: Rhetorical Nonverbal Communication*. JSOTSup 283. Sheffield: Sheffield Academic, 1999.

Friebel, Kelvin G. "Sign Acts." Pages 707–13 in *Dictionary of the Old Testament: Prophets*. Edited by Mark J. Boda and J. G. McConville. Downers Grove: InterVarsity Academic, 2012.

Frisch, Alexandria, and Lawrence H. Schiffman. "The Body in Qumran Literature: Flesh and Spirit, Purity and Impurity in the Dead Sea Scrolls." *DSD* 23.2 (2016): 155–82.

Frymer-Kensky, Tikva. "Pollution, Purification, and Purgation in Biblical Israel." Pages 399–414 in *The Word of the Lord Shall Go Forth: Essays in Honor of David Noel Freedman in Celebration of His Sixtieth Birthday*. Winona Lake, IN: Eisenbrauns, 1983.

Frymer-Kensky, Tikva. *Reading the Women of the Bible*. New York: Schocken, 2002.

García Martínez, Florentino. "The Prayer of Nabonidus: A New Synthesis." Pages 116–36 in *Qumran and Apocalyptic: Studies on the Aramaic Texts from Qumran*. STDJ 9. Leiden: Brill, 1992.

García Martínez, Florentino, and Eibert J. C. Tigchelaar. *The Dead Sea Scrolls Study Edition*. Leiden: Brill, 1997.

Garroway, Joshua. "The Invasion of a Mustard Seed: A Reading of Mark 5.1–20." *JSNT* 32.1 (2009): 57–75.

Geertz, Clifford. *The Interpretation of Cultures: Selected Essays*. New York: Basic Books, 1973.

Gibson, Marion. *Possession, Puritanism and Print: Darrell, Harsnett, Shakespeare and the Elizabethan Exorcism Controversy*. London: Pickering & Chatto, 2006.

Giercke-Ungermann, Annett. "Saul und der חרם: Beobachtungen zu den חרם-Konzepten in 1 Sam 15." *BN* 162 (2014): 47–65.

Giles, Linda L. "Possession Cults on the Swahili Coast: A Re-Examination of Theories of Marginality." *Africa* 57.2 (1987): 234–58.

Goldhill, Simon. "What Has Alexandria to Do with Jerusalem? Writing the History of the Jews in the Nineteenth Century." *HistJ* 59.1 (2016): 125–51.

Grabbe, Lester L. "Daniel: Sage, Seer … and Prophet?" Pages 87–94 in *Constructs of Prophecy in the Former & Latter Prophets & Other Texts*. Edited by Lester L. Grabbe and Martti Nissinen. ANEM 4. Atlanta: SBL Press, 2011.

Grabbe, Lester L. "Shaman, Preacher, or Spirit Medium?: The Israelite Prophet in the Light of Anthropological Models." Pages 117–32 in *Prophecy and the Prophets in Ancient Israel*. Edited by John Day. LHBOTS 531. New York: T & T Clark, 2010.

Greenspahn, Frederick E. "Why Prophecy Ceased." *JBL* 108.1 (1989): 37–49.

Griffin, Brandon J., Natalie Purcell, Kristine Burkman, Brett T. Litz, Craig J. Bryan, Martha Schmitz, Claudia Villierme, Jessica Walsh, and Shira Maguen. "Moral Injury: An Integrative Review." *JTrauSt* 32.3 (2019): 350–62.

Grimell, Jan. "Contemporary Insights from Biblical Combat Veterans through the Lenses of Moral Injury and Post-Traumatic Stress Disorder." *JPCC* 72.4 (2018): 241–50.

Grossman, Maxine L. "Religious Experience and the Disciple of Imagination: Tanya Luhrmann Meets Philo and the Dead Sea Scrolls." *DSD* 22.3 (2015): 308–24.

Gruenwald, Ithamar. *Apocalyptic and Merkavah Mysticism*. 2nd ed. AJEC 90. Leiden: Brill, 2014.

Grushcow, Lisa. *Writing the Wayward Wife: Rabbinic Interpretations of Sotah*. Leiden: Brill, 2006.

Gudme, Anne Katrine de Hemmer. "A Kind of Magic? The Law of Jealousy in Numbers 5:11–31 as Magical Ritual and as Ritual Text." Pages 149–68 in *Studies on Magic and Divination in the Biblical World*. Edited by Anne Katrine de Hemmer Gudme, Helen R. Jacobus, and Philippe Guillaume. Piscataway: Gorgias, 2013.

Gunkel, Hermann. *Die Wirkungen des heiligen Geistes, nach der populären Anschauung der apostolischen Zeit und nach der Lehre des Apostels Paulus: eine biblisch-theologische Studie*. Göttingen: Vandenhoeck & Ruprecht, 1888.

Gunkel, Hermann. *Schöpfung und Chaos in Urzeit und Endzeit: eine religionsgeschichtliche Untersuchung über Gen 1 und Ap Joh 12*. Göttingen: Vandenhoeck & Ruprecht, 1895.

Gunkel, Hermann. *The Influence of the Holy Spirit: According to the Popular View of the Apostolic Age and the Teaching of the Apostle Paul: A Biblical-Theological Study*. Translated by Roy A. Harrisville and Philip A. Quanbeck II. Philadelphia: Fortress Press, 1979.

Gunkel, Hermann. "The Secret Experiences of the Prophets." *The Expositor* 9.1 (1924): 356–66, 427–35.

Gunnel, André. "Ecstatic Prophecy in the Old Testament." Pages 187–200 in *Religious Ecstasy: Based on Papers Read at the Symposium on Religious Ecstasy Held at Åbo, Finland, on the 26th-28th of August 1981*. Edited by Nils G. Holm. SIDA 11. Stockholm: Almqvist & Wiksell, 1982.

Gyatso, Janet. *Apparitions of the Self: The Secret Autobiographies of a Tibetan Visionary*. Princeton: Princeton University Press, 1998.

Haber, Susan. "Ritual and Moral Purity and Impurity in Second Temple Judaism." Pages 31–46 in *They Shall Purify Themselves: Essays on Purity in Early Judaism*. Edited by Adele Reinhartz. Atlanta: SBL Press, 2008.

Haber, Susan. "Ritual and Moral Purity and Impurity in the Dead Sea Scrolls." Pages 47–74 in *They Shall Purify Themselves: Essays on Purity in Early Judaism*. Edited by Adele Reinhartz. Atlanta: SBL Press, 2008.

Haber, Susan. "Ritual and Moral Purity and Impurity in the Hebrew Bible." Pages 9–29 in *They Shall Purify Themselves: Essays on Purity in Early Judaism*. Edited by Adele Reinhartz. Atlanta: SBL Press, 2008.

Hale, William. *The Demon Murder Case.* Len Steckler Productions, Dick Clark Productions, 1983.
Hamori, Esther J. "The Spirit of Falsehood." *CBQ* 72.1 (2010): 15–30.
Hamori, Esther J. *Women's Divination in Biblical Literature: Prophecy, Necromancy, and Other Arts of Knowledge.* New Haven: Yale University Press, 2015.
Hanson, Paul D. *The Dawn of Apocalyptic: The Historical and Sociological Roots of Jewish Apocalyptic Eschatology.* Rev. ed. Philadelphia: Fortress, 1979.
Harding, James. "A Spirit of Deception in Job 4:15? Interpretive Indeterminacy and Eliphaz's Vision." *BibInt* 13.2 (2005): 137–66.
Harding, Rachel. "Afro-Brazilian Religions." *ER* 1:119–25.
Harkins, Angela Kim. *Reading with an "I" to the Heavens: Looking at the Qumran Hodayot through the Lens of Visionary Traditions.* Ekstasis 3. Berlin: De Gruyter, 2012.
Harkins, Angela Kim. "Ritual Mourning in Daniel's Interpretation of Jeremiah's Prophecy." *JCH* 2.1 (2015): 14–32.
Harkins, Angela Kim. "The Performative Reading of the Hodayot: The Arousal of Emotions and the Exegetical Generation of Texts." *JSP* 21.1 (2011): 55–71.
Harrington, Hannah K. "Purity and the Dead Sea Scrolls: Current Issues." *CBR* 4.3 (2006): 397–428.
Harrington, Hannah K. *The Purity Texts.* CQS 5. New York: T & T Clark, 2004.
Haustein, Jörg. "Embodying the Spirit(s): Pentecostal Demonology and Deliverance Discourse in Ethiopia." *Ethnos* 76.4 (2011): 534–52.
Hecker, Tobias, Eva Barnewitz, Hakon Stenmark, and Valentina Iversen. "Pathological Spirit Possession as a Cultural Interpretation of Trauma-Related Symptoms." *PTTRPP* 8.4 (2016): 468–76.
Hehn, Johannes. "Zum Problem des Geistes im Alten Orient und im Alten Testament." *ZAW* 43 (1925): 210–25.
Hempel, Charlotte. *The Qumran Rule Texts in Context: Collected Studies.* TSAJ 154. Tübingen: Mohr Siebeck, 2013.
Hempel, Charlotte. "The Treatise on the Two Spirits and the Literary History of the Rule of the Community." Pages 102–20 in *Dualism in Qumran.* Edited by Géza G. Xeravits. LSTS 76. London: T & T Clark, 2010.
Hendel, Ronald S. "Away from Ritual: The Prophetic Critique." Pages 59–79 in *Social Theory and the Study of Israelite Religion: Essays in Retrospect and Prospect.* Edited by Saul M. Olyan. Atlanta: SBL Press, 2012.
Henley, Paul. *The Adventure of the Real: Jean Rouch and the Craft of Ethnographic Cinema.* Chicago: University of Chicago Press, 2009.
Heschel, Abraham J. *The Prophets.* New York: Harper Collins, 1962.
Heschel, Susannah. "Ecstasy Versus Ethics: The Impact of the First World War on German Biblical Scholarship on the Hebrew Prophets." Pages 187–206 in *The First World War and the Mobilization of Biblical Scholarship.* Edited by Andrew Mein, Nathan MacDonald, and Matthew A. Collins. LHBOTS 676. London: Bloomsbury, 2019.
Hildebrandt, Wilf. *An Old Testament Theology of the Spirit of God.* Peabody: Hendrickson, 1995.
Himmelfarb, Martha. "Sexual Relations and Purity in the Temple Scroll and the Book of Jubilees." *DSD* 6.1 (1999): 11–36.

Hirschkind, Charles. *The Ethical Soundscape: Cassette Sermons and Islamic Counterpublics.* New York: Columbia University Press, 2006.
Hoffner Jr., Harry A. "Second Millennium Antecedents to the Hebrew 'ôb." *JBL* 86.4 (1967): 385–401.
Holland, Dorothy C., and Naomi Quinn, eds. *Cultural Models in Language and Thought.* Cambridge: Cambridge University Press, 1987.
Holland, Dorothy C., and Naomi Quinn. "Culture and Cognition." Pages 3–40 in *Cultural Models in Language and Thought.* Edited by Dorothy C. Holland and Naomi Quinn. Cambridge: Cambridge University Press, 1987.
Holmes, Brooke. *The Symptom and the Subject: The Emergence of the Physical Body in Ancient Greece.* Princeton: Princeton University Press, 2010.
Hornik, Heidi J., and Mikeal C. Parsons. *The Acts of the Apostles Through the Centuries.* WBBC. Chichester, UK: Wiley-Blackwell, 2016.
Howard Jr., David M. "The Transfer of Power from Saul to David in 1 Sam 16:13–14." *JETS* 32.4 (1989): 473–83.
Humphreys, W. Lee. "From Tragic Hero to Villain: A Study of the Figure of Saul and the Development of 1 Samuel." *JSOT* 7.22 (1982): 95–117.
Huskinson, Lucy. "Analytical Psychology and Spirit Possession: Towards a Non-Pathological Diagnosis of Spirit Possession." Pages 71–96 in *Spirit Possession and Trance: New Interdisciplinary Perspectives.* Edited by Bettina E. Schmidt and Lucy Huskinson. New York: Continuum, 2011.
Hutter, Manfred. "Religionsgeschichtliche Erwägungen zu *'elohîm* in 1 Sam 28:13." *BN* 21 (1983): 32–36.
Isaacs, Marie E. *The Concept of Spirit: A Study of Pneuma in Hellenistic Judaism and its Bearing on the New Testament.* HeyM 1. London: Heythrop College, 1976.
Jagel, Katie. "Half of Americans Believe in Possession by the Devil." *YouGov*, 17 September 2013. https://today.yougov.com/topics/lifestyle/articles-reports/2013/09/17/half-americans-believe-possession-devil.
James, William. "The Divided Self, and the Process of its Unification." Pages 132–49 in *Varieties of Religious Experience: A Study in Human Nature.* Centenary ed. New York: Routledge, 2002.
James, William. *Varieties of Religious Experience: A Study in Human Nature.* Centenary ed. New York: Routledge, 2002.
Janowski, Bernd. *Anthropologie des Alten Testaments: Grundfragen – Kontexte – Themenfelder.* Tübingen: Mohr Siebeck, 2019.
Janzen, J. Gerald. "Prayer and/as Self-Address: The Case of Hannah." Pages 113–28 in *God So Near: Essays on Old Testament Theology in Honor of Patrick D. Miller.* Edited by Brent A. Strawn and Nancy R. Bowen. Winona Lake, IN: Eisenbrauns, 2002.
Johnson, Aubrey R. *The Vitality of the Individual in the Thought of Ancient Israel.* 2nd ed. Cardiff: University of Wales Press, 1964.
Johnson, J. Cale. "The Stuff of Causation: Etiological Metaphor and Pathogenic Channeling in Babylonian Medicine." Pages 72–121 in *The Comparable Body: Analogy and Metaphor in Ancient Mesopotamian, Egyptian, and Greco-Roman Medicine.* Edited by John Z. Wee. SAM 49. Leiden: Brill, 2017.

Johnson, Paul C. "Toward an Atlantic Genealogy of 'Spirit Possession.'" Pages 23–45 in *Spirited Things: The Work of "Possession" in Afro-Atlantic Religions*. Edited by Paul C. Johnson. Chicago: University of Chicago Press, 2014.
Joseph Naveh. "Fragments of an Aramaic Magic Book from Qumran." *IEJ* 48.3/4 (1998): 252–61.
Joyce, Paul M. "The Prophets and Psychological Interpretation." Pages 133–48 in *Prophecy and Prophets in Ancient Israel: Proceedings of the Oxford Old Testament Seminar*. Edited by John Day. New York: T & T Clark, 2010.
Jung, Carl G. "Commentary on 'The Secret of the Golden Flower.'" Pages 1–56 in *Alchemical Studies*. Translated by R. F. C. Hull. Vol. 13 of *The Collected Works of C. G. Jung*. Princeton: Princeton University Press, 1967.
Kärkkäinen, Veli-Matti, Kirsteen Kim, and Amos Yong, eds. *Interdisciplinary and Religio-Cultural Discourses on a Spirit-Filled World: Loosing the Spirits*. New York: Palgrave Macmillan, 2013.
Katz, Steven T. "The Conservative Character of Mystical Experience." Pages 3–60 in *Mysticism and Religious Traditions*. Edited by Steven T. Katz. Oxford: Oxford University Press, 1983.
Kaufmann, Yeḥezkel. *The Religion of Israel: From its Beginnings to the Babylonian Exile*. Translated by Moshe Greenberg. Chicago: University of Chicago Press, 1960.
Kazen, Thomas. *Emotions in Biblical Law: A Cognitive Science Approach*. Sheffield: Sheffield Phoenix, 2011.
Kazen, Thomas. *Jesus and Purity Halakhah: Was Jesus Indifferent to Impurity?* Rev. ed. Winona Lake, IN: Eisenbrauns, 2010.
Keener, Craig S. "Spirit Possession as a Cross-Cultural Experience." *BBR* 20.2 (2010): 215–35.
Keith, Chris, and Loren T. Stuckenbruck, eds. *Evil in Second Temple Judaism and Early Christianity*. WUNT2 417. Tübingen: Mohr Siebeck, 2016.
Kelle, Brad E. *The Bible and Moral Injury: Reading Scripture alongside War's Unseen Wounds*. Nashville: Abingdon, 2020.
Kiboko, J. Kabamba. *Divining the Woman of Endor: African Culture, Postcolonial Hermeneutics, and the Politics of Biblical Translation*. LHBOTS 644. New York: T & T Clark, 2017.
Kim, Kirsteen. *The Holy Spirit in the World: A Global Conversation*. London: SPCK, 2007.
Kister, Menahem. "Body and Purification from Evil: Prayer Formulas and Concepts in Second Temple Literature and Their Relationship to Later Rabbinic Literature." *Megillot* (2010): 243–84.
Kitz, Anne Marie. "Demons in the Hebrew Bible and the Ancient Near East." *JBL* 135.3 (2016): 447–64.
Klass, Morton. *Mind Over Mind: The Anthropology and Psychology of Spirit Possession*. Lanham: Rowman & Littlefield, 2003.
Klatt, Werner. *Hermann Gunkel. zu seiner Theologie der Religiongeschichte und zur Entstehung der formgeschichtlichen Methode*. FRLANT 100. Göttingen: Vandenhoeck & Ruprecht, 1969.
Klawans, Jonathan. *Impurity and Sin in Ancient Judaism*. Oxford: Oxford University Press, 2000.

Klawans, Jonathan. "Josephus on Fate, Free Will, and Ancient Jewish Types of Compatibilism." *Numen* 56.1 (2009): 44–90.
Klawans, Jonathan. "Purity in the Dead Sea Scrolls." Pages 377–402 in *The Oxford Handbook of the Dead Sea Scrolls*. Edited by Timothy H. Lim and John J. Collins. Oxford: Oxford University Press, 2010.
Klein, Anja. "From the 'Right Spirit' to the 'Spirit of Truth': Observations on Psalm 51 and 1QS." Pages 171–91 in *The Dynamics of Language and Exegesis at Qumran*. Edited by Devorah Dimant and Reinhard Gregor Kratz. FAT2 35. Tübingen: Mohr Siebeck, 2009.
Klein, Anja. *Schriftauslegung im Ezechielbuch: redaktionsgeschichtliche Untersuchungen zu Ez 34–39*. BZAW 391. Berlin: De Gruyter, 2008.
Kluger, Rivkah Schärf. *Satan in the Old Testament*. Translated by Hildegard Nagel. Evanston: Northwestern University Press, 1967.
Klutz, Todd E. "The Grammar of Exorcism in the Ancient Mediterranean World: Some Cosmological, Semantic, and Pragmatic Reflections on How Exorcistic Prowess Contributed to the Worship of Jesus." Pages 156–65 in *The Jewish Roots of Christological Monotheism: Papers from the St. Andrews Conference on the Historical Origins of the Worship of Jesus*. Edited by Carey C. Newman, James R. Davila, and Gladys S. Lewis. Leiden: Brill, 1999.
Knibb, Michael A. "Rule of the Community." *EDSS* 1:793–97.
Koch, Robert. *Der Geist Gottes im Alten Testament*. Bern: Lang, 1991.
Koehler, Ludwig, Walter Baumgartner, and Johann Jakob Stamm. "רוח." *HALOT* 3:1195–1201.
Kosman, Admiel. "Breath, Kiss, and Speech as the Source of the Animation of Life: Ancient Foundations of Rabbinic Homilies on the Giving of the Torah as the Kiss of God." Pages 96–124 in *Self, Soul, and Body in Religious Experience*. Edited by Albert I. Baumgarten, Jan Assmann, and Guy G. Stroumsa. SHR 78. Leiden: Brill, 1998.
Kotzé, Zacharias. "A Cognitive Linguistic Approach to the Emotion of Anger in the Old Testament." *HTS* 60.3 (2004): 843–63.
Kratz, Reinhard G. *Historical and Biblical Israel: The History, Tradition, and Archives of Israel and Judah*. Oxford: Oxford University Press, 2015.
Kratz, Reinhard G. *The Composition of the Narrative Books of the Old Testament*. Translated by John Bowden. New York: T & T Clark, 2005.
Krippner, Stanley. "Learning from the Spirits: Candomble, Umbanda, and Kardecismo in Recife, Brazil." *AnthCon* 19.1 (2008): 1–32.
Krüger, Thomas. "Das menschliche Herz und die Weisung Gottes: Elemente einer Diskussion über Möglichkeiten und Grenzen der Tora-Rezeption im Alten Testament." Pages 65–92 in *Rezeption und Auslegung im Altem Testament und in seinem Umfeld: ein Symposion aus Anlass des 60. Geburtstags von Odil Hannes Steck*. Edited by Reinhard G. Kratz and Thomas Krüger. OBO 153. Göttingen: Universitätsverlag, 1997.
Kugel, James L. *A Walk through Jubilees: Studies in the Book of Jubilees and the World of Its Creation*. Leiden: Brill, 2012.
Kuhn, Karl G. "Die Sektenschrift und die Iranische Religion." *ZTK* 49.3 (1952): 296–316.
Kvalvaag, Robert W. "The Spirit in Human Beings in Some Qumran Non-Biblical Texts." Pages 159–80 in *Qumran between the Old and New Testaments*. Edited by Frederick H. Cryer and Thomas L. Thompson. JSOTSup 290. Sheffield: Sheffield Academic Press, 1998.

Lakoff, George, and Zoltán Kövecses. "The Cognitive Model of Anger Inherent in American English." Pages 195–221 in *Cultural Models in Language and Thought*. Edited by Dorothy C. Holland and Naomi Quinn. Cambridge: Cambridge University Press, 1987.

Lambek, Michael. "Afterword: Recognizing and Misrecognizing Spirit Possession." Pages 257–76 in in *Spirited Things: The Work of "Possession" in Afro-Atlantic Religions*. Edited by Paul C. Johnson. Chicago: University of Chicago Press, 2014.

Lambek, Michael. "From Disease to Discourse: Remarks on the Conceptualization of Trance and Spirit Possession." Pages 36–61 in *Altered States of Consciousness and Mental Health: A Cross Cultural Perspective*. Edited by Colleen Ward. CCRM 12. London: Sage, 1989.

Lambek, Michael. *Human Spirits: A Cultural Account of Trance in Mayotte*. CSCS 6. Cambridge: Cambridge University Press, 1981.

Lambek, Michael. *Knowledge and Practice in Mayotte: Local Discourses of Islam, Sorcery, and Spirit Possession*. AnthHor 3. Toronto: University of Toronto Press, 1993.

Lambek, Michael. "Nuriaty, the Saint and the Sultan: Virtuous Subject and Subjective Virtuoso of the Post-Modern Colony." *AnthT* 16.2 (2000): 7–12.

Lambek, Michael. "On Being Present to History: Historicity and Brigand Spirits in Madagascar." *HAU* 6.1 (2016): 317–41.

Lambek, Michael. "Taboo as Cultural Practice Among Malagasy Speakers." *Man* 27.2 (1992): 245–66.

Lambek, Michael. "The Sakalava Poiesis of History: Realizing the Past Through Spirit Possession in Madagascar." *AmEthno* 25.2 (1998): 106–27.

Lambek, Michael. *The Weight of the Past: Living with History in Mahajanga, Madagascar*. Basingstoke: Palgrave Macmillan, 2002.

Lambert, David A. *How Repentance Became Biblical: Judaism, Christianity, and the Interpretation of Scripture*. Oxford: Oxford University Press, 2015.

Lambert, David A. "Refreshing Philology: James Barr, Supersessionism, and the State of Biblical Words." *BI* 24.3 (2016): 332–56.

Lapsley, Jacqueline E. *Can These Bones Live?: The Problem of the Moral Self in the Book of Ezekiel*. BZAW 301. Berlin: De Gruyter, 2000.

Leavenworth, Jesse. "Was the 12-Year-Old Connecticut Boy Featured in 'Conjuring 3' Really Possessed? His Brother Says 'No' –and the True Horror Story Has Been His Family's Exploitation." *Hartford Courant*, 2 June 2021. https://www.courant.com/news/connecticut/hc-news-ct-demon-defense-conjuring-3-glatzel-20210602-bmugjsuihndixog222mub2lfaa-story.html.

Lehnart, Berhnard. "Saul unter den 'Ekstatikern' (I Sam 19, 18–24)." Pages 205–23 in *David und Saul im Widerstreit: Diachronie und Synchronie im Wettstreit: Beiträge zur Auslegung des ersten Samuelbuches*. Edited by Walter Dietrich. Göttingen: Vandenhoeck & Ruprecht, 2004.

Lemke, Werner E. "Circumcision of the Heart: The Journey of a Biblical Metaphor." Pages 299–319 in *A God So Near: Essays on Old Testament Theology in Honor of Patrick D. Miller*. Edited by Brent A. Strawn and Nancy R. Bowen. Winona Lake, IN: Eisenbrauns, 2003.

Leuchter, Mark. "The Rhetoric of Convention: The Foundational Saul Narratives (1 Samuel 9–11) Reconsidered." *JRH* 40.1 (2016): 3–19.

Leven, Karl-Heinz. "'At Times These Ancient Facts Seem to Lie before Me like a Patient on a Hospital Bed'—Retrospective Diagnosis and Ancient Medical History." Pages 369–86 in *Magic and Rationality in Ancient Near Eastern and Graeco-Roman Medicine*. Edited by H. F. J. Horstmanshoff, Marten Stol, and C. R. van Tilburg. SAM 27. Leiden; Boston: Brill, 2004.

Levenson, Jon D. *Creation and the Persistence of Evil: The Jewish Drama of Divine Omnipotence*. 2nd ed. Princeton: Princeton University Press, 1994.

Levenson, Jon D. *Resurrection and the Restoration of Israel: The Ultimate Victory of the God of Life*. New Haven: Yale University Press, 2006.

Levenson, Jon D. "The Hebrew Bible, the Old Testament, and Historical Criticism." Pages 1–32 in *The Hebrew Bible, the Old Testament, and Historical Criticism: Jews and Christians in Biblical Studies*. Louisville: Westminster John Knox, 1993.

Levenson, Jon D. *The Love of God: Divine Gift, Human Gratitude, and Mutual Faithfulness in Judaism*. Princeton: Princeton University Press, 2016.

Levine, Baruch A. *In the Presence of the Lord: A Study of Cult and Some Cultic Terms in Ancient Israel*. Leiden: Brill, 1974.

Levison, John R. "Did the Spirit Withdraw from Israel? An Evaluation of the Earliest Jewish Data." *NTS* 43.1 (1997): 35–57.

Levison, John R. *Filled with the Spirit*. Grand Rapids: Eerdmans, 2009.

Levison, John R. "Prophecy in Ancient Israel: The Case of the Ecstatic Elders." *CBQ* 65.4 (2003): 503–21.

Levison, John R. *The Holy Spirit before Christianity*. Waco: Baylor University Press, 2019.

Levison, John R. *The Spirit in First Century Judaism*. AGJU 29. Leiden: Brill, 1997.

Lewis, Ioan M. *Ecstatic Religion: A Study of Shamanism and Spirit Possession*. 3rd ed. New York: Routledge, 2003.

Lewis, Theodore J. *Cults of the Dead in Ancient Israel and Ugarit*. HSM 39. Atlanta: Scholars Press, 1989.

Lienhardt, R. Godfrey. *Divinity and Experience: The Religion of the Dinka*. Oxford: Oxford University Press, 1961.

Lilly, Ingrid. "A Moral Voice from a Spirit-Possessed Body?: Babylonian Medical Cosmology in the Hebrew Prophet Ezekiel." Paper presented at the Biennial Meeting of the Society for the Anthropology of Religion. San Diego, CA, 17 Apr 2015.

Lilly, Ingrid. "Conceptualizing Spirit: Supernatural Meteorology and Winds of Distress in the Hebrew Bible and the Ancient Near East." Pages 826–44 in *Sibyls, Scriptures, and Scrolls: John Collins at Seventy*. Edited by Joel Baden, Hindy Najman, and Eibert Tigchelaar. 2 vols., 2018.

Lilly, Ingrid. "Rûaḥ Embodied: Job's Internal Disease from the Perspective of Mesopotamian Medicine." Pages 323–36 in *Borders: Terminologies, Ideologies, and Performances*. Edited by Annette Weissenrieder. WUNT 366. Tübingen: Mohr Siebeck, 2016.

Lim, Timothy H., and John J. Collins, eds. *The Oxford Handbook of the Dead Sea Scrolls*. Oxford Handbooks. The Oxford Handbook of the Dead Sea Scrolls. Oxford: Oxford University Press, 2010.

Lincicum, David. "Greek Deuteronomy's 'Fever and Chills' and Their Magical Afterlife." *VT* 58.4 (2008): 544–49.

Littlemore, Jeannette. *Metonymy: Hidden Shortcuts in Language, Thought and Communication*. Cambridge: Cambridge University Press, 2015.

Loewenthal, Kate M. *Religion, Culture, and Mental Health*. Cambridge: Cambridge University Press, 2007.
Luhrmann, Tanya M. *When God Talks Back: Understanding the American Evangelical Relationship with God*. New York: Vintage Books, 2012.
Lundbom, Jack R. "Burning Anger in the Old Testament: Hebrew *Ḥrh*, *Yṣt*, and *Yqd*." *Theology in Language, Rhetoric, and Beyond: Essays in Old and New Testament*. Cambridge, UK: Lutterworth, 2014.
Lys, Daniel. *"Rûach": Le Souffle Dans l'Ancien Testament*. Études d'Histoire et de Philosophie Ireligieuses 56. Paris: Presses universitaires de France, 1962.
Ma, Wonsuk. *Until the Spirit Comes: The Spirit of God in the Book of Isaiah*. London: Bloomsbury, 2009.
MacDonald, Nathan. *Not Bread Alone: The Uses of Food in the Old Testament*. Oxford: Oxford University Press, 2008.
MacDonald, Nathan. "The Spirit of YHWH: An Overlooked Conceptualization of Divine Presence in the Persian Period." Pages 95–119 in *Divine Presence and Absence in Exilic and Post-Exilic Judaism*. Edited by Nathan MacDonald and Izaak J. de Hulster. 2 vols. FAT2 61. Tübingen: Mohr Siebeck, 2013.
Machinist, Peter. "On Self-Consciousness in Mesopotamia." Pages 183–201 in *The Origins and Diversity of Axial Age Civilizations*. Edited by S. N. Eisenstadt. Albany: State University of New York Press, 1986.
Mahmood, Saba. *Politics of Piety: The Islamic Revival and the Feminist Subject*. Princeton: Princeton University Press, 2011.
Maiden, Brett. "Psychological Essentialism in Serek Ha-Yaḥad and the Two Spirits Treatise." *DSD* 25.1 (2018): 39–56.
Mainwaring, Simon. *Mark, Mutuality, and Mental Health: Encounters with Jesus*. SemeiaSt 79. Atlanta: SBL, 2014.
Manigault-Bryant, LeRhonda S. *Talking to the Dead: Religion, Music, and Lived Memory among Gullah-Geechee Women*. Durham: Duke University Press, 2014.
Marchand, Suzanne L. *German Orientalism in the Age of Empire: Religion, Race, and Scholarship*. PGHI. Cambridge: Cambridge University Press, 2009.
Martin, Dale B. "When Did Angels Become Demons?" *JBL* 129.4 (2010): 657–77.
Martin, Lee Roy. "Power to Save!?: The Role of the Spirit of the Lord in the Book of Judges." *JPT* 16.2 (2008): 21–50.
Martin, Lee Roy. *The Unheard Voice of God: A Pentecostal Hearing of the Book of Judges*. JPTSup 32. Blandford Forum: Deo, 2008.
Martínez, Florentino García. *The Dead Sea Scrolls Translated: The Qumran Texts in English*. Translated by Wilfred G. E. Watson. 2nd ed. Leiden: Brill, 1996.
Masquelier, Adeline. "From Hostage to Host: Confessions of a Spirit Medium in Niger." *Ethos* 30.1/2 (2002): 49–76.
Maston, Jason. "Anthropological Crisis and Solution in the Hodayot and 1 Corinthians 15." *NTS* 62.4 (2016): 533–48.
McCarter Jr., P. Kyle. "Evil Spirit of God." *DDD*, 319–20.
McCarter Jr., P. Kyle. *I Samuel: A New Translation with Introduction, Notes, and Commentary*. AB 8. Garden City, NY: Doubleday, 1980.
McDonald, Joseph, ed. *Exploring Moral Injury in Sacred Texts*. Philadelphia: Jessica Kingsley, 2017.

Mercer, Jean. "Deliverance, Demonic Possession, and Mental Illness: Some Considerations for Mental Health Professionals." *MHRC* 16.6 (2013): 595–611.

Michaelsen, Peter. "Ecstasy and Possession in Ancient Israel: A Review of Some Recent Contributions." *SJOT* 3.2 (1989): 28–54.

Míguez, Daniel. *Spiritual Bonfire in Argentina: Confronting Current Theories with an Ethnographic Account of Pentecostal Growth in a Buenos Aires Suburb*. LAS 81. Amsterdam: CEDLA, 1998.

Milgrom, Jacob. "Israel's Sanctuary: The Priestly 'Picture of Dorian Gray.'" *RB* 83.3 (1976): 390–99.

Milgrom, Jacob. *Leviticus 1–16: A New Translation with Introduction and Commentary*. AB 3. New York: Doubleday, 1991.

Milgrom, Jacob. "Systemic Differences in the Priestly Corpus: A Response to Jonathan Klawans." *RB* 112.3 (2005): 321–29.

Miller, James E. "A Critical Response to Karin Adams's Reinterpretation of Hosea 4:13–14." *JBL* 128.3 (2009): 503–6.

Miller, Shem. "The Role of Performance and the Performance of Role: Cultural Memory in the Hodayot." *JBL* 137.2 (2018): 359–82.

Mittermaier, Amira. "Dreams from Elsewhere: Muslim Subjectivities beyond the Trope of Self-Cultivation." *JRAI* 18.2 (2012): 247–65.

Moberly, R. W. L. "Does God Lie to His Prophets?: The Story of Micaiah Ben Imlah as a Test Case." *HTR* 96.1 (2003): 1–23.

Moberly, R. W. L. "Micaiah Ben Imlah: The Costs of Authenticity and Discernment." Pages 100–129 in *Prophecy and Discernment*. CSCD 14. Cambridge: Cambridge University Press, 2006.

Morris, Michael J. *Warding Off Evil: Apotropaic Tradition in the Dead Sea Scrolls and Synoptic Gospels*. WUNT2 451. Tübingen: Mohr Siebeck, 2017.

Moss, Candida R. "The Man with the Flow of Power: Porous Bodies in Mark 5:25–34." *JBL* 129.3 (2010): 507–19.

Moss, Candida R., and Jeremy Schipper, eds. *Disability Studies and Biblical Literature*. New York: Palgrave Macmillan, 2011.

Moss, Candida R., and Jeremy Schipper. "Introduction." Pages 1–11 in *Disability Studies and Biblical Literature*. New York: Palgrave Macmillan, 2011.

Mowinckel, Sigmund. "'The Spirit' and the 'Word' in the Pre-Exilic Reforming Prophets." *JBL* 53.3 (1934): 199–227.

Mülller, Hans-Peter. "נָבִיא." *TDOT* 9:129–50.

Najman, Hindy. "Imitatio Dei and the Formation of the Subject in Ancient Judaism." *JBL* 140.2 (2021): 309–23.

Nasrallah, Laura S. *An Ecstasy of Folly: Prophecy and Authority in Early Christianity*. HTS 52. Cambridge, MA: Harvard University Press, 2003.

Neiman, Susan. *Evil in Modern Thought: An Alternative History of Philosophy*. Princeton: Princeton University Press, 2002.

Neuner, Frank, Anett Pfeiffer, Elisabeth Schauer-Kaiser, Michael Odenwald, Thomas Elbert, and Verena Ertl. "Haunted by Ghosts: Prevalence, Predictors and Outcomes of Spirit Possession Experiences among Former Child Soldiers and War-Affected Civilians in Northern Uganda." *SSM* 75.3 (2012): 548–54.

Neusner, Jacob. *The Idea of Purity in Ancient Judaism*. Leiden: Brill, 1973.

Neve, Lloyd. *The Spirit of God in the Old Testament*. Tokyo: Seibunsha, 1972.
Newsom, Carol A. "Apocalyptic Subjects: Social Construction of the Self in the Qumran Hodayot." *JSP* 12.1 (2001): 3–35.
Newsom, Carol A. "Models of the Moral Self: Hebrew Bible and Second Temple Judaism." *JBL* 131.1 (2012): 5–25.
Newsom, Carol A. *The Self as Symbolic Space: Constructing Identity and Community at Qumran*. STDJ 52. Leiden: Brill, 2004.
Newsom, Carol A. *The Spirit Within Me: Self and Agency in Ancient Israel and Second Temple Judaism*. New Haven: Yale University Press, 2021.
Newsom, Carol A. "Toward a Genealogy of the Introspective Self in Second Temple Judaism." Pages 63–79 in *Functions of Psalms and Prayers in the Late Second Temple Period*. Edited by Mika S. Pajunen and Jeremy Penner. BZAW 486. Berlin: De Gruyter, 2017.
Ngong, David. "African Pentecostal Pneumatology." Pages 77–90 in *Pentecostal Theology in Africa*. Edited by Clifton Clarke. ACSS 6. Eugene: Pickwick, 2014.
Nickelsburg, George W. E. "Enoch, Books of." *EDSS* 1:249–53.
Nicklas, Tobias. "'Food of Angels' (Wis 16:20)." Pages 83–100 in *Studies in the Book of Wisdom*. Edited by Géza G. Xeravits and József Zsengellér. JSJSup 142. Leiden: Brill, 2010.
Nicklas, Tobias, Karin Schöpflin, and Friedrich V. Reiterer. *Angels: The Concept of Celestial Beings: Origins, Development and Reception*. Deuterocanonical and Cognate Literature Yearbook. Berlin: De Gruyter, 2007.
Niditch, Susan. *The Responsive Self: Personal Religion in Biblical Literature of the Neo-Babylonian and Persian Periods*. New Haven: Yale University Press, 2015.
Niditch, Susan. *War in the Hebrew Bible: A Study in the Ethics of Violence*. Oxford: Oxford University Press, 1993.
Nihan, Christophe. "1 Samuel 28 and the Condemnation of Necromancy in Persian Yehud." Pages 23–54 in *Magic in the Biblical World: From the Rod of Aaron to the Ring of Solomon*. Edited by Todd Klutz. JSNTSup 245. New York: T & T Clark, 2003.
Nihan, Christophe. "Saul Among the Prophets (1 Sam 10:10–12 and 19:18–24): The Reworking of Saul's Figure in the Contexts of the Debate on 'Charismatic Prophecy' in the Persian Era." Pages 88–118 in *Saul in Story and Tradition*. Edited by Carl S. Ehrlich and Marsha C. White. FAT 47. Tübingen: Mohr Siebeck, 2006.
Nissinen, Martti. *Ancient Prophecy: Near Eastern, Biblical, and Greek Perspectives*. Oxford: Oxford University Press, 2017.
Nissinen, Martti. "Biblical Prophecy from a Near Eastern Perspective: The Cases of Kingship and Divine Possession." Pages 441–68 in *Congress Volume Ljubljana 2007*. Edited by André Lemaire. VTSup 133. Leiden: Brill, 2010.
Nissinen, Martti. "Prophecy and Ecstasy." *Ancient Prophecy: Near Eastern, Biblical, and Greek Perspectives*. Oxford: University Press, 2017.
Nissinen, Martti. ed. *Prophecy in its Ancient Near Eastern Context: Mesopotamian, Biblical, and Arabian Perspectives*. SBLSS 13. Atlanta: SBL Press, 2000.
Nissinen, Martti. "Prophetic Madness." *Ancient Prophecy: Near Eastern, Biblical, and Greek Perspectives*. Oxford: University Press, 2017.
Nissinen, Martti. "Prophetic Madness: Prophecy and Ecstasy in the Ancient Near East and in Greece." Pages 3–29 in *Raising Up a Faithful Exegete: Essays in Honor of Richard D.*

Nelson. Edited by Kurt L. Noll and Brooks Schramm. University Park: Penn State University Press, 2010.
Nisula, Tapio. *Everyday Spirits and Medical Interventions: Ethnographic and Historical Notes on Therapeutic Conventions in Zanzibar Town*. SAST 43. Helsinki: Finnish Anthropological Society, 1999.
Noll, K. L. "The Deconstruction of Deuteronomism in the Former Prophets: Micaiah Ben Imlah as Example." Pages 325–34 in *Far from Minimal: Celebrating the Work and Influence of Philip R. Davies*. Edited by Duncan Burns and John W. Rogerson. LHBOTS 484. New York: T & T Clark, 2014.
Olyan, Saul M. *Disability in the Hebrew Bible: Interpreting Mental and Physical Differences*. Cambridge: Cambridge University Press, 2008.
Orlinsky, Harry Meyer. "The Plain Meaning of *Ruah* in Gen 1:2." *JQR* 48.2 (1957): 174–82.
Otto, Rudolf. *The Idea of the Holy: An Inquiry into the Non-Rational Factor in the Idea of the Divine and Its Relation to the Rational*. 2nd ed. Oxford: Oxford University Press, 1958.
Pagels, Elaine H. *The Origin of Satan*. New York: Random House, 1995.
Papaioannou, Kim. "The Sin of the Angels in 2 Peter 2:4 and Jude 6." *JBL* 140.2 (2021): 391–408.
Parker, Jonathan Deane. "Moses and the Seventy Elders: Mosaic Authority in Numbers 11 and the 'Legend of the Septuagint.'" PhD Diss., Durham University, 2015.
Parker, Simon B. "Possession Trance and Prophecy in Pre-Exilic Israel." *VT* 28.3 (1978): 271–85.
Paul, Shalom M. "Job 4:15 – a Hair Raising Encounter." *ZAW* 95.1 (1983): 119–21.
Penney, Douglas L., and Michael O. Wise. "By the Power of Beelzebub: An Aramaic Incantation Formula from Qumran (4Q560)." *JBL* 113.4 (1994): 627–50.
Petersen, David L. "Ecstasy and Role Enactment." Pages 279–88 in *"The Place Is Too Small for Us": The Israelite Prophets in Recent Scholarship*. Edited by R. P. Gordon. SBTS 5. Winona Lake, IN: Eisenbrauns, 1995.
Poirier, John C. *The Tongues of Angels: The Concept of Angelic Languages in Classical Jewish and Christian Texts*. WUNT2 287. Tübingen: Mohr Siebeck, 2010.
Pola, Thomas. "Ekstase im Alten Testament." Pages 1–77 in *Gott fürchten und lieben: Studien zur Gotteserfahrung im Alten Testament*. BThSt 59. Neukirchen-Vluyn: Neukirchener, 2007.
Popović, Mladen. "Apocalyptic Determinism." Pages 225–70 in *The Oxford Handbook of Apocalyptic Literature*. Edited by John J. Collins. Oxford: Oxford University Press, 2014.
Popović, Mladen. "Light and Darkness in the Treatise on the Two Spirits (1QS III 13–IV 26) and in 4Q186." Pages 148–65 in *Dualism in Qumran*. Edited by Géza G. Xeravits. LSTS 76. London: T & T Clark, 2010.
van de Port, Mattijs. "Circling around the Really Real: Spirit Possession Ceremonies and the Search for Authenticity in Bahian Candomblé." *Ethos* 33.2 (2005): 149–79.
Porter, Roy. "Witchcraft and Magic in Enlightenment, Romantic, and Liberal Thought." Pages 193–282 in *Witchcraft and Magic in Europe: The Twentieth Century*. Edited by Bengt Ankarloo and Stuart Clark. 6 vols. Philadelphia: University of Pennsylvania Press, 1999.
Proudfoot, Wayne. *Religious Experience*. Berkeley: University of California Press, 1987.
Qimron, Elisha. "Qumran Corner: Notes on the 4Q Zadokite Fragment on Skin Disease." *JJS* 42.2 (1991): 256–59.

Reed, Annette Yoshiko. *Demons, Angels, and Writing in Ancient Judaism*. Cambridge: Cambridge University Press, 2020.
Reed, Annette Yoshiko. *Fallen Angels and the History of Judaism and Christianity: The Reception of Enochic Literature*. Cambridge: Cambridge University Press, 2005.
Reiling, Jannes. "Holy Spirit." *DDD*, 419–20.
Reimer, Andy M. "Rescuing the Fallen Angels: The Case of the Disappearing Angels at Qumran." *DSD* 7.3 (2000): 334–53.
Reis, Pamela Tamarkin. "Eating the Blood: Saul and the Witch of Endor." *JSOT* 73 (1997): 3–23.
Reuter, Eleonore. "קנא." *TDOT* 13:47–58.
Reventlow, Henning Graf. *History of Biblical Interpretation, Volume 4: From the Enlightenment to the Twentieth Century*. Translated by Leo G. Perdue. RBS 63. Atlanta: SBL Press, 2009.
Ricoeur, Paul. *The Symbolism of Evil*. Translated by Emerson Buchanan. Boston: Beacon, 1967.
Rogan, Wil. "Purity in Early Judaism: Current Issues and Questions." *CBR* 16.3 (2018): 309–39.
Rosen-Zvi, Ishay. *Demonic Desires: "Yetzer Hara" and the Problem of Evil in Late Antiquity*. Philadelphia: University of Pennsylvania Press, 2011.
Rouch, Jean. *Les Maîtres Fous ("The Mad Masters")*. France, Les Films de la Pléiade, 1955.
Sands, Kathleen R. *An Elizabethan Lawyer's Possession by the Devil: The Story of Robert Brigges*. Westport: Praeger, 2002.
Sands, Kathleen R. *Demon Possession in Elizabethan England*. Westport: Praeger, 2004.
Sands, Kathleen R. "John Foxe: Exorcist." *History Today* 51.2 (2001): 37–43.
Schaper, Joachim. "Elements of a History of the Soul in North-West Semitic Texts: Npš/Nbš in the Hebrew Bible and the Katumuwa Inscription." *VT* 70.1 (2020): 156–76.
Scheepers, Johannes H. *Die Gees van God En Die Gees van Die Mens in Die Ou Testament*. Kampen: Kok, 1960.
Schiffman, Lawrence H., and Michael D. Swartz. *Hebrew and Aramaic Incantation Texts from the Cairo Genizah: Selected Texts from Taylor-Schechter Box K1*. STS 1. Sheffield: JSOT Press, 1992.
Schiffman, Lawrence H., Emanuel Tov, James C. VanderKam, and Galen Marquis, eds. "Implanting Pious Qualities as a Theme in the Barkhi Nafshi Hymns." *The Dead Sea Scrolls Fifty Years after Their Discovery: Proceedings of the Jerusalem Congress, July 20–25, 1997*. Jerusalem: Israel Exploration Society, 2000.
Schipper, Jeremy. *Disability Studies and the Hebrew Bible: Figuring Mephibosheth in the David Story*. LHBOTS 441. New York: T & T Clark, 2006.
Schmidt, Bettina E., and Lucy Huskinson. "Introduction." Pages 1–15 in *Spirit Possession and Trance: New Interdisciplinary Perspectives*. Edited by Bettina E. Schmidt and Lucy Huskinson. New York: Continuum, 2011.
Schmidt, Bettina E., and Lucy Huskinson, eds. *Spirit Possession and Trance: New Interdisciplinary Perspectives*. New York: Continuum, 2011.
Schmidt, Brian B. "The 'Witch' of En-Dor, 1 Samuel 28, and Ancient Near Eastern Necromancy." *Ancient Magic and Ritual Power*. Edited by Marvin W. Meyer and Paul Allan Mirecki. RGRW 129. Leiden: Brill, 1995.

Schmidt, Ludwig. *Menschlicher Erfolg und Jahwes Initiative: Studien zu Tradition, Interpretation und Historie in Überlieferungen von Gideon, Saul und David.* WMANT 38. Neukirchen-Vluyn: Neukirchener, 1970.

Schofield, Alison. *From Qumran to the Yaḥad: A New Paradigm of Textual Development for The Community Rule.* STDJ 77. Leiden: Brill, 2009.

Schuller, Eileen M. "Petitionary Prayer and Religion at Qumran." Pages 29–45 in *Religion in the Dead Sea Scrolls.* Edited by John J. Collins and Robert A. Kugler. SDSSRL. Grand Rapids: Eerdmans, 2000.

Schwartz, Baruch J., ed. *Perspectives on Purity and Purification in the Bible.* LHBOTS 474. New York: T&T Clark, 2008.

Scurlock, Jo Ann. *Magico-Medical Means of Treating Ghost-Induced Illnesses in Ancient Mesopotamia.* AMD 3. Leiden: Brill, 2006.

Seebass, Horst. "נפשׁ." *TDOT* 9:497–519.

Seely, David Rolph. "Barkhi Nafshi." *EDSS* 1:76–77.

Seely, David Rolph. "The Barki Nafshi Texts (4Q434–439)." Pages 194–214 in *Current Research and Technological Developments on the Dead Sea Scrolls: Conference on the Texts from the Judean Desert, Jerusalem, 30 April, 1995.* Edited by D. W. Parry and S. D. Rick. Leiden: Brill, 1996.

Seely, David Rolph. "The 'Circumcised Heart' in '4Q434 Barki Nafshi.'" *RevQ* 17.1–4 (1996): 527–35.

Segal, Michael. *The Book of Jubilees: Rewritten Bible, Redaction, Ideology and Theology.* JSJSup 117. Leiden: Brill, 2007.

Segal, Michael. "The Literary Relationship between the Genesis Apocryphon and Jubilees: The Chronology of Abram and Sarai's Descent to Egypt." *AS* 8.1–2 (2010): 71–88.

Segal, Robert A. "Myth and Ritual." Pages 372–96 in *The Routledge Companion to the Study of Religion.* Edited by John R. Hinnells. 2nd ed. London: Routledge, 2010.

Sekki, Arthur Everett. *The Meaning of Ruaḥ at Qumran.* SBLDS 110. Atlanta: SBL Press, 1989.

Sellars, Dawn Maria. "An Obedient Servant?: The Reign of King Saul (1 Samuel 13–15) Reassessed." *JSOT* 35.3 (2011): 317–38.

Sered, Susan Starr. *Priestess, Mother, Sacred Sister: Religions Dominated by Women.* Oxford: Oxford University Press, 1996.

Shaked, Shaul. "Qumran and Iran: Further Considerations." *IOS* 2 (1972): 433–46.

Shantz, Colleen. "Opening the Black Box: New Prospects for Analyzing Religious Experience." Pages 1–15 in *Experientia, Volume 2: Linking Text and Experience.* Edited by Colleen Shantz and Rodney A. Werline. Atlanta: SBL Press, 2012.

Shantz, Colleen. *Paul in Ecstasy: The Neurobiology of the Apostle's Life and Thought.* Cambridge: Cambridge University Press, 2009.

Shantz, Colleen, and Rodney A. Werline. *Experientia, Volume 2, Linking Text and Experience.* EJL 35. Atlanta: SBL Press, 2012.

Sharf, Robert H. "Experience." Pages 94–116 in *Critical Terms for Religious Studies.* Edited by Mark C. Taylor. Chicago: University of Chicago Press, 1998.

Sharp, Lesley A. "Exorcists, Psychiatrists, and the Problems of Possession in Northwest Madagascar." *SSM* 38.4 (1994): 525–42.

Sharp, Lesley A. "Playboy Princely Spirits of Madagascar: Possession as Youthful Commentary and Social Critique." *AQ* 68.2 (1995): 75–88.

Sharp, Lesley A. "Royal Difficulties: A Question of Succession in an Urbanized Sakalava Kingdom." *JRAf* 27.1–4 (1997): 270–307.

Sharp, Lesley A. *The Possessed and the Dispossessed: Spirits, Identity, and Power in a Madagascar Migrant Town*. CSHSMC 37. Berkeley: University of California Press, 1993.

Shay, Jonathan. *Odysseus in America: Combat Trauma and the Trials of Homecoming*. New York: Scribner, 2002.

Sherwood, Yvonne. "Modern Trails and Tests of 'Experience': Plastic Commonplace and Managed Exception." Pages 30–56 in *Religious Experience Revisited: Expressing the Inexpressible?* Edited by Thomas Hardtke, Ulrich Schmiedel, and Tobias Tan. Leiden: Brill, 2016.

Smith, Frederick M. *The Self Possessed: Deity and Spirit Possession in South Asian Literature and Civilization*. New York: Columbia University Press, 2006.

Smith, Mark S. *The Genesis of Good and Evil: The Fall(out) and Original Sin in the Bible*. Louisville: Westminster John Knox, 2019.

Smith, Mark S. "The Heart and Innards in Israelite Emotional Expressions: Notes from Anthropology and Psychobiology." *JBL* 117.3 (1998): 427–36.

Snaith, Norman H. *Distinctive Ideas of the Old Testament*. Eugene: Wipf and Stock, 2009.

Somer, Eli. "Culture-Bound Dissociation: A Comparative Analysis." *PCNA* 29.1 (2006): 213–26.

Sommer, Benjamin D. "Reflecting on Moses: The Redaction of Numbers 11." *JBL* 118.4 (1999): 601–24.

Sorensen, Eric. "Possession and Exorcism in Ancient Israel and Early Judaism." Pages 47–74 in *Possession and Exorcism in the New Testament and Early Christianity*. WUNT2 157. Tübingen: Mohr Siebeck, 2002.

Sperling, S. David. "Belial." *DDD*, 169–71.

Stagis, Julie. "Killer's Defense Was Demon Possession." *Hartford Courant*, 12 April 2014. https://www.courant.com/news/connecticut/hc-250-arne-johnson-20140412-story.html.

Stein, George. "The Voices That Ezekiel Hears." *BRJ* 196.2 (2010): 101.

Steiner, Richard C. *Disembodied Souls: The Nefesh in Israel and Kindred Spirits in the Ancient Near East, with an Appendix on the Katumuwa Inscription*. ANEM 11. Atlanta: SBL, 2015.

Steinmann, Andrew. "The Chicken and the Egg: A New Proposal for the Relationship Between the Prayer of Nabonidus and the Book of Daniel." *RevQ* 20.4 (80) (2002): 557–70.

Stendahl, Krister. "The Apostle Paul and the Introspective Conscience of the West." *HTR* 56.3 (1963): 199–215.

Steven Engler. "Umbanda and Africa." *NovaRel* 15.4 (2012): 13–35.

Stökl, Jonathan. *Prophecy in the Ancient Near East: A Philological and Sociological Comparison*. Leiden: Brill, 2012.

Stuckenbruck, Loren T. "Origins of Evil in Jewish Apocalyptic Tradition: The Interpretation of Genesis 6:1–4." Pages 1–33 in *The Myth of Rebellious Angels: Studies in Second Temple Judaism and New Testament Texts*. WUNT 335. Tübingen: Mohr Siebeck, 2014.

Stuckenbruck, Loren T. "The Human Being and Demonic Invasion: Therapeutic Models in Ancient Jewish and Christian Texts." Pages 161–86 in *The Myth of Rebellious Angels: Studies in Second Temple Judaism and New Testament Texts*. WUNT 335. Tübingen: Mohr Siebeck, 2014.

Stuckenbruck, Loren T. "The Interiorization of Dualism within the Human Being in Second Temple Judaism: The Treatise of the Two Spirits (1QS III:13–IV:26) in its Tradition-

Historical Context." Pages 145–68 in *Light against Darkness: Dualism in Ancient Mediterranean Religion and the Contemporary World*. Edited by Armin Lange. Göttingen: Vandenhoeck & Ruprecht, 2011.

Stuckenbruck, Loren T. *The Myth of Rebellious Angels: Studies in Second Temple Judaism and New Testament Texts*. WUNT 335. Tübingen: Mohr Siebeck, 2014.

Stuckenbruck, Loren T. "The Need for Protection from the Evil One and John's Gospel." Pages 187–215 in *The Myth of Rebellious Angels: Studies in Second Temple Judaism and New Testament Texts*. WUNT 335. Tübingen: Mohr Siebeck, 2014.

Sturdy, John. "The Original Meaning of 'Is Saul Also Among the Prophets?' (1 Samuel X 11, 12; XIX 24)." *VT* 20.2 (1970): 206–13.

Sulzbach, Carla. "When Going on a Heavenly Journey, Travel Light and Dress Appropriately." *JSP* 19.3 (2010): 163–93.

Taussig, Michael T. *The Devil and Commodity Fetishism in South America*. Chapel Hill: University of North Carolina Press, 1980.

Taves, Ann. *Religious Experience Reconsidered: A Building-Block Approach to the Study of Religion and Other Special Things*. Princeton: Princeton University Press, 2009.

Taylor, Charles. *A Secular Age*. Cambridge, MA: Harvard University Press, 2007.

Teeter, D. Andrew. "The Hebrew Bible and/as Second Temple Literature: Methodological Reflections." *DSD* 20.3 (2013): 349–77.

Tengström, Sven, and Heinz-Josef Fabry. "רוח." *TDOT* 13:365–402.

Thiessen, Matthew. *Jesus and the Forces of Death: The Gospels' Portrayal of Ritual Impurity within First-Century Judaism*. Grand Rapids: Baker Academic, 2020.

Tibbs, Clint. *Religious Experience of the Pneuma: Communication with the Spirit World in 1 Corinthians 12 and 14*. WUNT2 230. Tübingen: Mohr Siebeck, 2007.

Tigchelaar, Eibert. "The Evil Inclination in The Dead Sea Scrolls, with a Re-Edition of 4Q468I (4QSectarian Text?)." Pages 347–55 in *Empsychoi Logoi: Religious Innovations in Antiquity; Studies in Honour of Pieter Willem van Der Horst*. Edited by Alberdina Houtman, Albert de Jong, and Magda Misset-van de Weg. AJEC 73. Brill: Leiden, 2008.

Tropper, Josef. *Nekromantie: Totenbefragung im Alten Orient und im Alten Testament*. AOAT 223. Neukirchen-Vluyn: Neukirchener, 1989.

Tropper, Josef. "Spirit of the Dead." *DDD*, 806–9.

Tropper, Josef. "Wizard." *DDD*, 907–8.

Twelftree, Graham H. *Jesus the Exorcist: A Contribution to the Study of the Historical Jesus*. WUNT2 54. Tübingen: Mohr Siebeck, 1993.

VanderKam, James C. "The Angel of the Presence in the Book of Jubilees." *DSD* 7.3 (2000): 378–93.

VanGemeren, William, and Andrew Abernethy. Pages 321–45 in "The Spirit and the Future: A Canonical Approach," in Presence, Power, and Promise: The Role of the Spirit of God in the Old Testament. Edited by David G. Firth and Paul D. Wegner. Downers Grove: IVP Academic 2011.

Volz, Paul. *Das Dämonische in Jahwe*. Tübingen: Mohr, 1924.

Volz, Paul. *Der Geist Gottes und die verwandten Erscheinungen im Alten Testament und im anschliessenden Judentum*. Tübingen: Mohr, 1910.

Vreugdenhil, Gerrit C. *Psalm 91 and Demonic Menace*. OtSt 77. Leiden: Brill, 2020.

Wacholder, Ben Zion. *The New Damascus Document: The Midrash on the Eschatological Torah of the Dead Sea Scrolls: Reconstruction, Translation and Commentary.* STDJ 56. Leiden: Brill, 2007.
Wagner, Andreas. "Speech Acts: Biblical Hebrew," *EHLL*, 605–10.
Waldman, Nahum M. "The Imagery of Clothing, Covering, and Overpowering." *JANES* 19 (1989): 161–70.
Ward, Colleen A., and Michael H. Beaubrun. "The Psychodynamics of Demon Possession." *JSSR* 19.2 (1980): 201–7.
Wee, John Z., ed. *The Comparable Body: Analogy and Metaphor in Ancient Mesopotamian, Egyptian, and Greco-Roman Medicine.* SAM 49. Leiden: Brill, 2017.
Wellhausen, Julius. *Prolegomena to the History of Israel: With a Reprint of the Article Israel from the "Encyclopaedia Britannica."* Translated by John Sutherland Black and Allan Menzies. Edinburgh: Adam & Charles Black, 1885.
Werline, Rodney A. "Assessing the Prophetic Vision and Dream Texts for Insights into Religious Experience." Pages 1–15 in *"I Lifted My Eyes and Saw": Reading Dream and Vision Reports in the Hebrew Bible.* Edited by Elizabeth R. Hayes and Lena-Sofia Tiemeyer. LHBOTS 584. London: Bloomsbury, 2014.
West, Benjamin. *Saul and the Witch of Endor.* Oil on Canvas, 1777. London, Victoria and Albert Museum. http://collections.vam.ac.uk/item/O134041/saul-and-the-witch-of-oil-painting-west-benjamin/.
Westermann, Claus. "Geist im Alten Testament." *Evangelische Theologie* 41.3 (1981): 223–30.
William Ross Schoemaker. "The Use of רוּחַ in the Old Testament, and of Πνεῦμα in the New Testament: A Lexicographical Study." *JBL* 23.1 (1904): 13–67.
Williams, Gillian Patricia, and Magdel Le Roux. "King Saul's Mysterious Malady." *HTS* 68.1 (2012).
Williams, Ronald J., and John C. Beckman. *Williams' Hebrew Syntax.* 3rd ed. Toronto: University of Toronto Press, 2007.
Wilson, Robert R. "Prophecy and Ecstasy: A Reexamination." *JBL* 98.3 (1979): 321–37.
Wilson, Robert R. *Prophecy and Society in Ancient Israel.* Philadelphia: Fortress Press, 1980.
Wilson, Stephen M. "Fear, Love, and Leadership: Posing a Machiavellian Question to the Hebrew Bible." *JBL* 139.2 (2020): 233–53.
Wolde, Ellen van. "Sentiments as Culturally Constructed Emotions: Anger and Love in the Hebrew Bible." *BI* 16 (2008): 1–24.
Wolfe, Michael C. *The Abundant Life Prevails: Religious Traditions of Saint Helena Island.* Waco: Baylor University Press, 2000.
Wolff, Hans Walter. *Anthropology of the Old Testament.* Translated by Margaret Kohl. Philadelphia: Fortress, 1974.
Wright, Archie T. *The Origin of Evil Spirits: The Reception of Genesis 6:1–4 in Early Jewish Literature.* 2nd ed. Minneapolis: Fortress, 2015.
Wright, David P. "The Spectrum of Priestly Impurity." Pages 150–81 in *Priesthood and Cult in Ancient Israel.* Edited by Gary A. Anderson and Saul M. Olyan. Sheffield: Sheffield Academic, 1991.
Yamaguchi, Masataka, Dennis Tay, and Benjamin Blount, eds. *Approaches to Language, Culture, and Cognition: The Intersection of Cognitive Linguistics and Linguistic Anthropology.* London: Palgrave Macmillan, 2014.

Young, Jason R. *Rituals of Resistance: African Atlantic Religion in Kongo and the Lowcountry South in the Era of Slavery*. Baton Rouge: Louisiana State University Press, 2007.

Zahn, Molly. *Genres of Rewriting in Second Temple Judaism: Scriptural Composition and Transmission*. Cambridge: Cambridge University Press, 2020.

Index of Ancient Sources

Hebrew Bible

Genesis
- 1:22   103n36
- 1:28   103n36
- 2:7   95
- 5:18–24   88n83
- 6:1–4   80, 88
- 6:3a   106n42
- 6:4, 5–7, 12   88
- 6:17   95, 106n42
- 7:15, 22   95, 106n42
- 9:1   103n36
- 11:1–9   80
- 12   79
- 12:10–20   135
- 12:17   135
- 14:13   79
- 15:5   79
- 22   89n85
- 22:15–18   79
- 30:2   66
- 39:19   67
- 41:8   67, 104
- 41:38   103n34, 107
- 41:38–39   104
- 42:24   66
- 43:30   66
- 45:2   66
- 45:14   66
- 45:27   104
- 46:29   66

Exodus
- 6:12   143
- 17:8–16   35
- 18   114n73
- 22:18   50
- 24   114n73
- 28:1–3   103n34
- 28:3   102
- 30:24   66
- 30:34–35   103n36
- 31:1–6   103n34
- 31:2–3   107
- 31:3   102, 103
- 33:22   66
- 34:7   131
- 35:30–35   103n34
- 35:31   102, 103
- 40:34   103, 104
- 40:35   104

Leviticus
- 13–15   134
- 13:33   134
- 16:8, 10, 26   133
- 17:7   133
- 19–20   47
- 19:31   48, 53n94
- 19:32   47
- 20:6   48, 53n94
- 20:27   53n94
- 26:41   142, 143n61

Numbers
- 5:11–31   70–71, 74
- 5:14, 30   70, 133
- 6:1–21   58
- 6:24–26   77n56
- 11   113, 114n73
- 11:16–30   74
- 11:25   120
- 11:25–27   110n56
- 11:25–29   155n95
- 11:29   120, 156n96
- 14:18   131
- 14:24   107n43
- 24:2   74n46, 156n96
- 24:2–3a   106, 116
- 24:10   66
- 26:55   50n84
- 27:16   121
- 27:16–23   74
- 27:18   120
- 27:18–23   103n34

Deuteronomy
- 2:30 68, 149n77
- 5–11 142
- 10 143
- 10:12–13, 16 142
- 10:12–16 126, 142
- 10:16 143
- 15:10 68n30
- 18 47
- 18:10 50
- 18:11 53n94
- 18:12 85n76
- 21:17 120
- 25:17–19 35
- 30 142, 143, 151
- 30:1–2a 142
- 30:6 126, 142
- 34:9 102, 103, 103n34, 104, 120

Joshua
- 2:11a 106n42
- 5:1 106n42

Judges
- 3:10 74, 74n46, 103, 106, 156n96
- 6:34 74, 74n46, 108, 156n96
- 9:23 107, 114, 115, 156n96
- 11:29 74, 106, 156n96
- 13:25 108
- 14:6 74, 74n46, 108
- 14:6, 19 35, 156n96
- 14:19 108
- 15:14 35, 108, 156n96
- 19:6 68n30

1 Samuel
- 1–2 34
- 1:14 112n64
- 1:15 67
- 1:22–28 34
- 2:19 34
- 8 37n32
- 9:5–10 33
- 9:9 33
- 10 44, 113, 114, 147
- 10:5 76
- 10:5–6, 10, 13 110n56, 111
- 10:5b–6, 9–10 32
- 10:6 33, 74n46, 76, 111, 156n96
- 10:6, 10 108
- 10:9 33, 147
- 10:10 147, 156n96
- 10:11, 12 110n55
- 10:12 113
- 10:12a 120
- 11:6 35, 108, 156n96
- 13–15 41
- 13:8 37
- 13:8–15a 36
- 13:12 37
- 13:13–14 37
- 14:2 112n64
- 14:24 47
- 14:24, 43–44 37
- 14:24–45 36x
- 14:31–35 37
- 14:37 37, 50
- 14:41 50n84, 75
- 14:45–46 37
- 14:47–48 37
- 14:52 36–37
- 15 35, 35n37, 47
- 15:3 35
- 15:21 35
- 15:22–23 35
- 15:35 58
- 16 44
- 16:2 26
- 16:13 108
- 16:13–14 15, 36, 36n30, 85
- 16:14 114, 156n96
- 16:14–15, 23 43
- 16:14–23 32, 156n96
- 16:15, 23 29
- 16:15–16, 23 156n96
- 16:15–19, 23 44
- 16:16 106
- 16:23 116
- 18:10 29, 32n14, 43, 108, 110n56, 111, 114, 156n96
- 18:10–11 111
- 18:12 15
- 19 114
- 19:9 29, 43, 108, 156n96
- 19:20 76, 106
- 19:20–21, 23–24 110n56, 111
- 19:20, 23 156n96

- 19:20–24   111
- 19:23   106
- 19:24   113
- 20:33   43
- 21   42
- 21:11–16   42
- 22:5   50n84
- 23:9   50n84
- 25   48
- 28   24, 29, 30, 46, 47, 47n74, 48, 49, 53, 55n102, 75
- 28:1–2   47n70
- 28:3   48
- 28:3, 7–9   55n105
- 28:4–7   50
- 28:6   50
- 28:7   50, 51
- 28:8–9   51
- 28:10–11   53
- 28:10–15   52
- 28:11–12   53, 54
- 28:12   53, 54
- 28:12–13   53n95
- 28:12–14   54
- 28:13   54
- 28:13–14   55
- 28:14   47
- 28:15   56
- 28:15–19   55, 59
- 28:16–19   55, 58
- 28:20   57
- 28:20–25   56
- 28:21   56, 57
- 29:1   47n70
- 30   47n70

2 Samuel
- 12:1–7   87
- 12:7   87n80
- 14:16   54
- 23:2   106n43, 156n96

1 Kings
- 3:5–15   50n84
- 8:10–11   103n36
- 8:15   103n36
- 17:17   95
- 18   119
- 18:12   156n96
- 18:12a   109
- 18:17–46   85n75
- 18:27–29   118
- 18:29   76, 110n56
- 18:36–38   119
- 18:46   109n50
- 22   25, 62, 81, 83, 87, 107, 112
- 22:6–28   84
- 22:6b   85
- 22:8, 10, 18   110n56
- 22:8a   111
- 22:10   76
- 22:10–12   85
- 22:13–18   85
- 22:15–16   86
- 22:18   111
- 22:19–23   85
- 22:20–23   114
- 22:21   86, 110n53
- 22:23   156n96
- 22:24   85, 87, 120, 156n96

2 Kings
- 2:9   107n43, 120
- 2:11   109n50
- 2:15a   109
- 2:16   109
- 3:13   117
- 3:15   32, 44
- 3:15–16a   117
- 19:7   74, 107, 115
- 21:6   53n94
- 23   47, 87n80
- 23:24   53n94

Isaiah
- 1:10–17   149
- 1:14   68n30
- 4:4   156n96
- 6   86
- 6:1   103n36
- 8:19   48, 53n94, 54
- 11:1–5   75
- 11:2   109, 156n96
- 19:3   48
- 19:14   74, 120, 156n96
- 26:9   68
- 27:1   80
- 28:6   156n96

- 29:4   53n94
- 29:9–10   74
- 29:10   114, 120, 156n96
- 32:15   120
- 32:15–18   74
- 34:11–15   109n51
- 34:16b   109
- 37:7   74, 107
- 38:16   96
- 40:13   156n96
- 42:1   115
- 42:5   95, 106n42
- 44:3   96, 120
- 48:16   115
- 51:9–11   80
- 57:15   67, 145
- 59:21   75, 106, 116, 156n96
- 61:1   106, 116
- 61:1–4   76
- 63   155
- 63:7–11   117
- 63:10–11   117, 155
- 63:11   96
- 63:14   156n96
- 63:14a   109
- 66:14   66

Jeremiah
- 4:4   143
- 5:13   118
- 6   143
- 6:10   143, 144
- 9   143
- 9:17   66
- 9:24   143
- 9:25   143
- 14:14   110n56, 112
- 16:18   103n36
- 19:4   103n36
- 23:13   110n56, 112
- 26:20   110n56, 112, 113n71
- 27–28   87
- 29:26–27   111
- 29:27   110n56
- 31   147, 151
- 31:33–34   126, 143–44
- 32:37–41   144
- 44:25   103n36
- 51:11   67, 74, 107, 115
- 51:11b   115

Ezekiel
- 1:3   117n77
- 2:2   107, 109
- 3:7   68n33
- 3:12   109
- 3:12, 14   109n50
- 3:14   109
- 3:22   117n77
- 3:22–27   74
- 3:24   107, 109
- 6:11–12   74
- 8:1   117n77
- 8:3   109, 109n50
- 8:17   103n36
- 10:3–4   103n36
- 11:1   109
- 11:1, 24   109n50
- 11:5   109, 116, 156n96
- 11:19   96, 156n96
- 11:19–20   126, 146
- 11:19a   107
- 11:24   109, 156n96
- 12:1–16   74
- 13:17   110n56
- 18:31   96, 107, 126, 146
- 21:23–29   74
- 24:25–27   74
- 30:11   103n36
- 33:21–22   74
- 36   147, 151
- 36:26   148, 151, 156n96
- 36:26–27   96, 107, 126, 146, 147
- 36:26b–32   146n70
- 36:27   148
- 37:1   64, 109n50, 117n77, 156n96
- 37:1–14   63–64
- 37:4–6   64
- 37:5, 10, 14   106n42
- 37:9a   64
- 37:9b   64
- 37:10   76, 110n56, 113n71, 114
- 37:14   64
- 40:1   117n77
- 43:5   109, 109n50

Hosea
- 4:12   69, 96
- 5:4   69, 96
- 6:6   149
- 7:15   66
- 9:7a–b   118

Joel
- 3:1   15, 75, 119, 121
- 3:1–2   96

Amos
- 5:21–24   149

Micah
- 3:8   76, 102, 103n36, 156n96
- 6:6–8   149

Habakkuk
- 2:4   103n36

Haggai
- 1:14   74, 96
- 2:5   96
- 2:5b   106n42

Zechariah
- 3:2   151n84
- 4:6   115
- 7:12   115, 116, 145
- 7:12a   115
- 12:1   106n42
- 12:10   75, 96, 120, 156n96

Psalms
- 6:2   66
- 13:2   68n30
- 31:6   95
- 32:2   68
- 34:1   42
- 34:19   104
- 51   26, 147, 148, 148n73, 149, 150, 151, 155
- 51:12   107, 147, 148
- 51:12–14   147, 149
- 51:13   148, 155
- 51:14   148
- 51:18–19   149
- 51:19   148
- 63:2   66, 68n33
- 73:21   68n30
- 74:10–22   80
- 77:4   104
- 77:7   145
- 78:8   145
- 82   86
- 91   77, 77n56
- 91:3–6   77
- 116:8   66
- 143:4   145
- 143:10   96, 109

Proverbs
- 15:13   67
- 16:12   69n35
- 16:32   69, 116
- 17:27   69n35
- 19:15   68n33
- 25:28   69
- 29:11   69n35, 116

Job
- 1–2   80, 86
- 4:15   110
- 6:4   129
- 6:12   129
- 7:7   67, 95
- 7:11   104
- 7:20   129
- 10:12   96
- 12:10   106n42
- 15:12–13   96
- 26:12   80
- 27:3   156n96
- 29:14   108n45
- 32:8   95n9
- 32:8, 18   106n42
- 33:4   95n9, 156n96
- 34:14–15   95n9

Lamentations
- 2:11   68n30

Qohelet
- 11:5   95

Daniel
- 4   130
- 4:5, 6, 15   103n34
- 9:3   57
- 10:2–3   57

Ezra
- 1:1   107, 115

Nehemiah
- 1:6–11   143n60
- 9:20, 30   115

- 9:30   115

1 Chronicles
- 10:13   53n94
- 12:19   74n46, 108

2 Chronicles
- 5:14   103n36
- 6:4   103n36
- 7:1–2   103n36
- 15:1   74n46, 106, 156n96

- 18   84n72
- 18:7   111
- 18:7, 9, 17   110n56
- 18:17   111
- 18:22   156n96
- 18:23   156n96
- 20:14   106, 156n96
- 20:37   110n56, 113n71
- 24:20   108, 156n96

New Testament

Matthew
- 4:1–11   93
- 8:28–34   3, 23
- 12:43–45   154
- 17:14–21   3
- 17:18   132

Mark
- 1:24   93
- 1:40–45   132
- 3:21–22   42
- 3:22, 30   133
- 5:1–20   3, 23
- 5:3–4   93
- 6   132
- 9:14–29   3
- 9:18   93
- 9:25   132
- 9:38–41   92

Luke
- 1:15, 41, 67   102n30
- 4:1–13   93
- 4:14   102n30
- 6:18   132
- 7:21   132
- 8:2   132
- 8:26–39   3, 23
- 8:27, 29   133
- 9:37–43   3
- 9:42   132
- 11:24–26   154
- 13:11   132

John
- 19:37   120n83

Acts
- 2   79, 80, 80n64, 111
- 2:4   102n30
- 2:16–17   15
- 4:8, 31   102n30
- 5:16   132
- 7:55   102n30
- 8:7   132
- 9:17   102n30
- 13:9   102n30
- 13:52   102n30
- 16:16–18   9n19

Romans
- 2:29   144

2 Corinthians
- 12:7   42n53

Ephesians
- 4:4   117
- 4:30   117
- 5:18   102n30

Titus
- 3:6   121

Hebrews
- 2:4   121

2 Peter
- 2:4   88

Jude
- 6   88

Revelation
- 12:1–12   81

Dead Sea Scrolls

Genesis Apocryphon (1QapGen ar)
- 20:16–18   135
- 20:27–29   136, 151

Hodayot/Thanksgiving Hymns (1QH^a)
- 4:29   100
- 4:35–36   101n27
- 4:38   138
- 5:35b–36a   107, 139
- 6:22–24   121
- 6:36   139
- 7:26   100n23
- 7:35a   100
- 8:26–30   101
- 8:28   101
- 8:29   101
- 8:29–31   139
- 8:30   156
- 9:10c–11a   100
- 9:17   100n23
- 9:30–31   100n23
- 9:34   138
- 10:9, 20   144
- 11:22–24   138
- 15:6b–8   138
- 15:9   100n23
- 18:24a–b   100
- 18:24   100n23
- 21:6   144

The War Scroll (1QM)
- 14:10   151

Pesher Habakkuk (1QpHab)
- 11:12–13   144

Community Rule (1QS)
- 3:6–9   156
- 3:6b–12   97
- 3:7   155n94
- 3:13–4:26   127, 156–58
- 3:17b–23a   157
- 3:23   157
- 3:24   158
- 4:2–8   158
- 4:21   156
- 5:3b–6a   127
- 5:4b–5   144
- 5:25–26   144
- 8:16   156
- 8:19   115

Serek Damascus (4QSD)
- 4Q265   144n65

4QBarkhi Nafshi
- 4Q434 1 i 10–11   151n85
- 4Q435 2 i 1–5   151
- 4Q436 1 i 5b–6   150
- 4Q436 1 i–ii   152
- 4Q436 1 i 10–ii 4   151, 156
- 4Q436 1 ii.1   152
- 4Q418 8:6   155n94

The Prayer of Nabonidus (4Q242)
- 1 3:2   130
- 1 3:4   130

Damascus Document (CD)
- 2:12   156
- 12   70
- 12:2b–3a   70
- 12:3b–6a   131–32

4Q Zadokite Fragments (4Q266, 4Q268, and 4Q272)   134–36

4QMMT
- 4Q398 13:1–7   143n60

4QWords of the Luminaries^a (4Q504)
- 4 11   144n64

4QExorcism ar
- 1 i 4   131

11QPsalms Scroll^a (11Q5)   19:15–16   152
11QApocryphal Psalms^a (11Q11)   77, 130

Other Early Jewish Literature

Sirach
- 39:6   102
- 48:12   120

2 Baruch
- 9:2, 4   57

1 Enoch
- 1–36   81
- 12   88
- 15–16   88

4 Ezra
- 5:13   57

Jubilees
- 10:8–9   88
- 10:22–26   80
- 12   78

- 12:16   79
- 12:17–18   79
- 12:19–20   78
- 12:25–27   79
- 16:25   80
- 16:26   79
- 17:15–18:16   81

Jewish Antiquities (Josephus)
- 8.45   132

Ancient Near Eastern Texts

The Poem of the Righteous Sufferer (Ludlul bēl nēmeqi)   129

Enuma Elish   129

Early Christian Literature

Epistle of Barnabas
- 9:1–8   144
- 10:12   144

Shepherd of Hermas   9n19

Cyril of Jerusalem
- Catechetical Lectures 17:17   80n64

Augustine
- Enarrations on the Psalms (Ps 55)   80n64

Subject and Author Index

Abram/Abraham 78–79, 135–37
Adam, Klaus-Peter 111n55, 112–115, 118n78
Agency 21, 29, 35, 58–59, 69, 94, 99–102, 121, 144, 148–49
Alexander, Philip S. 131n21
Altered States of Consciousness (ASCs) 7–8 75n72
Anderson, Gary A. 20n56
Angel(s): fallen 80, 88–90; in visions 57; of the presence, 78–79
Apotropaism (apotropaic) 76–80, 130–32, 155
Arnold, Bill T. 46n67
Assmann, Jan 65n22
Avalos, Hector 139n53
Azazel 133

Baden, Joel S. 137n46
Barr, James 14n37, 21n61
Baumgarten, Joseph M. 134n39
Bazzana, Giovanni B. 8–9, 11, 16n45, 42n54, 58n115, 133n32
Beelzebul 42
Belial, *see* Satan
Ben Zvi, Ehud 85n76
Berman, Joshua 35n25, 47
Bernstein, Richard J. 161
Bezalel (biblical figure) 74, 107
Bibb, Bryan D. 149n76
Blenkinsopp, Joseph 50, 54n97, 55n102, 55n105
Blischke, Mareike Verena 15, 32n12, 63n6, 108n48
Block, Daniel I. 64n18, 94n6, 109n52
Blood 56, 134–35
Boddy, Janice 23, 34, 72
Body *see* Spirits, part of the body
Boase, Elizabeth 40n46
Bori 43–44
Bourguignon Erika 10, 119
Brand, Miryam T. 20n56, 77n56, 150n78, 152, 157
Brettler, Marc 142

Briggs, Richard S. 71n42
Brock, Rita Nakashima 40n47
Broida, Marian W. 77n57
Brooke, George J. 150n78, 151n80
Brown, Diana DeGroat 123–26
Brown, Karen McCarthy 51n90
Brueggemann, Walter 85n73
Bush, Stephen S. 17n47
Bynum, William Randolph 120n84

Caciola, Nancy Mandeville 5n10, 57n113
Cambers, Andrews 92n4
Carlson, Reed 34n23, 89n85
Carter, Warren 23n69
Charismaticism *see* Pentecostalism/Charismaticism (religion)
Childs, Brevard S. 77n54
Circumcision 141–45
Clines David, 110n53
Clothing 49, 53, 82, 108n45, 124–25
Craffert, Pieter F. 11
Crawford, Sidnie White 130n18
Crenshaw, James L. 87n81
Cogan, Mordechai 46n67, 52n92
Cohen, Emma 125, 149
Collins, Adela Yarbro 42n53
Collins, John J. 88n83, 130n19
Colonization 8–9, 58
Compatibilism *see* agency
Csordas, Thomas J. 71n41, 127–28, 154
Cultural model(s) 65–67, 70, 80, 140, 145

David (biblical figure) 31, 36, 42, 44, 87, 139
Determinism *see* Agency
Deuteronomists (deuteronomistic) 47
De Vries, Simon J. 84n72
Di Vito, Robert A. 30n9
Diagnostic and Statistical Manual of Mental Disorders 38–39
Disability Studies 26, 40, 139–40
Dissociation 38–40
Divination 36, 49n8, 50

Divine Council 86
Dobroruka, Vicente 11n24, 76n53
Douglas Mary, 137n45
Duling, Dennis C. 132n28

Eagleton, Terry 20n58
Elijah (biblical figure) 85, 109, 118–120
Engberg-Pedersen, Troels 11
Eshel, Esther 20n55, 77n55
Ethnography 6–7, 10–11, 23–24, 34, 43–44, 55, 57–58, 61, 71, 82, 89–90, 153–54
Espiritismo 24, 27–29, 44–46, 59, 93
Espírito Santo, Diana 24, 27–29, 44–46
Evil *see* Theodicy
Exorcism 3, 92–93, 124, 130, 132, 135, 151–52
Experience *see* Religious Experience
Ezekiel (biblical figure) 41n53, 63–64, 74, 76, 140

Falk, Daniel K. 150n78
Fasting 57
Fee, Gordon D. 11n25
Feinstein, Eve Levavi 71n42
Ferber, Sarah 91n4
Fischer, Irmtraud 11n24, 54n100
Fischer, Stefan 46n67
Fisher, Philip 68n34
Foucault, Michel 21n60, 25, 37n34, 98–99
Frankfurter, David 75
Frechette, Christopher G. 40n46
Freeman, Thomas 93n5
Freud, Sigmund 37
Friebel, Kelvin G. 74n48
Frymer-Kensky, Tikva 56n106, 136n45

Garroway, Joshua 23n69
Ghosts *see* spirits
Gibson, Marion 91n4
Giercke-Ungermann, Annett 35n27
Giles, Linda L. 49
Glossolalia 32, 111, 154
Göttingen School 81n67
Grabbe, Lester L. 10n24
Grimell, Jan 40n47
Grossman, Maxine L. 16n45

Grushcow, Lisa 71n42
Gudme, Anne Katrine de Hemmer 71n42
Gullah/Geechee 25, 60–62, 90, 93
Gunnel, André 118n78
Gunkel, Hermann 12–14, 32, 111n62
Gyatso, Janet 21n60

Haber, Susan 136n44, 137n48
Hamori, Esther J. 49n78, 50n85, 51, 53n95, 54n99, 69n37, 86n77
Haugstein, Jörg 153–54
Hannah (biblical figure) 34
Harding, Rachel 124
Harkins, Angela Kim 21n60, 100n19
Harrington, Hannah K. 138n50
Heart (לבב) 26, 67, 90, 141–44, 151, 153
Hempel, Charlotte 96n10, 157n97
Hendel, Ronald S. 149n76
Heschel, Abraham J. 43n58
Holland, Dorothy C. 67
Holmes, Brooke 105
Holy Spirit *see* Spirits, holy
Hutter, Manfred 46n67

Inclination (יצר) 127, 144–45, 151–53
Islam 34, 49, 58n118

James, William 21n60
Janowski, Bernd 62, 66n23, 68n31
Jealousy 70–71, 133
Job (biblical figure) 129
Johnson, Aubrey R. 63n6
Johnson, Paul Christopher 8–9
Joseph (biblical figure) 66–67, 104, 107
Jung, Carl 38

Kardec, Allan (Kardecism) 27, 45
Katz, Steven T. 17n49
Kaufmann, Yeḥezkel 50n84, 56n106, 133n33
Kazen, Thomas 132n29, 137n47
Keener, Craig S. 11n25
Keith, Chris 19n55
Kelle, Brad E. 40n47, 41
Kiboko, J. Kabamba 46n68
Kitz, Anne Marie 43n57
Klass, Morton 40n44

Klawans, Jonathan   100–01, 136–37
Klein, Anja   97n12, 97n13, 146n70, 147
Klutz, Todd E.   133
Knibb, Michael A.   96n10
Kratz, Reinhard G.   5–6n12, 32n12, 85n74, 108n48
Krippner, Stanley   39n37
Krüger, Thomas   141n58
Kugel, James L.   78n58, 79

Lambek, Michael   7n13, 9, 22, 25, 58n117, 73, 82–83, 89n87, 90, 99n18
Lambert, David A.   20n56, 21n61, 57n111, 142n59
Lapsley, Jacqueline E.   21n60, 146
Legion (demon)   23
Lên đồng   53
Lemaire, André   76n52
Lemke, Werner E.   141n58, 143n61
Levenson, Jon D.   5n11, 20n55, 20n59, 64n18, 144n63
Levine, Baruch   133n35
Levison, John R.   14–15, 43n58, 64n18, 74n47, 94, 102–03, 111n63, 113–115, 155n93
Leuchter, Mark   32n12
Lewis, Ioan   10, 22, 43n59, 51n89, 51n90, 58
Lewis, Theodore J.   46n67
Lilly, Ingrid   10n24, 25, 65, 68, 128–29, 140n57
Lincicum, David   131n24
Loewenthal, Kate M.   38n37, 39
LXX see Old Greek

MacDonald, Nathan   18n50, 109n50, 111n55, 120n84, 145–46
Madness see Mental Illness
Magic   75, 88, 131
Manigault-Bryant, LeRhonda S.   25, 60–62, 90
Martin, Dale B.   79n61
Masquelier, Adeline   44n60, 140n55
Mastema see Satan
Maston, Jason   100n19
Martin, Lee Roy   11n25, 108n45, 108n47, 109

Martínez, Florentino Garcia   130n18
Material (materiality)   7, 16–17, 95, 142
McCarter Jr., P. Kyle   47, 51
Medicine see Spirits, medical notions of
Medium (mediums/mediumship)   24, 28–29, 30, 31, 34, 4447, 50–59, 75, 82–83, 131
Mental Illness   31, 37–46, 59, 118
Micaiah son of Imlah (biblical figure)   62, 81, 83–88
Milgrom, Jacob   133, 137n45
Miller, Shem   100n19
Mittermaier, Amira   98–99
Moberly, R. W. L.   85n74, 86
Moral Injury (MI)   24, 30, 40–41, 59
Morris, Michael J.   77n54
Moss, Candida   40n46, 137n46
Mowinckel, Sigmund   118n78
Mercer, Jean   40n45
Metonymy   66
Mroczek, Eva   5–6n12
Music   44, 117
Muslims see Islam
Mysticism   17, see Religious Experience
Myth see Spirits, myths about

Najman, Hindy   21n60
Nasrallah, Laura   43n58
Naveh, Joseph   131n21
Neiman, Susan   20n57
Neusner, Jacob   137n45
Newsom, Carol A.   18n51, 21n60, 21n61, 30n9, 62, 65n19, 94, 95n9, 100n19, 138, 139n52
Nicklas, Tobias   57n112
Niditch, Susan   21n60, 35n26
Nihan, Christophe   47, 111n55
Nissinen, Martti   10n24, 33, 43n58, 75n72, 111n55, 118n79
Noll, K. L.   85n76

Old Greek (OG)   48–49, 55n103, 55n105
Olyan, Saul   40n46, 42n56
Otto, Rudolf   17n48

Pagels, Elaine H.   20n55
Parker, Jonathan Deane   112n64

Parker, Simon 118n78
Paul (New Testament figure) 41n53
Paul, Shalom 110n53
Penney, Douglas L. 130n21, 131
Pentecost (New Testament) 79–80
Pentecostalism/Charismaticism (religion) 127–28, 153–54, 158
Petersen, David L. 76n5
Pneumatology 13–15, 62, 139, 147–48, 153, 160–61
Poirier, John C. 79n63
Pokomo (people) 58n118
Pola, Thomas 43n58
Popović, Mladen 100n21, 157n98
Possession (spirit):
- as discourse 22–24, 72–73
- as other 69–71, 147, 149
- by demons 1–2
- corporate 32, 74, 96–97
- cultivated 32, 54
- descriptions of 62, 72–73, 105, 110–15, 128–29, 145
- executive and pathogenic 125–26
- in popular culture 2–4
- self- 6, 116–17
- polemics against 118
- terminology of 7–10

Post-Traumatic Stress Disorder (PTSD) 24, 31, 41, 59
Priestly (sources) 133, 136–37
Prophecy (prophets) 32–33, 106, 110–115, 147, 149
Proudfoot, Wayne 16n44
Purity 134–37, 147–48

Qimron, Elisha 134n37
Quinn, Naomi 67
Qur'an 49

Reed, Annette Yoshiko 20n55, 88n83
Reimer, Andy M. 79n61
Reis, Pamela Tamarkin 54n101, 56–57
Religious Experience 16–19, 80, 99
Repentance 142–43, 148–49
Ricoeur, Paul 82
Rogan, Wil 137n45

Rosen-Zvi, Ishay 20n55, 70n40, 150n78, 152
Rouch, Jean 57, 58n116

Sakalava (people) 25, 81, 82–83, 87, 89–90, 93
Samson (biblical figure) 34, 108
Sar 43–44
Satan (Belial, Mastema) 20, 70, 91, 131, 138–39
Sands, Kathleen R. 25, 91–93
Samuel (biblical figure) 31, 32–33, 34–36, 48, 52–56, 58–59
Saul (biblical figure) 24, 29–30, 31–37, 41–46, 46–59, 75–76, 111, 139, 147
Schipper, Jeremy 40n46, 140n54
Schuller, Eileen M. 100
Schofield, Alison 96n10
Seely, David Rolph 150n78, 151
Segal, Michael 78n58, 135n41
Segal, Robert A. 89n86
Self:
- conceptions of in antiquity 21;
- cultivation 26, 97–102, 138–39
- porous and buffered 30–31, 59, 129
- technologies of 26; 98
- unfamiliar 126, 141

Septuagint *see* Old Greek
Shantz, Colleen, 11, 16
Sharf, Robert H., 16n44,
Sharp, Lesley A., 40n45
Shay, Jonathan, 40n47
Sherwood, Yvonne, 16n44
Sign acts, 74, 85, 87
Smith, Frederick M., 18
Smith, Mark S., 19n55
Speech acts, 77n54
Speaking-in-tongues *see* glossolalia
Spirit(s):
- abiding 25, 94, 95–97, 121, 141
- confusing 74
- deceiving 86–87
- discernment of 154, 158
- empowering 74
- evil 43, 136, 154–56, 160–61
- filled with 102–05
- harmful 29, 43, 44, 153–54

- holy   13, 26, 127, 148, 150, 153–59
- in measure   119–21
- language for   62–66, 68, 100–01, 105, 146
- medical notions of   26, 125, 126, 127–29, 130–32; 134–37, 159
- migrating   25, 94, 105 121–22, 141
- myths about   62, 80–81, 87
- of the dead   24
- part of the body   25, 62, 66–68, 126, 128, 129, 140, 148
- rituals   31, 54
- spouse   51

Spiritism *see* Kardec, Allan
Stendahl, Krister   21n61
Stökl, Jonathan   33n20
Stars   79
Steinmann, Andrew   130n20
Stuckenbruck, Loren T.   19n55, 20n55, 20n59, 78n60, 88n83, 157n98, 158
Sulzbach, Carla   57n112
Swahili (people)   49

Taboo (behavior)   22, 58
Taussig, Michael   5
Taves, Ann   16n43, 19
Taylor, Charles   30–31
Teeter, D. Andrew   5–6n12
Tigchelaar, Eibert J. C.   150n78, 151n84
Theodicy   20

Therapy *see* Spirit(s), medical notions of
Thiessen, Matthew   133n30
Throat (נפש)   67–68, 97, 101, 104, 115, 142
Tropper, Josef   46n67, 49n77
Twelftree, Graham H.   11n25

Umbanda (religion)   26, 123–26

VanderKam, James C.   78n59, 79n61
Volz, Paul   14n36
Vreugdenhil, Gerrit C.   77n55

Wagner, Andreas   77n54
Warren, Ed and Lorraine   2
Wellhausen, Julius   33, 47n70
Werline, Rodney A.   16n45
Wilson, Robert R.   10, 43n58, 113n70
Wisdom   98, 102–104, 116, 156n96
Wise, Michael O.   130n21, 131
Witch: in the Bible   48; Trials, 4, 5n10, 50
Wolff, Hans Walter   63n6, 66n23, 68n31
Wright, Archie T.   19n55, 81n68, 88n83, 88n84
Wright, David P.   136n45

Yeṣer *see* Inclination
Yoruba (religion)   27

Zahn, Molly   5–6n12
Zār   34, 154

www.ingramcontent.com/pod-product-compliance
Lightning Source LLC
Chambersburg PA
CBHW020231170426

43201CB00007B/385